D1596717

Lyricality in English Literature

University of Nebraska Press
Lincoln and London

LYRICALITY in English Literature

Daniel Albright

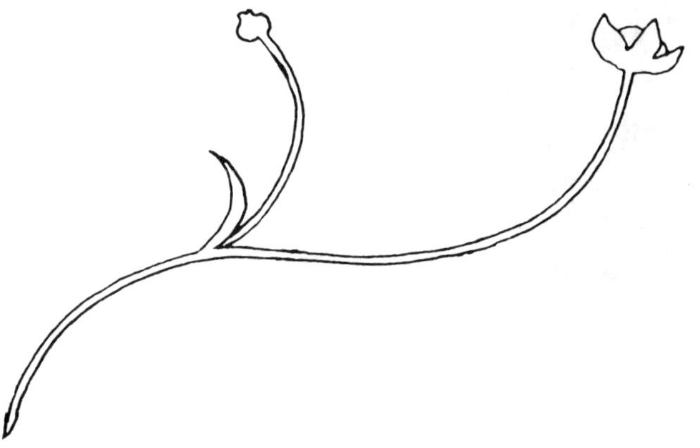

Manufactured in the
United States of America
The paper in this book meets
the guidelines for permanence
and durability of the Committee
on Production Guidelines for
Book Longevity of the Council
on Library Resources.
*Library of Congress
Cataloging in Publication Data*
Albright, Daniel, 1945–
Lyricality in English literature.
Bibliography: p.
Includes index.
1. English poetry—History
and criticism. 2. Lyric
poetry—History and criticism.
I. Title.
PR351.A4 1984 821'.04'09 84-10455
ISBN 0-8032-1019-1 (alk. paper)

Contents

Preface

THIS is a book about a species of delight, but it is a book conceived in drudgery. Over the years I have been asked many times to give oral examinations to Ph.D. candidates on the topic of the lyric genre—this is no instructor's favorite task—and I have never been certain what to do. At first I would walk into the examining room and ask the poor examinee, "What is a lyric?" I always began in this fashion because it was the only question I could think of; but even in later years, after I had thought of other questions I could have used instead—such as "What is a genre?" or "What is your favorite poem?"—I still began with "What is a lyric?" simply because I had received such an astonishing collection of answers over the years. One said a lyric was something that could be sung; but he admitted upon close interrogation that he did not know the tune to the "Ode on a Grecian Urn." Another said a lyric was an unusually personal and heartfelt poem; I asked him how he would reply to yesterday's candidate, who had been confident that the lyric was the most anonymous and universalized of literary forms. I became more and more adept at puncturing every trial definition that came my way; but as that happened my own grasp of what a lyric was—which had never been strong—grew weaker and weaker. Finally I could put it off no longer; I had to ask myself the tormenting question, "What is a lyric?" Every hypothesis I tried, of course, was vitiated by some opposing hypothesis; the lyric seemed definable only as a tissue of paradoxes.

There were times, in the course of my research, when I feared that every method for distinguishing the lyrical from the nonlyrical might fail. But I believe that, as Shelley says, hope creates from its own wreck the thing it contemplates, for the very indeterminacy that exasperated me in the quest to define the lyrical may turn out to be the long-missing criterion: a lyric is that which resists definition. A lyric is a poem in which one notices a certain shiftiness or instability, a certain slipping and sliding of things, a certain tendency to equate a thing with its antiself, a certain evasiveness of being. In other words, a lyric is magical, and the proper history of the lyric is the history of incantation.

We do not usually think of Shakespeare and Shelley and Eliot as magicians, but their most characteristically lyrical utterances can be taken as sophisticated versions of magic spells. A spell is a document that commands mutation, that effects a change of identity; and if we examine many lyrics we see that the lyrical is the domain not of solid entities but of half-formed hovering things. As we shall see, sometimes the magic is so intense and incoherent that everything seems poised on the brink of becoming everything else; lyricality can approach a condition of complete bewilderment. If I am right in thinking that the lyric is the literary mode that requires metamorphosis, mutation, it is not surprising that a theory of the lyric is hard to come by, ridden with paradoxes; for every attempt to grasp what a lyric is will be an attempt to seize Proteus in the midst of his changings or to confine Ariel in a cloven pine tree.

But if lyric poetry is magical, its magic can operate exclusively within the confines of the poem; it is a magic turned inward. The myth of Amphion, who built Thebes by means of singing, alleges that art is capable of telekinesis; but, as Swift notes in "Vanbrug's House," few architects nowadays employ poets in their construction crews. This involution, this nonreferential quality, is an important aspect of the lyric mode. Nonlyric poetry, like Crabbe's *The Village* or Milton's *Paradise Lost*, is essentially referential in character: it posits the existence of a world that may have more dimensions than our own or may have a more settled character, a world that may be a vivid simulacrum of our own or may be invisible and fantastical; but always a world that is real, unusually real. Nonlyric poetry is constitutive, creative. Lyric poetry, on the other hand, as Coleridge and Wordsworth began to understand, is a dissolving and an uncreating; it posits a half-world or metaworld where there exists no author, no reader, no commonplace earth, only a writhe of feelings and notions, sensations attributable to no one in particular. These sensations may ascribe themselves to the poem, as if a poem could generate its own little organs of sense, or they may ascribe themselves to nightingales, stars, spooks, men of clay, as if feelings and ideas were spirits that could improvise a body.

Of all the literary genres, the lyric has proved the most frustrating. It is so difficult to characterize that sometimes it seems as if the lyric genre consists of what is left over when all other genres are subtracted from the corpus of literature. The intention of this book is partly to provide a definition of the lyric and partly to tell why such a definition is at best provisional; that is, to sculpt a cloud and to explain why clouds resist sculpture.

A lyric was originally a poem sung or chanted; and, as poetry evolved away from actual accompaniment by a harp or psaltery, poets had to supply a musical effect by means of purely verbal resources. I believe that lyric poetry is fundamentally an attempt to approximate the condition of music within the slightly alien and prosaic domain of words, whether through phonemic intricacies or through the frustrating of semantic reference or through the presentation of transcendental ideas or of absolute feelings. Therefore the lyric is not truly a genre; no one can hope to compile a set of criteria, a questionnaire that, when answered, would confidently tell us whether a poem was or was not a lyric; rather one should say that the lyric is a mode, discoverable in odes and dramas and novels and possibly the telephone directory, through which the reader becomes aware of the illusion of music beyond the sense of the language.

In the study of English poetry—Spenser, Shakespeare, Jonson,

Dryden, Gray, Blake, Wordsworth, Coleridge, Shelley, Joyce, Eliot, and Auden are among the chief heroes of this book—I have tried to show how the representations of the poet, nature, and society become distorted under the pressure of the command to be musical. Because musical notes have no denotation, no "meaning," but only internal relations, lyric poetry tends to treat the objective world as something inherently unstable, subject to incantation, not especially real; and many lyrics describe processes of metamorphosis comparable to chord progressions in music. I have tried to be a sort of anthropologist and explorer in the peculiar world posited by lyric poetry, in which the poet and his landscape are essentially inseparable and juvenile, not quite born, and society consists not of responsible workmen and farmers but of kings, fools, freaks, fetuses, idle shepherds, and the mighty dead.

Lyricality in English Literature

Chapter 1

LYRICALITY AS A MODE

IN one sense there is no such thing as a lyric. No poem can be a piece of music, though it may approximate musicality in many ways. But any poem can be lyrical, to the degree that it can seem the sort of poem that the reader is used to hearing accompanied by music, or to the degree that it can evoke some phantom of a tune, a time signature, a harmony. It is no difficult trick to write a poem that reminds one of other poems always conjoined to melodies; every culture has a vocabulary of useful singables, words that denote simple passions, and landscapes comfortable to young love, and the names of famous birds. The second sort of lyric presents a greater challenge to the poet and the critic: to the poet because he must supply through some literary artifice the illusion of pitch, volume, thick overtone, all those charms that music could give his text; to the critic because his paraphrases, his thematic catalogs, his articulations of categories—his whole body of resources for description, analysis, and speculation—grow irrelevant to a poetry that is attempting to supersede its own verbal nature, attempting to lose itself in music. There is a discipline of literary criticism; there is a theory of language; there is a theory of music. But what can a critic do with a dissembling art that seems to deny what it is in order to have the pleasure of being what it is not?

It is wrong, I believe, to speak of the lyric as a genre. A genre must have an evolving corpus of rules governing composition, a huge storehouse of literary expectations that allow precise measurement of the licentiousness of any license. A genre must be a kind of contract between author and reader in which the author agrees to provide a certain sort of enjoyment or instruction, if only the reader will sharpen the experience of his reading by remembering other texts that belong to the same genre. Therefore generic constraints are clear to the degree that a given work resembles its predecessors in its genre, and generic constraints are strong to the degree that a given work will be unintelligible without knowledge of its genre-mates. But what do we expect when we are told that a work is a lyric? We do not expect any particular structure, though we may guess that the structure will somehow call attention to itself. We do not imagine that any special mood or persona will greet us in the text—tragedy has its frowning and comedy its smiling mask, epic offers its sober and strenuous paradigms of culture, but no passion or tenor is more lyrical than any other. No Aristotle has ever composed a manual prescribing the parts and proper sequences of the lyric. What invention could a writer proffer, besides a Defoe novel, that would be grounds for demanding our money back if it had been sold to us as a lyrical book? Where nothing can frustrate expectation, there is no genre.

During recent times there has arisen a better model for describing lyricality than the old tripartite generic scheme of lyric-epic-dramatic. W. H. Auden, in his essay on Robert Frost, says that every poem exists in a state of tense equilibrium between two competing tendencies, which he calls Ariel and Prospero, the spirit of unearthly fantasy and the spirit of unflinching truthfulness, fidelity to our actual miserable state. Ariel, says Auden, presides over the realm of imagination, in which images keep shifting and sliding effortlessly, beautifully, into other images, but in which nothing serious can happen. Ariel, then, is simply a disengaged, dispassionate, almost contentless creativity, an imagination so engrossed in the continual play of images that it cannot be bothered to attend to the real. In this study I shall test the adequacy of Ariel as the presiding genius of lyricality; if it can be shown that he is such, then the lyric is not a genre equal in rank to the dramatic or the epic, but a moment of all poetry, a swerving aside, a lifting at right angles from the usual axis of narrative or logical discourse—the antimimetic principle. The mere absence of a phenomenal world is almost enough to achieve the feeling of private intensity, internality, music; it is for this reason that a work that seems to discourage musical setting in every conceivable way—Beckett's *The Unnamable*—is nevertheless often called poetic or lyric. And though its grossness, its dissipation, its self-interruptedness, its incomprehensibility all seem unmusical, portions of it have in fact been set to music, in Earl Kim's *Earthlight*. Beckett strives as best he can to vitiate the illusion that his words constitute a world; and whatever tends to destroy reference also tends to enhance the musical purity of language, the feeling that all words, even the most erudite and meaningful, are only solmization syllables—do re mi fa. Composers have always been especially excited by texts of a frivolous, raving, arbitrary, or nonsensical character; as Auden remarks, Rossini should have scandalized no one when he said he could set a laundry list to music, for a laundry list is eminently suitable for musical setting. If some modern poet were to present a laundry list not as a tabulation of real clothes, but as a poem, it would be a lyric. Whenever we read a text and say to ourselves *Something is missing*, whether that something is a recognizably human author, or a customary world representation, or simply sense, we are in the domain of the lyrical. Ever since poets ceased believing that a composer was likely to set their lyrical poems to music, they have had to compensate for the missing melodies; and therefore poets have built into their poems, where music would be if music there was, a feeling of absence, as if silence made extant could supply the illusion of the unhearable music. The composer Lukas Foss has written a piece called *Phorion* by subtracting certain notes and parts from well-known baroque compositions; this technique gives the auditor the spidery feeling that he is hearing silence, a silence given an audible melodic shape. I take this as a metaphor for the practice of lyric poets, who everywhere suppress, omit, delete, touching their fingers to the strings without actually plucking a note.

LYRIC PARADOXES

When we study old and new ideas about the nature of the lyric mode, everywhere we find puzzles and contradictions. This is perhaps appropriate, for the lyric in its disguise as a genre is such a ragbag of panegyrics, eclogues, elegies, epicedes, obsequies that it invites a corresponding desire in critics simply to mourn, declaim, flatter, or emote, in the absence of a finite body of material to be dissected. Because the individual lyric poem often treats the breakdown of discursive categories, the lyric mode as a whole demonstrates an essential categorilessness. As T. S. Eliot says, a goose with no bones can be carved any way one likes.

1. *The Prehistoric versus the Oversophisticated*

No idea about the lyric has more prestige than the notion that the lyric poet was the original agent of human civilization. Horace's discussion in the *Ars Poetica* of Orpheus and Amphion, whose music uplifted man from his archaic bestiality, built him cities with stones obedient to melody, at last enabled him "Things sacred from prophane to separate; / The publicke from the private . . . Build townes, and carve the lawes in leaves of wood" (Jonson's translation, lines 565–66, 568) is remembered in most of the early, and many of the late, defenses of poetry and disquisitions on the art. For example, William Webbe, in *A Discourse of English Poetrie* (1586), says that

> the best wryters agree that it was *Orpheus*, who by the sweet gyft of his heavenly Poetry, withdrew men from raungyng uncertainly, and wandring brutishly about, and made them gather together, and keepe company, made houses, and kept fellowshippe together, who therefore is reported (as *Horace* sayth) to asswage the fiercenesse of Tygers, and moove the harde Flynts. After him was *Amphion*, who was the first that caused Citties to bee

> builded, and men therein to live decently and orderly according to lawe and right. (p. 25)

As the first great treatise in English on poetry, *The Arte of English Poesie* (1589), whose author is traditionally said to be George Puttenham, expresses this idea, "Poets were the first . . . Legislators and polititians in the world" (p. 6); and if Shelley is right, poets are the last legislators in the world as well. Webbe takes so seriously the notion that the function of poetry is to civilize the beasts that he seems to value poetry in direct proportion to its sententiousness, to the amount of useful wisdom that can be extracted from it. Indeed, the reader of Webbe might believe that Plautus's chief excellence is his praise of virtue, Ovid's his advice "Flye thou from idlenes and ever be stable," and Martial's his precept "Set in no one person all wholly thy pleasure" (pp. 43–44). Most of Webbe's citations from modern poets—by *modern* I mean a span of twenty years, for that is how long memorable poetry had been written in English, according to Webbe (p. 30)—concern such matters as the suitability of poetry as a means for teaching proper speech to children (p. 42, quoted from "that learned and famous knight, Sir *Thomas Elyot*"), as if every generation had to undergo all over again the progress from the beastly to the civil and amiable; as if the work of Orpheus and Amphion were never quite complete. Though Webbe conceives Orpheus and Amphion as little more than players of musical saws, his emphasis on the educational functions of poetry reminds us that in its archetype poetry is addressed to the ungoverned, the unlettered, the uncitied, the formless, the obscure and bestial; that poetry has an ongoing mission to rectify and to heave into light. Most lyric poets do not forget that beyond the boundaries of their verse there lies a penumbra of anarchy, the dumb host of all those not yet incorporated into the charmed circle of the poem—that every lyric poem is a spell that transforms the barbarous and uncouth, whose vestiges are felt everywhere in the text, into the bright and clearly incised.

And yet, if the lyric is always set in 4000 B.C., there is another sense in which it is the most modish, even the most effete sort of poem. This aspect did not escape the attention of Puttenham (for so I will always call the author of *The Arte of English Poesie*), who notices that, while some are of the opinion that pastoral poetry came before every other genre, because language itself arose in the casual babble found at the primeval assemblies of shepherds, and singing arose in their "first idle wooings," it seems more likely that eclogues are a much later invention, because they do not intend

> to counterfait or represent the rusticall manner of loves and communication: but under the vaile of homely persons, and in rude speeches to insinuate and glaunce at greater matters, and such as perchance had not bene safe to have beene disclosed in any other sort, which may be perceived by the Eglogues of *Virgill*, in which are treated by figure matters of greater importance then the loves of *Titirus* and *Corydon*. These Eglogues came after to containe and enforme morall discipline, for the amendment of mans behavior, as be those of *Mantuan* and other moderne Poets. (pp. 38–39)

If there is any sort of poem in which we ought to be able to see in pure form the archetypal lyric act, whereby homely rude folk are enlightened by the power of song, brought into the consoling orbit of human community by the virtue of shared delight and shared instruction, it is the eclogue, where shepherd singers embody and shape their feelings in the act of song, where a lyrical economic system, according to which singers receive some tribute, a lamb or a kid, in proportion to the admiration they can excite in their fellow shepherds, begins to replace the primitive economy of barters and dowries, a sophistication of primary appetites into an exchange of emotion. But the closer we seem to approach to Orpheus in the very act of civilizing, the further we seem to get from that primal lyric drama, which reveals itself as a court masque in which dukes and duchesses dress up as shepherds for spectacular delight; and Orpheus himself is but a hired singer brought onstage for the sake of effortless coloratura. It is as if the overcivilized and the undercivilized meet in the lyric, which spans the whole gamut from ape to castrato.

2. *Temporality versus Atemporality*

If in the lyric mode beginnings and endings seem to meet, so also do the momentary and the eternal. Often a lyric attempts to contract its time span to the briefest instant, to refine its action to a single throb or spasm or flash of light:

"Thank you, whatever comes." And then she turned
And, as the ray of sun on hanging flowers
Fades when the wind hath lifted them aside,
Went swiftly from me. Nay, whatever comes
One hour was sunlit and the most high gods
May not boast of any better thing
Than to have watched that hour as it passed.
(Pound, "Erat Hora," 1911)

In this species of lyric, the poem attempts to construct an exceedingly intense and defective world in which space has thinned itself into a single dazzling photograph and all the numerals have been scrubbed off the clock face except one marker denoting the important moment. This moment is what Wordsworth called the spot of time, Joyce the epiphany, Eliot the moment in and out of time. It is one tick asked to stand in place of the entire temporal continuum. In the world of prose everything we value turns to dust or sludge, and if we know anything at all we know loss; but lyricality posits another place and time, always at the fringes of our place, our time—a metaphysis, a metachrony:

THE LEADEN ECHO

How to keep—is there any any, is there none such, nowhere
known some, bow or brooch or braid or brace, lace,
latch or catch or key to keep
Back beauty, keep it, beauty, beauty, beauty, . . . from vanishing away? . . .

THE GOLDEN ECHO

Spare!
There is one, yes I have one (Hush there!);
Only not within seeing of the sun . . .
One. Yes I can tell such a key, I do know such a place,
Where whatever's prized and passes of us, everything that's
    fresh and fast and flying of us, seems to us sweet of
    us and swiftly away with, done away with, undone . . .
Never fleets more, fastened with the tenderest truth
To its own best being and its loveliness of youth . . .
See; not a hair is, not an eyelash, not the least lash lost . . .
(Hopkins, "The Leaden Echo and the Golden Echo," 1881)

The Golden Echo offers lyric consolation to our unlyric selves. Heaven is a vast treasure-house of lost valuables, the backstage to which all we love must exit. Here time works not by mutation but by accretion, for no precious thing changes, although more precious things keep pouring in from the domain of the temporal. Hopkins has displayed an asylum for every lyric poet's dream of prolonging his cherished instant, as if every lyric poem alluded to some great receptacle where keen evanescent sensations were embalmed, pickled, made eternal in all their keenness, all their trembling on the brink of dissolution. In this elysium no steady time sequence can exist, for each saved moment is incommensurable, unrelated to any other moment, an inhabitant of its own private forever; what we have is a heap of separate eternities, an anthology of Standing Nows.

3. *Structure versus Amorphousness*

Not only is the time span of a lyric unsteady, difficult to measure, but the proper nature of its own internal organization is hard to classify. Which is more musical—a poem with a highly visible structure, a firmly determined meter and rhyme scheme, or a more amorphous poem? A musical composition usually has a time signature, a regular pattern of stress; and so many poets imitate music by enforcing a clear beat, by showing phrase lengths with the cadences of rhyme, by using consonance and assonance to provide the illusion of the attacks and timbre of a single musical instrument. However, it is easy to show that there is a limit to how far structural rigor can go toward endowing a poem with the feeling of musicality:

> "Life is the lust of a lamp for the light that is dark till
> the dawn of the day when we die."

This is from Swinburne's famous self-parody "Nephelidia" (1880). If obedience to a predetermined form could make a line seem musical, this would be the most musical line in English: the accented syllables are strikingly accented, the unaccented syllables are as faint as possible, the alliteration lollops along with level tread, it is all a faultless model of dactylic octameter. Indeed, it is far too faultless to be lyrical.

Because a poem cannot actually sing, cannot actually be music, every poetic device used to enhance the feeling of musicality is an illusion; and so when these devices are overstressed, overstuffed, they necessarily call attention to their illusory character and start to fail. A poem that insists too emphatically on its rhythm will cease to seem rhythmical—anyone who listens long enough to bad Augustan poetry will find that the meter of the couplets soon recedes into a general singsong, unobtrusive but annoying. Verse that is too regular starts to seem mechanical, thumpy, the opposite of musical; melodiousness vanishes in rigid piston pounding or the sewing machine's yatter.

To equate rigid angularity of structure with musicality is also to make an error about the nature of music. Symmetry of phrase length, rhythmical tidiness, is indeed an aspect of music; but music has another aspect as well, a certain flexibility, impetuosity, freedom from prior constraint, open rein to impulse. Music becomes lively, expressive, vivid when it makes calculated departures from the bar lines, from the notated pitches, by means of *rubato*, *portamento*, agogic subtleties; and poetry too will seem most lyrical when it is sinuous and lithe, tensile, deviant. Ezra Pound may have gone too far when he suggested that the most musical poetry, what he called *melopoeia*, ought to avoid traditional verse forms; Eliot described better how poetry ought to orient itself on the boundary line between free verse and traditional meters:

> the most interesting verse which has yet been written in our language has been done either by taking a very simple form, like the iambic pentameter, and constantly withdrawing from it, or taking no form at all, and constantly approximating to a very simple one. It is this contrast between fixity and flux, this unperceived evasion of monotony, which is the very life of verse. ("Reflections on *Vers Libre*," 1917)

Musical verse is restless, instinct with its own measure, instinct with the urge to escape its measure.

Every age of English poetry has esteemed lyric poetry according to its own formula, its own sense of the proper mixture of regular and irregular elements. And what one age considers a liberation from the old constraints, a finely modulated and pleasingly asymmetrical style of verse, will often seem to the next age hopelessly stiff, plodding, foursquare. Keats thought himself part of a movement to smash Augustan metronomic rigidity:

> . . . with a puling infant's force
> They sway'd about upon a rocking horse,
> And thought it Pegasus.
> ("Sleep and Poetry," 1816, lines 185–87)

And a century later D. H. Lawrence would in turn feel the need to take a hammer to the verse of Keats:

> This completeness, this consummateness, the finality and the perfection are conveyed in exquisite form: the perfect symmetry, the rhythm which returns upon itself like a dance . . . these are the treasured gem-like lyrics of Keats and Shelley.
>
> But there is another kind of poetry: the poetry of that which is at hand: the immediate present. In the immediate present there is no perfection, no consummation, nothing finished. The strands are all flying, quivering, intermingling into the web, the waters are shaking the moon. . . . There are no gems of the living plasm. ("Poetry of the Present," 1918)

To each generation the work of the previous generation ossifies into metrical orthodoxy, so each must invent its own style of evading it, of approaching the singing line that glides above the halting tum-pum.

What is true of the individual line is also true of larger structures. The vessel that easily holds the matter contained in it is not necessarily a good lyrical structure; the lyric poet often prefers a structure that is overcomplicated, in danger of collapse. Something like the Pindaric ode, in which irregularities multiply into a general structural giddiness, may be ideally lyrical, despite Samuel Johnson's denunciation of Gray's two Pindaric efforts:

> His stanzas are too long . . . the ode is finished before the ear has learned its measures, and consequently before it can receive pleasure from their consonance and recurrence. (*Life* of Gray, 1781, 2:462)

It is possible, however, that a lyric poet might find especially congenial an unlearnable or only half-learnable structure, a teasing structure that permitted only the ghosts of expectations to be felt, a structure of suspensions, arrests, surprises, artful graces, a structure so complex and curvilinear, eccentric, that it seemed to deviate in every limb from some well-known regular design. It is easy to deviate; but to make of deviation a general law takes ingenuity. A poetic structure will seem lyrical if it appears to take an organic form of its own, a kinetic shapeliness at some meeting of extremes between the robot's jerky rigor and the utter laxness of plasm. And a complex and self-entertaining structure, ramified almost beyond its ability to hold its shape, like the Pindaric ode, seems to enforce a certain musicality by its suggestion of some irregular, urgent, or anfractuous melody that lies behind the text and seems to contort the words to fit it.

4. *Personality versus Impersonality*

There is no more often cited nor often doubted conviction about the lyric than that it is an unusually personal form of literature. C. Day Lewis, in *The Lyric Impulse,* notes that, though most of us think of the lyric as "the most personal, intimate kind of poem," a study of English lyrics from 1560 to 1620 shows that we are only rarely, as in the case of Wyatt's "They flee from me," aware of the "individual personality and experience" of the poet; in the usual case the poet and his emotions seem general and conventional, and Day Lewis attributes this to "the discipline imposed . . . by music" (p. 5). Auden also doubts that the lyric has any necessarily personal aspect; his example of a poem that seems almost entirely written by Ariel, the spirit of lyricality, is Peele's "Bathsabe's Song":

> Hot sun, cool fire, tempered with sweet air,
> Black shade, fair nurse, shadow my white hair:
> Shine, sun; burn, fire; breathe, air, and ease me;
> Black shade, fair nurse, shroud me and please me:
> Shadow, my sweet nurse, keep me from burning,
> Make not my glad cause, cause for mourning,
>   Let not my beauty's fire
>   Inflame unstaid desire,
>   Nor pierce any bright eye
>   That wandereth lightly.

Auden comments that the *I* of this poem

> seems anonymous, hardly more than a grammatical form; one cannot imagine meeting Bathsabe at a dinner party. . . . Take away what Bathsabe says and she vanishes, for what she says does not seem to be a response to any specific situation or event. If one asks what her song is about, one cannot give a specific answer, only a vague one: —a beautiful young girl, any beautiful girl, on any sunny morning, half-awake and half-asleep, is reflecting on her beauty, with a mixture of self-admiration and pleasing fear . . . a girl who was really afraid of a Peeping Tom would sing very differently. If one tries to explain why one likes the song, or any poem of this kind, one finds oneself talking about language, the handling of the rhythm, the pattern of vowels and consonants, the placing of caesuras, epanorthosis, etc. (*The Dyer's Hand*, p. 339)

If Auden is right, a purely lyrical poem should be read deconstructively, for any personal authority is a tenuous illusion that readily disperses into language, a field of neutral inflectibles; and if Bathsabe is a nearly perfect avatar of the lyric subject, then it seems that narcissism is the ideal character trait for such a subject, as if the person Bathsabe were but a metaphor for language's own self-engrossment. There is no immediate textual justification for Auden's assertion that Bathsabe is half-asleep, but perhaps few readers would think this wholly unwarranted: in extremely lyrical lyrics there is often this feeling of dreamy inconsequence, of highly patterned verse structures oddly combined with a nearly random movement from one topic or image to the next; the greatest possible tightness combined with the greatest possible looseness. Again we see how structure and amorphousness tend to coexist strangely in a single lyric poem.

In his essay "Interlude: The Wish Game" Auden suggests that "The kind of enjoyment the fairy tale can provide is similar, I believe, to that provided by the poems of Mallarmé or by abstract painting" (*The Dyer's Hand*, p. 214). Auden seems to imagine that all abstract or fanciful or unreal or *lyrical* experiences converge, constitute a single aesthetic phenomenon, the delectation of play; and Ariel is playfulness given a name, impersonality impersonated. Yet Auden is far from advocating a theory of poetical impersonality, in the matter of the lyric or in any other matter. Auden's essays on poetry, while often implying a certain disengagement of the poet from the poem, frequently use a body of all-too-human metaphors to describe what a poem is: for example, in "The Virgin and the Dynamo," he says that

> The subject matter of a poem is comprised of a crowd of recollected occasions of feeling, among which the most important are recollections of encounters with sacred beings or events. This crowd the poet attempts to transform into a community by embodying it in a verbal society. Such a society, like any society in nature, has its own laws; its laws of prosody and syntax are analogous to the laws of physics and chemistry. (*The Dyer's Hand*, p. 67)

Soon thereafter Auden is referring to the poem as a "pseudo-person"; what had been a small society has become a single man. It seems, then, that a lyric poem is impersonal to the extent that it is an uncanny transformation of the poet's feelings into some autonomous domain, an independent city-state from which the poet is henceforth excluded, and to the extent that this transformation is governed by inhuman, almost mathematically rigid rules. And a lyric poem is personal to the extent that the poet may conclude all manner of cozy treaties with this city-state, whose Amphion he is, for it has become a verbal analogue to a human sensibility—though not *his* sensibility—a little eidolon or golem with its own vowel bones and consonant skin. The imagination, Ariel, seems the most impersonal of faculties, for the poet cannot explain whence it plucks its images; but its finished products, once settled and established, grow warm and intimate, personal.

T. S. Eliot's theory of the lyric is also complicated by the puzzle of the personal versus the impersonal. Everyone remembers Eliot as the champion of impersonality because of his remarks, later somewhat embarrassing to him, in his 1919 essay "Tradition and the Individual Talent"; but his important late essay "The Three Voices of Poetry" (1953) gives a fuller account of the poet's relation to his poem. There the difficulty of defining the lyric—he claims that "the word cannot be satisfactorily defined"—drives him to quoting the *Oxford English Dictionary*:

> *Lyric:* Now the name for short poems, usually divided into stanzas or strophes, and directly expressing the poet's own thoughts and sentiments. (*On Poetry and Poets*, p. 105)

Eliot then makes the usual refutation, pointing out that "Come unto these yellow sands" (Ariel's song, *The Tempest* 1.2) and "Hark! hark! the lark" can scarcely be said to be direct expression of a poet's own thoughts and sentiments, while Samuel Johnson's "London" and "The Vanity of Human Wishes," which no one thinks lyrical, do appear to be such expressions. Eliot then offers as a tentative substitute for the *OED*'s definition of the lyric what he calls the *first voice* of poetry, that of the poet talking to himself, or to nobody. This is the sort of poetry in which, unlike the second voice, that of the poet talking to an audience, or the third voice, that of the dramatist, the poet assumes no public persona whatever; his text is only *overheard* (p. 109) by readers to whom the poem is in no sense addressed. Eliot elaborates his notion of the first voice with the help of Gottfried Benn's lecture "Probleme der Lyrik," in which the German poet said that the origin of the lyric poem was "an inert embryo or 'creative germ' " (p. 106), something within him for which he must find words:

> When you have the words for it, the "thing" for which the words had to be found has disappeared, replaced by a poem. What you start from is nothing so definite as an emotion, in any ordinary sense; it is still more certainly not an idea; it is—to adapt two lines of Beddoes to a different meaning—a
>
> *bodiless childful of life in the gloom*
> *Crying with frog voice, "what shall I be?"*
>
> I agree with Gottfried Benn, and I would go a little further. In a poem which is neither didactic nor narrative . . . the poet may be concerned solely with expressing in verse—using all his resources of words, with their history, their connotations, their music—this obscure impulse. He does not know what he has to say until he has said it. . . . He is oppressed by a burden which he must bring to birth in order to obtain relief. Or, to change the figure, he is haunted by a demon, a demon against which he feels powerless, because in its first manifestation it has no face, no name, nothing; and the words, the poem he makes, are a kind of form of exorcism of this demon. (*On Poetry and Poets,* pp. 106–7)

A poem, then, displays underneath itself what it was before it was made into words, its own preexistence, a state of incoherent irritation that disturbs the poet until he takes the trouble to articulate it, to give it reality. This myth of the origin of the poem has many features in common with Auden's, but whereas Auden takes intuitions of the sacred, then decrees that these feelings be given civil rights, Eliot seems to think of the stuff poetry is made on as a tapeworm or tubal pregnancy, something alien and almost malign growing within him, which must be excised, exorcised, and allowed to assume its own strange being. A few pages later he calls this prepoem "the octopus or angel with which the poet struggles"; and this whole line of imagery is central to Eliot's thought and work. In his dissertation he speaks of the novelist's "really 'vital' characters" as "a sort of parasitic growth upon the author's personality, developing by internal necessity" (*Knowledge and Experience in the Philosophy of F. H. Bradley*, p. 124); and perhaps the most terrifying moment in *Murder in the Cathedral* is the chorus's announcement that "I have tasted / The living lobster, the crab, the oyster, the whelk and the prawn; and they live and spawn in my bowels, and my bowels dissolve in the light of dawn" (*Complete Poems and Plays*, p. 207). It seems that the measure of the lyricality of a poem is the fullness of its allusion to that state anterior to its writing, to its being brought into the light of words. Seen in this perspective, many of Eliot's most powerful passages can be interpreted as allegories of the process by which demon, octopus, or angel—the prepoem—is given verbal form; for example, the third part of *Ash-Wednesday* records a struggle with a demon:

> At the first turning of the second stair
> I turned and saw below
> The same shape twisted on the banister
> Under the vapour in the fetid air
> Struggling with the devil of the stairs who wears
> The deceitful face of hope and of despair.
>
> At the second turning of the second stair
> I left them twisting, turning below;
> There were no more faces and the stair was dark,
> Damp, jaggèd, like an old man's mouth drivelling,
> beyond repair,
> Or the toothed gullet of an agèd shark.

It is as if the poet is meditating upon the perplexities of the process of composition, the difficult passage from the state of vague self-inquisition, confrontation with the demon, to the finite achieved image: the doubtful specters wrestling on a turning stair vanish, and what take their place are the potent images of the old man's mouth and the shark's gullet, satisfying objective correlatives to the feelings behind the poem. In the next stanza other, lovelier images clarify themselves in the poet's imagination—a Maytime flutist in a pastoral scene—only to be dismissed, as if the process of lyrical composition ought to complete itself in a resorption of the images back into the indistinctness from which they came. But this final collapse of the lyrical into its creative germ is no part of Eliot's official theory, only a hint we may wish to take from his poetical practice.

Eliot's account of the development of the lyric discusses and to some extent attempts to reconcile all the paradoxes we have seen so far: the lyric is a highly structured thing that everywhere appeals to some profound shapelessness, to that octopus or state of amoebic dysentery out of which it springs; the lyric is up-to-date, indeed aggressively modern, yet it begins "with a savage beating a drum in a jungle, and it retains that essential of percussion and rhythm; hyperbolically one might say that the poet is *older* than other human beings" (*The Use of Poetry and the Use of Criticism*, p. 155); and the lyric is at once impersonal, in that it dispenses with every mask or pretense of dramatic character, and personal, in that it is the product of the most intense sort of self-communion.

Of the great modern authors, James Joyce perhaps takes the strongest stand on the personalness of the lyric; yet we will see that his theory does not differ greatly from Eliot's. In the famous disquisition on genre in *A Portrait of the Artist as a Young Man*, Stephen Dedalus asserts that literature originates in undifferentiated lyric energy:

> The lyrical form is in fact the simplest verbal vesture of an instant of emotion, a rhythmical cry such as ages ago cheered on the man who pulled at the oar or dragged stones up a slope. He who utters it is more conscious of the instant of emotion than of himself as feeling emotion. The simplest epical form is seen emerging out of lyrical

> literature when the artist prolongs and broods upon himself as the centre of an epical event and the form progresses till the centre of emotional gravity is equidistant from the artist himself and from others. The narrative is no longer purely personal. The personality of the artist passes into the narration itself, flowing round and round the persons and the action like a vital sea. This progress you will see easily in that old English ballad *Turpin Hero* which begins in the first person and ends in the third person. The dramatic form is reached when the vitality which has flowed and eddied round each person fills every person with such vital force that he or she assumes a proper and intangible esthetic life. The personality of the artist, at first a cry or a cadence or a mood and then a fluid and lambent narrative, finally refines itself out of existence, impersonalises itself, so to speak. (*A Portrait*, pp. 214–15)

It is well known that Joyce was influenced by Yeats, and I believe that Stephen's word *mood* here carries the full implications of Yeats's usage. Yeats's doctrine of the moods specified that human emotion is not, as we commonly imagine, something private, our own personal property, but instead is something given to us from outside: "moods are the labourers and messengers of the Ruler of All, the gods of ancient days still dwelling on their secret Olympus, the angels of more modern days ascending and descending upon their shining ladder" (*Essays and Introductions*, p. 195). By ourselves we can feel nothing; our feelings belong to some alien deity or are gods themselves. For Yeats such speculations belong to his project of affiliating himself as intimately as possible with an exterior *anima mundi*, the warehouse of symbols; and while Stephen Dedalus is not quite so strict an aesthete, he nevertheless emphasizes here that in the lyric it is not the man that speaks but the emotion—an individuated speaker belongs to a later, "epical" phase in the progress of literature. The rowers and stone haulers of this passage are not beasts to be humanized by Orpheus, nor are they savages to be hypnotized by the poet's tom-tom; they are similarly figments of the prehistoric, half-embodied creatures of pure mindless feeling. The lyric mode addresses itself to feeling before it has entered the province of the human, the complex. According to Joyce's historical myth, the lyric is literature before it has descended to earth, grown weighty and acute from observation and rich knowledge of things. According to the hydrodynamic metaphor, the lyric is vaporous, cloudy, not yet precipitated into rain or congealed into fixed form. The lyric, then, is not so much personal as prepersonal, pertinent to some fantastic antiquity when feelings were not yet fully human.

But of course Joyce does not imagine that any modern lyric would closely resemble the song of the Volga boatmen; and shortly after defining the lyric, Stephen Dedalus writes a new one to show us how a refined sensibility would approach this task. He is inspired with the desire to write when he wakes at dawn, "conscious of faint sweet music," feeling on himself the passionless breathing of some seraphic spirit, "An enchantment of the heart":

> The instant of inspiration seemed now to be reflected from all sides at once from a multitude of cloudy circumstances of what had happened or of what might have happened. The instant flashed forth like a point of light and now from cloud on cloud of vague circumstance confused form was veiling softly its afterglow. O! In the virgin womb of the imagination the word was made flesh. . . . An afterglow deepened within his spirit, whence the white flame had passed, deepening to a rose and ardent light. That rose and ardent light was her strange wilful heart, strange that no man had known or would know, wilful from before the beginning of the world: and lured by that ardent roselike glow the choirs of the seraphim were falling from heaven.
>
> *Are you not weary of ardent ways,*
> *Lure of the fallen seraphim?*
> *Tell no more of enchanted days.*
>
> The verses passed from his mind to his lips and, murmuring them over, he felt the rhythmic movement of a

> villanelle pass through them. The roselike glow sent forth its rays of rhyme; ways, days, blaze, praise, raise. Its rays burned up the world, consumed the hearts of men and angels: the rays from the rose that was her wilful heart. (*A Portrait*, p. 217)

This account of the operations of the imagination is also an imitation of them, for almost every word of the finished villanelle exists in an unstructured form, as if the account were a prose matrix not yet constellated into a poem, all the members spread out for critical inspection like a patient etherized upon a table; and the villanelle itself is an imitation of the operations of the imagination, for it describes the descent to earth of images that could have kept their celestial indeterminateness if only Stephen's girl friend E. C. had not tempted them, made them fall into poetry, a *felix culpa.* The texture of the prose account is at once incantatory and jumbled, with inchoate meters felt on the edges as words fall through the allotropic states of their rhymes. To this extent the prose account is more lyrical than the poem, or perhaps one should say it is an attempt to prove the poem's lyricality by showing the *mood,* the angel of the poem, before it entered the sublunary sphere of verbal composition. The terms "enchantment of the heart" and "afterglow" recall Stephen's elucidation of creative process to Lynch, where he quoted with approval both Volta's phrase and Shelley's description of the mind as a fading coal. The original passage in Shelley reads like an outline or summary of Stephen's prose account of his poem:

> the mind in creation is as a fading coal, which some invisible influence, like an inconstant wind, awakens to transitory brightness: this power arises from within, like the colour of a flower which fades and changes as it is developed, and the conscious portions of our natures are unprophetic either of its approach or its departure. Could this influence be durable in its original purity and force, it is impossible to predict the greatness of the results; but when composition begins, inspiration is already on the decline, and the most glorious poetry that has ever been

> communicated to the world is probably a feeble shadow of the original conception of the Poet. (*A Defence of Poetry*, ed. John E. Jordan, p. 71)

The critic M. T. Solve has suggested that Shelley accepts here Plotinus's "notion of creation as a falling-away from the perfection of the ideal" (*Shelley: His Theory of Poetry*, p. 43); and it is the purpose of Joyce's prose account to make dim suggestions of that preimaginative glory from which the poem, with its clear structures and definite images, is a falling away. Joyce is even Shelleyan in his choice of colors, for the original inspiration is white light, while the afterglow is rose and ardent, colorful, like the "dome of many-colored glass" that "Stains the white radiance of eternity" (*Adonais*, lines 462–63); and the colors remind Stephen of E. C.'s lurid heart, of all the mire and intricacy of human passion. A lyrical poem, of course, is embedded in the texture of personal relations—Stephen imagines E. C. reading it at the breakfast table and perhaps letting its author be mocked—but it resonates with those transpersonal originalities that brought it into being, that it is a shadow of. At either end of the progress of literature there is impersonality, for in the beginning there is lyric indefiniteness and at the end there is dramatic overrefinement; but after reading *A Portrait* we feel not that there are three different kinds of literary works, but that there are three moments to an ongoing literary process, the first of which is called the lyric and contains in itself the momentum to pass onward into the epic and the dramatic, the increasingly stiff and sharp-edged forms. Every lyric poem recapitulates the whole history of literature; similarly, the prose account of the villanelle echoes the opening pages of *A Portrait*, as if every poet became an infant at the moment of inspiration. The actual villanelle is less lyrical than that from which it came, and indeed anything with real verbal or material existence is to some extent contaminated, heavy, unlyrical in the gnostic theory of Shelley and Joyce, and Yeats too:

> I can see nothing plain; all's mystery.
> Yet sometimes there's a torch inside my head
> That makes all clear, but when the light is gone

I have but images, analogies,
The mystic bread, the sacramental wine,
The red rose . . .
(*The Shadowy Waters*, lines 131–36)

The ideal lyric, being pure music and pure feeling and yet words, cannot be written at all.

5. *Embodiment versus Disembodiment*

I have been speaking as if the lyric were a species of ether, having no commerce with the low world of solid forms. But this assertion, like many assertions about the lyric, is only a partial truth, and we must consider its antithesis. Surely many lyric poems are notably physical, corporeal, showing the surges, the spurtings, the muscularities, the thrusts of the body:

Awe bleteth after lomb,
Lhouth after calve cu,
Bulluc sterteth, bucke verteth–
Murie sing, cuccu!
Cuccu, cuccu.
Wel singes thu, cuccu.
Ne swik thu naver nu!

In a great many lyrics of the thirteenth to fifteenth centuries, we can see a deep embodiedness, a clinging to the carnal, as if medieval poets were drunk on their own blood:

Beware, therefore: the blind eateth many a fly.

The whins shall prick thee to the bare bane.

And in that bed there lieth a knight,
His woundes bleeding day and night. . . .
And by that bed's side there standeth a stone,
Corpus Christi written thereon.

Here is a general looming of the body. If from one point of view it seems that the lyric is that which resists embodiment, then from another point of view it seems that the lyric is that which demands embodiment; which has no existence other than as an immanence, a physical presence. On one hand the lyric aspires to be a wordless melody; on the other hand it is verbal, nothing but verbal, exclusively a matter of verbal color, clamor, birdcalls, farts, grunts, yodels. Wordsworth identified this paradox exactly in the course of a discussion of the affinity between religion and poetry:

> religion—whose element is infinitude, and whose ultimate trust is in the supreme of things, submitting herself to circumscription, and reconciled to substitutions; and poetry—ethereal and transcendent, yet incapable to sustain her existence without sensuous incarnation. ("Essay, Supplementary to the Preface")

Elsewhere in his work, when Wordsworth considered this topic, he was more disturbed by the downward tendency of poetry, its sensuous and incarnate, carnal, nature:

> I select these writers [Milton and Spenser] in preference to those of ancient Greece and Rome, because the anthropomorphitism of the Pagan religion subjected the minds of the greatest poets in those countries too much to the bondage of definite form; from which the Hebrews were preserved by their abhorrence of idolatry. This abhorrence was almost as strong in our great epic Poet. . . . Imagination . . . recoils from everything but the plastic, the pliant, and the indefinite. (1815 Preface)

By Wordsworth's standards, the Cuckoo Song and the other old lyrics cited above, despite the fact of their Christian provenance, are idolatrous; possibly none of their authors would have understood this charge, but it is perhaps true that every demonstration of words delighting in their own verbality tends to erect a little autonomous kingdom of art, neither man's world nor God's.

Wordsworth's distinction between idolatrous and sublime poetry, between the definite and the indefinite, will help us distinguish the former species of lyric from true mimesis, from anthropology and Zola. Mimetic art aspires to transparency: every deftness of language, every revel in the colors and textures of words, tends to defeat its goal, which is to endow the shadowy world of reference behind the words with the illusion of mass, gravity, depth of focus. The embodied lyric, on the other hand, aspires to opacity: it does not represent, it *is*. Through this uncontingency of being it becomes the Golden Calf, splendid, bellowing, locomotive. A representation of the song of a cuckoo is a different matter from an attempt to sing cuckoowise; as onomatopoeia keeps growing denser and more insistent, we become increasingly aware of the poem itself as the source of noise, not some unreal bird or buck behind the poem. As the lyric gains its own verbal heft and coil its referential functions grow debilitated: the Cuckoo Song does not show Spring; it Springs. Similarly the sense of penetration into the body's pith, in a certain species of lyric, attempts not to imitate a shudder but to make the reader shudder:

> The whins shall prick thee to the bare bane.
> ("A Lyke-Wake Dirge," fifteenth century)

> A bracelet of bright hair about the bone.
> (Donne, "The Relic," 1633)

> But never met this Fellow
> Attended, or alone
> Without a tighter breathing
> And Zero at the Bone—
> (Dickinson, #986, 1866)

> He knew the anguish of the marrow
> The ague of the skeleton;
> No contact possible to flesh
> Allayed the fever of the bone.
> (Eliot, "Whispers of Immortality," 1918)

> Their [Donne's and Webster's] words have often a network of tentacular roots reaching down to the deepest terrors and desires. (Eliot, "Ben Jonson," 1919)

> He that sings a lasting song
> Thinks in a marrow-bone;
> (Yeats, "A Prayer for Old Age," 1934)

In these lines there is an investigation of the innermost nervous system, a probing into the quick. The more immediately we respond to such bold inquisition into our bodies, the more there is a breakdown between poet, poem, and reader: we do not feel that we are reading a sober clinical report of a certain sensation, we feel that stab, that burn, ourselves. The poem seems to have its own body and to be manipulating our nerves through a kind of voodoo; and indeed in many lyric poems we find words that seem to generate a little body around themselves, thrashing legs, a smiling or scowling face. In this way the lyric tends either to violent disembodiment or to some state inextricable from the words that constitute it.

One sophistication of this lyric carnality occurs when a poem starts to show physical responses to its own stanza form, its own technical apparatus:

> RIme the rack of finest wits,
> That expresseth but by fits,
>   True Conceipt.
> Spoyling Senses of their Treasure,
> Cosening Judgement with a measure,
>   But false weight.
> Wresting words, from their true calling;
> Propping Verse, for feare of falling
>   To the ground.
> Joynting Syllabes, drowning Letters,
> Fastning Vowells, as with fetters
>   They were bound! . . .
> He that first invented thee,
> May his joynts tormented bee,
>   Cramp'd forever . . .
> (Jonson, "A Fit of Rime against Rime," 1640)

It seems that the poem's sense has its own sensibility, a frail, suffering intelligence racked and deformed by the torsion of the rhyme scheme, the poem's structure; the poet, the poem, and the inventor of rhyme are all consigned to an infernal torture chamber. Auden likes to speak of a poem as a pseudoperson, and Jonson too seems to personify the poem, or almost personify it, for it is as if the poem were a crustacean trapped in a too-tight exoskeleton, or a hermit crab that had outgrown its borrowed shell. Insofar as the embodied lyric manages to constitute its own world instead of referring to our world, it is proper for this domain to be populated not with human beings like ourselves, but with technical figments, half-personifications of its structural attributes, King Rhyme, Queen Meter, various attendant vowels and consonants. One of the charms of Puttenham's *The Arte of English Poesie* is his habit of treating figures of speech as little people:

> the figure [*Zeugma*] we call him the [*single supply*] because by one word we serve many clauses of one congruitie, and may be likened to the man that serves many maisters at once, but all of one country or kindred. . . .
>
> . . . then is he called by the Greeks *Prozeugma,* by us the Ringleader . . . it is by the Greeks called *Mezozeugma,* by us the [*Middlemarcher*]. . . .
>
> . . . the Greekes call him *Prolepsis,* we the Propounder . . . we ought rather to call him the forestaller, for like as he that standes in the market way, and takes all up before it come to the market in grosse and sells it by retaile, so by this maner of speach our maker setts down before all the matter by a brief proposition, and afterward explanes it by a division more particularly. (3, chapter 12)

Like many early grammarians Puttenham never forgets that figures of speech exert an intelligent control on discourse, behave quasi-mentally, or that meters are best conceived as dance steps, characteristic gaits by which poems walk or run or stride or saunter or step haltingly; that meters are legs, or the nerves and muscles that guide legs. It is a sign of our modern distance from the notion of the poem as a genuinely embodied thing that many students can recognize a dactyl, or a trochee, or an iamb, or a spondee; but few seem to know that a dactyl is a finger, a three-jointed, flexible beckoning member; or that a trochee is a tripping run; or that an iamb, originally a satirical foot, comes from a verb meaning "to wound" or "to smite one's breast"; or that the spondee, slow and solemn, is derived from the libation ceremony at which it was chanted. All these suggestions, whether of fingers, feet, blood, or drinking, pertain to the body, the body's will, the body's exertion.

6. *Brevity*

Here it seems there is no paradox, for all writers and lexicographers are agreed that lyrics should be short; but perhaps here there ought to be a paradox even if there is not. It is certainly true that in any poem, no matter how musical, other, nonlyrical constraints will start to be felt after a certain length: a particular historical author will make himself known, and the heft, the shape, of a particular world will begin to reveal itself in the midst of lyric worldlessness. But there are strategies for neutralizing these tendencies, as we will see in a later chapter, and there are certain effects of lyricality that can be created only in long poems. In the Elizabethan sonnet sequences of Spenser, Sidney, Drayton, and Daniel, for example, we see two contrary movements at work as the number of sonnets begins to grow large: first, the lady grows particular, predictable, human, and the poet's relation to her takes on certain discursive, novelistic qualities—both lovers descend out of Petrarchan musicality into time and space; but second, the mere fact of the excessive and incredible verbality of this manner of courtship, the fact that the lover seems to be spending all his time writing sonnets, the fact that he seems to woo the muse more ardently than his lady, tend to unrealize poet and beloved, to disintegrate the illusion of a historical situation. The rhetoric may grow more and more desperate and impassioned, but this desperation, this passion, seems less and less to admit of any human solution; the sequence turns itself inward, becomes self-engrossed and world-exclusive, and the massive and unwieldly instruments of persuasion are elaborated to such a degree that the poet is surrounded by the thick walls of the poem, unable even to catch a glimpse of his lady. This is the movement back into the lyrical. But the greatest maker of the extended lyric is Shakespeare, the true master of Ariel.

ARIEL

One strategy for isolating the lyrical component of poetry is to study those poems that seem supremely lyrical, those poems in which the admixture of nonlyrical elements is kept to a minimum. This was Auden's goal when he chose Peele's "Bathsabe's Song" as an example of a poem in which Ariel's contribution, the delight in abstract patterns for their own sake, was as little as possible disturbed by Prospero's will to verisimilitude. But most students, when asked to name an ideally lyrical lyric, would probably say something else; many might say "Kubla Khan" or "Lycidas" or something by the early Yeats, and not a few might pick Ariel's own most famous song:

Full fathom five thy father lies;
  Of his bones are coral made;
Those are pearls that were his eyes;
  Nothing of him that doth fade
But doth suffer a sea-change
Into something rich and strange.
Sea-nymphs hourly ring his knell:
Burden. Ding-dong.
Ari. Hark! now I hear them,—ding-dong, bell.
(*The Tempest*, 1.2.396–404)

A notable feature of this song is the combination of the theme of unnaturalness with a certain metrical phenomenon, the line of seven syllables in catalectic trochaic tetrameter (not every line is of this sort, but it is the predominant meter). This combination also appears in certain modern poems, such as Yeats's "Under Ben Bulben," in several other songs by Shakespeare, and in his strange lyric "The Phoenix and the Turtle," which treats the unnatural theme of a childless, sexless marriage—insofar as any intelligible theme can be discerned—and in which the emphatic beat of the seven-syllable line, with its cymbal clash between the end of each line and the beginning of the next, its heightened contrast between stressed and unstressed syllables, makes for a fierce incantation:

Let the bird of loudest lay,
On the sole Arabian tree,
Herald sad and trumpet be,
To whose sound chaste wings obey.

But thou shrieking harbinger,
Foul precurrer of the fiend,
Augur of the fever's end,
To this troop come thou not near!

From this session interdict
Every fowl of tyrant wing,
Save the eagle, feath'red king;
Keep the obsequy so strict!

Let the priest in surplice white,
That defunctive music can,
Be the death-divining swan,
Lest the requiem lack his right.
(lines 1–16)

It is as if the poem were itself the charm that excludes the improper species of birds, itself the liturgy of the requiem for Love and Constancy, the phoenix and the turtle. This powerful metrical form—"To this troop come thou not near!"—is also used in *A Midsummer Night's Dream* as an invocation to protect the sleeping Titania:

You spotted snakes with double tongue,
  Thorny hedgehogs, be not seen;
Newts and blind-worms, do no wrong
  Come not near our fairy queen.
(2.2.9–12)

The seven-syllable line is especially magical, useful for delimiting the charmed circle in which art operates, for making the circle inviolable by lower, coarser creation, and for dissolving and refining the separate elements in the circle into a single purity:

Here the anthem doth commence:
Love and Constancy is dead;
Phoenix and the turtle fled
In a mutual flame from hence.

So they lov'd as love in twain
Had the essence but in one:
Two distincts, division none:
Number there in love was slain.
("The Phoenix and the Turtle," lines 21–28)

Fillet of a fenny snake,
In the cauldron boil and bake;
Eye of newt and toe of frog,
Wool of bat and tongue of dog,
Adder's fork and blind-worm's sting,
Lizard's leg and howlet's wing,
For a charm of pow'rful trouble,
Like a hell-broth boil and bubble.
(*Macbeth*, 4.1.12–19)

In the imagination of Shakespeare, the seven-syllable line is appropriate for the subject of transcendence, the shivery isolation and immunity of the supernatural; but at the fringes of heavenly uniqueness and ineffability there teems a puzzling throng of primitive and slimy living things, bats, snakes, newts, small horrors. Yeats was impressed by the vision of a friend of his in which Absolute Being appeared in the image of a slug, as if the lowest, least organized form of life were somehow like God (*A Vision*, p. 284); and Shakespeare too seems to have had an intuition of the convergence of the high and the low, the Nilotic mud and the sun that breeds maggots from it. It is as if he needs to summon up the energies of the catalectic meter to chase away the frogs, the lizards, the harbingers of the fiend, precisely because amorphous, swarming nocturnal life was so intimate with, so inseparable from, his vision of the supernal and the single, the timeless and spaceless.

When we turn back to Ariel's song, we see that its theme is also the theme of banishing. What is excluded here is not the unpleasant host of reptiles and raptors, but the fact of death. In real life a drowned man grows soft and swollen, a dissipated thing; but Ariel says that exactly the opposite is happening, that King Alonso is becoming harder, more impervious than a living man; in death he is turning into his own monument, a statue of himself, a physical image of the immutability and perfection of the soul in heaven. In the neo-Platonic mythology of which Yeats and other poets have been fond, water is associated with the generation of images, partly because a film of water will, when smooth, reflect, when agitated, disperse; and so it is right that Ariel, as the spirit of imagination, should dwell with water as well as air, that the sea should be the agent of sea change. What Ariel is announcing, though Ferdinand is not yet supposed to understand, is that King Alonso has departed from earth not into the afterlife, but into the province of the lyrical, where one of the governing principles is the easy transmutability of images, their refusal to stay in any usual shape.

The study of Shakespeare's incantatory songs suggests that the lyric is a tense joining of two modalities: an unnatural stasis and a too natural excess of flow. It seems that the lyric is fascinated with the notion of a metamorphosis that happens once and for all, whether it is the conflagration of the phoenix and the turtle that reduces them to one changeless self-contained emblem of perfection, or it is the translation of Alonso into coral and pearls. In fact, though, the very impulse that drives human beings into statues, trees, and other immortalities will also tend to resist any final resting place; the imagination, freed of all constraint except the constraint of song, of design, will demand, no matter how lovely the attained shape, a further flux of images. The ear is avid for novelty, and the hearer is restless for a change of harmony, for variation. Metamorphosis is to poetry what variation is to music, just as the static image is to poetry what a continuous tonic, a pedal point, is to music. Here is the reason newts and worms keep threatening the peripheries of lyrical heaven: the amphibian and the larval are emblems for the further encroachment of the metamorphic principle upon the stable satisfying image. At the end of "Full fathom five" a chorus of sea nymphs exsurges to ring a bell, just as at the end of Ariel's previous song, "Come unto these yellow sands," a chorus of barking dogs and crowing roosters joined in the celestial invitation; again there is a tendency for low animal vitality, the aggressively natural, to rise up at the moment when it seems that all commonplace things are hushed, quelled, by the potent operations of supernature. But what passes for nature in the lyric mode is not much like nature as it is beheld by botanists, zoologists, anthropologists, Zola. Lyrical nature is simply a clamor of indistinct shapes and sounds, a ceaseless transshifting of theriomorphs through the whole domain of the sensible, a condition of dreamy lability in which nothing alights on solid form. Lyrical nature is like the witches' stew in *Macbeth*, in which severed limbs and fins and fur all swirl together in a viscid mass, work down toward protoplasm. When one is inside a song, that is what outer nature looks like: a welter of buzzing half-created things.

Ariel tells Ferdinand that his father has fossilized, become a statue; but of course his father is really still alive, struggling toward his destiny on another part of the island. One of the great themes of Shakespeare's late romances is this theme of false death, of the veering of father, mother, wife, or sister into a state of suspended animation. In *Cymbeline*, for example, King Cymbeline's sons Guiderius and Arviragus come across what seems to be the corpse of a fair young man, though it is really their still-living sister Imogen; they decide to bury "him" next to the grave of their mother, and they sing a burying song that is the second best of Shakespeare's seven-syllable-line songs, though the meter is lightened and smoothed by a number of acatalectic lines:

Gui. Fear no more the heat o' th' sun,
        Nor the furious winter's rages;
Thou thy worldly task hast done,
        Home art gone, and ta'en thy wages.
Golden lads and girls all must,
As chimney-sweepers, come to dust.

Arv. Fear no more the frown o' th' great;
        Thou art past the tyrant's stroke.
Care no more to clothe and eat;
        To thee the reed is as the oak.
The sceptre, learning, physic, must
All follow this, and come to dust.

(4.2.258–69)

What is notable about lyrical death is that it represents a loss of variety. Life is rich and carefully discriminated; but to a dead man the reed and the oak look the same, and summer and winter, gold and dirt, joy and moaning, the raw and the cooked, all those patterns of opposition by which we make sense of the world, have collapsed into a singleness. All the vectors of living things have converged at one point, dust, into which all frantic action vanishes. It is the same lyric fascination with the immobile that beguiles Ferdinand in *The Tempest*, but here the singers do not know that this death is unnatural, strictly lyrical, that no real infection of mortality has made itself felt at all. The song, with its famous pun that might seem heartless in real life, with its peculiar undercurrent of exuberance, of delight in the manifold, imposes upon the scene its own lyric unreality; a place appropriate for such a song is a place in which any strangeness, any shape change may occur, in which the truth of surrogates is so fully established that the charms sung over a dead mother's grave may bring an actual sister back to life. This poem, like other poems with seven-syllable lines, is a lyric of exclusion: not only does it announce that the heat of the sun, the furious winter's rages, the all-dreaded thunderstone are excluded from the realm of the dead, it also ends (as Shakespeare's career as a poet ends, if the verse on his tombstone is the last thing he wrote) with a prayer against disturbance of a grave—"Ghost unlaid forbear thee!" But the lyric of exclusion secretly demands the inclusion of all that it seems to push away, and the replete world of summer and winter, tyrants and lightning, that seems to have been tamed into a monotony, is made to retreat only so that its liveliness, its juiciness, may flow back in the final comic movement of the play. The sister seems to turn to dust, the father to coral and pearls, only for the sake of further refreshment; they are invigorated, made healthy, by their sojourn in the lyrical. Having been pushed into an anti-world by some contamination in common life, they return all the more beautiful as soon as common life can develop some of the patternedness, the symmetry, of a lyric.

If the usual movement of a lyric is a sort of experimentation in the satisfactoriness of images, as though the poet were a doting mother who was never content until her daughter had tried on every hat in the store—it is typical for the poet to dismiss even the loveliest image after it has been perfected, to readjust his unworldly topics back into the domain of the ordinary—then the Shakespearean romance is a single lyric writ large. In *Pericles* and *The Winter's Tale* one can find songs, but not of the incantatory sort with seven-syllable lines; it seems the play as a whole has to work to provide a silent or purely instrumental equivalent to "Full fathom five" or "Fear no more." Ariel sings of a father who turns into a statue; in *The Winter's Tale* a mother is disguised as a statue, by tricks of makeup and theatrical presentation, though she too will thaw back into human flesh as the play ends. To enter the mode of the lyrical is a desperate strategy, not to be embarked upon lightly; Hermione has to spend sixteen years of unliving, of residence in an antiworld, because of Leontes' pathological and random jealousy; similarly, Daphne and Philomela underwent their lyrical metamorphoses into laurel and nightingale only under the extreme provocation of rape and mutilation. But once someone has been converted into an image, he or she falls under the rules of the imagination, becomes rigid or plastic in the memory of lovers, brothers, sons—Leontes cannot understand how a statue of a long-dead woman could have wrinkles unknown in experience, and indeed her whole petrification, her false death, was the response of a woman menaced by a malign attempt to freeze her in an unnaturally juvenile dream, to force her to exclude all but her husband from her affection. She becomes susceptible to odd events dictated by a logic in which a nearly contentless will to design is the operant principle. The rhythm of lyricality, with its sudden haltings and suspensions, its half-suppressed wealth of interchangeabilities, its final abandonment of song for speech, determines the development of such characters as Alonso, Marina, Hermione. They attain for a while the quality of pure artifice; and if Shakespeare sometimes speaks of them as if they were statues, it is because no dramatist can display the ideal lyric transformation, that of man into song.

So far it has seemed that high lyricality in Shakespeare is a condition of struggling out of exterior messiness into aesthetic exaltation, but there is another kind of lyricality in his work in which ecstasy is notably unpleasant, ugly. "Full fathom five" and "The Phoenix and the Turtle" are poems in which the metamorphic energies of the lyric are concentrated on one supreme act of translation. At the other extreme the energies of metamorphosis run wild; everything changes into everything else, and chaos swallows every finite image. The list of ingredients in the witches' stew in *Macbeth* is clearly working in this direction, but the purest example of this modality in Shakespeare is the great ranting scene in *Timon of Athens:*

> *Timon.* Wouldst thou have thyself fall in the confusion of men, and remain a beast with the beasts?
> *Apemantus.* Ay, Timon.
> *Tim.* A beastly ambition, which the gods grant thee t' attain to! If thou wert the lion, the fox would beguile thee. If thou wert the lamb, the fox would eat thee. If thou wert the fox, the lion would suspect thee, when peradventure thou wert accus'd by the ass. If thou wert the ass, thy dulness would torment thee, and still thou liv'dst but as a breakfast to the wolf. If thou wert the wolf, thy greediness would afflict thee. . . . What beast couldst thou be, that were not subject to a beast? And what a beast art thou already, that seest not thy loss in transformation!
> (4.3.325–37, 346–49)

> The sun's a thief, and with his great attraction
> Robs the vast sea; the moon's an arrant thief,
> And her pale fire she snatches from the sun;
> The sea's a thief, whose liquid surge resolves
> The moon into salt tears; the earth's a thief,
> That feeds and breeds by a composture stol'n
> From gen'ral excrement; each thing's a thief;
> (4.3.439–45)

Though the bewilderment here almost exceeds the power of meter to contain it, I am not sure that these passages are not as *lyrically* impressive as any song of Ariel's. All steady grasp on a particular image has been lost; Timon can only exuberate into ever more dizzy ravings against the universe. This is the lyric of exclusion carried about as far as it can go; and in this vast revulsion the lyric principle seeks to exclude the whole human, the animal, the cosmic, finally even the lyric. This is Ariel with a case of self-hatred; for Timon, though he perceives all things as intermetamorphosable, hates that very alterability, wishes that mankind did not have every sort of idiot frantic beast latent within it—he tells Apemantus he has nothing to gain by becoming an animal. He wishes too that the heavenly bodies were discrete, uninvasive, not subject to the general contagion of greed. The scene in which these speeches occur begins with the tableau of Timon digging for roots, and this digging seems to show an appetite for reality much appalled by the profusion of false appearances in his former life as magnifico; it is as if he seeks to force the earth, the "gen'ral excrement," to yield up the secret principles by which dirt assumes the many likenesses of virtue. As in "Fear no more the heat o' th' sun," the lyric mode attempts to find some basic formlessness that subsists before or after any particular form. It is right that at the heart of his great tirade Timon should revile a poet and a painter—a panegyrist and a maker of flattering portraits—for in him we see the imagination loathing its own immense powers of invention, its capacity to confuse man and lion and lamb and ass, sun and moon and sea and earth. Before he reviles the painter, Timon indulges in the following sarcasm:

> Good honest men! Thou draw'st a counterfeit
> Best in all Athens; thou'rt, indeed, the best;
> Thou counterfeit'st most lively.
>
> (5.1.83–85)

Every image is a violation of what it is an image of, and representation is itself theft. Indeed the speech about the planets as thieves almost suggests that metaphor is a kind of theft, in that the properties of one thing are dubiously appropriated by something else. To Timon, tropes are the diseases of speech.

When Timon urges the bandits to further robbery—"Nothing can you steal, / But thieves do lose it"—at the end of his impressive denunciation of the solar system as a gang of thieves, the bandits are so awestricken that they nearly vow to give up crime. This is the opposite of what Timon is ostensibly urging; and though it would go too far to say that Timon's fury is completely converted into artful speech, it is certainly true that the bandits suddenly, strangely, discover that they have become the audience of a magnificent orator rather than the robbers of a helpless victim. By sheer verbal power Timon has changed the situation from commonplace rascality to a theater of misanthropy. In this lyrical energy, this flurry of mutation, there is a sort of inner hilarity. T. S. Eliot said that Othello delivers himself of his lovely death speech, in which he compares himself to the Turk who threw away a pearl worth more than all his tribe, in order to cheer himself up (*Selected Essays*, p. 111); and Timon too, though here there is no inexplicable intrusion of beauty into the discourse, seems to exercise his imaginative powers to the utmost as a nearly final act of self-dismissal, a preparation for suicide. The rage against mankind deflects into endless chains of likenesses, and emotion seems to grow more interested in the lyrical delirium it provokes than in itself. This tendency is clearer in another passage concerned with universal derangement:

> But with thy brawls thou hast disturb'd our sport.
> Therefore the winds, piping to us in vain,
> As in revenge, have suck'd up from the sea
> Contagious fogs; which, falling in the land,
> Hath every pelting river made so proud
> That they have overborne their continents.
> The ox hath therefore stretch'd his yoke in vain,
> The ploughman lost his sweat, and the green corn
> Hath rotted ere his youth attain'd a beard. . . .
> And thorough this distemperature we see
> The seasons alter: hoary-headed frosts
> Fall in the fresh lap of the crimson rose,
> And on old Hiems' thin and icy crown
> An odorous chaplet of sweet summer buds
> Is, as in mockery, set; the spring, the summer,
> The childing autumn, angry winter, change

Their wonted liveries; and the mazèd world,
By their increase, now knows not which is which.
And this same progeny of evils comes
From our debate, from our dissension;
We are their parents and original.
(*A Midsummer Night's Dream* 2.1.87–95, 106–17)

This passage begins as an irritable reproach to Oberon about the disturbances that his frustrated obsession with Titania's changeling boy have wrought in the mortal world; his jealousy and his neglect of his fairy duties have caused a wobbling in the seasonal rhythms. It seems at first to be an effective, well-calculated piece of rhetoric; Titania emphasizes the blights, the plagues, the miseries inflicted on mankind; but as she works up speed and vehemence the whole texture changes, grows lyrical, lovely; the images of incongruity, Winter's wreath of buds and the glazed rose, grow settled and striking, a sudden swerve into beauty, until at last the passage sinks back into the rhetorical, into Titania's attempt to persuade Oberon of his guilt. This unforeseeable discovery of form in the midst of formlessness, this odd realization that Chaos has a precisely outlined, lithe young body, like Blake's Los, is crucial to the development of the sense of the lyrical; sweet music is most startling when it is a surprise, most effective when it seems to reconcile the discordant. Timon's ranting is, by contrast, prelyrical or sublyrical, not yet enfolded into that condition in which language grows self-engrossed and dispassionate, though it is moving in that direction. Titania's description of seasonal confusion has moved a good deal further along that path, but it needed a later poet to push it to complete lyricality:

What is the late November doing
With the disturbance of the spring
And creatures of the summer heat,
And snowdrops writhing under feet
And hollyhocks that aim too high
Red into grey and tumble down
Late roses filled with early snow?
Thunder rolled by the rolling stars

Simulates triumphal cars
Deployed in constellated wars
Scorpion fights against the Sun
Until the Sun and Moon go down
Comets weep and Leonids fly
Hunt the heavens and the plains
Whirled in a vortex that shall bring
The world to that destructive fire
Which burns before the ice-cap reigns.
("East Coker," lines 1–17)

This lyric seems closely based on Titania's speech; and the whole lyrical movement of T. S. Eliot's *Four Quartets* is based on a series of careful temporal derangements, as if time had to be pulled apart, or displayed in its most botched state, to reveal those sempiternals that Eliot is seeking. The rose filled with snow, the rose made of flames in "East Coker" 4, the hedgerow blanched with a transitory blossom of snow in "Little Gidding" 1 all suggest an attempt to encompass the timeless by the most evanescent images; the flower triumphs over what would shrivel or scorch it; fire and ice confront each other—it is the old Petrarchan "I burn, I freeze" elaborated into a cosmos of oxymoron—and in the outrageous joining the temporal collapses and the eternal is glimpsed. As in Shakespeare's incantatory lyrics, there is a movement to exclude what is not sacred, coupled with an effort to hoist up something impervious to time, some free-floating loveliness that must yet be embedded in a temporal context—"Only through time time is conquered" ("Burnt Norton" 2). It is generally true that the lyric presupposes some stress in the low, natural world and that out of that stress there emerges an unnaturalness, song, a man made of coral, a glacial rose. This principle is elevated into a mythology of literary history by Yeats, in book 5 of *A Vision*, where he tries to account for the phenomenon that political chaos, the instant of culture he calls Phase One, invariably coincides with some achievement of supreme beauty, what he calls Phase Fifteen, even though his chronological scheme suggests that these moments ought to be a millennium or so apart: "Aphrodite rises from a stormy sea . . . Helen could not be Helen but for a beleaguered Troy" (pp. 267–68). Out of strength there comes forth sweetness; Samson's riddle, as Yeats knew well (see "Vacillation" 8), will serve as a definition of a lyric principle.

But it is better to think of the lyric's tendency to stasis as moving not necessarily toward the sweet or the conventionally beautiful but toward the striking. In the heart of lyric stasis there is a peculiar indifference to the emotional content, although a kind of general suggestiveness, suggestive of nothing in particular, is usually desirable. What is a man to feel when he hears in the course of a song that his father has turned to coral and pearls? No simple response is possible; the image is at once grisly and consoling: grisly because one's father seems to have entered into a marine parody of a living man, consoling because something of him seems to have survived, achieved a sort of transfiguration. Again, the analogy with music is helpful in explaining the emotional slipperiness of the lyric: everyone knows that a piece of music can move our feelings, sometimes to the point of distraction, but it is hard to assign even the most general emotional category to the music. To hear Rossini's opera *Elisabetta, Regina d'Inghilterra* for the first time is always a shock, for this tearjerker begins with the same overture used for *Il Barbiere di Siviglia*, where it seems to represent the friskiest sort of blustering delight; yet it does not take long to readjust one's perspective, to reorient the music into the realm of the tragic. Not even those relations of music and mood that seem almost physiologically ordained, such as the association of fast tempos with excitement and the minor mode with sadness, will in fact stand much scrutiny; similarly part of the ethos of the lyric is its resistance to the usual nomenclature of feeling.

We can see this characteristic clearly when we look at the curious history of the responses that two of the great writers of the twentieth century made to the song "Full fathom five." T. S. Eliot was obsessed with it; not only does "Those are pearls that were his eyes" keep glimmering through *The Waste Land*, but Eliot uses that same line in an essay to stand for the secret processes of Coleridge's transmutation of psychic material into "Kubla Khan":

> The imagery of that fragment, certainly, whatever its origins in Coleridge's reading, sank to the depths of Coleridge's feeling, was saturated, transformed there—"those are pearls that were his eyes"—and brought up into daylight again. But it is not *used:* the poem has not been written. . . . again and again the right imagery, saturated while it lay in the depths of Shakespeare's memory, will rise like Anadyomene from the sea. (*The Use of Poetry and the Use of Criticism,* pp. 146–47)

According to Eliot, the demon or octopus or angel with which Coleridge wrestled—I am returning to the vocabulary of "The Three Voices of Poetry"—was never resolved into its proper verbal equivalent but rose like a kraken shapeless from the deep, whereas Shakespeare managed the sea change so excellently that the dark psychic material was transmogrified into something like Botticelli's *Birth of Venus.* Eliot disparages Coleridge for writing a nonpoem, but Eliot's own work everywhere shows a certain fascination with inchoate things before any coalescence into form. Similarly, he derogates *Hamlet* in a famous essay, taking Shakespeare to task for his inability to find an objective correlative to an unreasonable emotion swollen beyond any possible provocation, and yet he used "The horror! the horror!" from Conrad's *Heart of Darkness* as the epigraph to the first draft of *The Waste Land,* as if infinite and objectless emotion were exactly what Eliot wished to offer the reader of his poem. It is as if Eliot the critic wished to extirpate from Eliot the poet his deep preoccupation with the undone, the indefinite, the jejune, wished to drive him from the flux of metamorphosis, the inconsequence that is one pole of the lyric to the sharply demarcated static forms that constitute its other pole.

But Eliot was not content simply to allude to "Full fathom five" in his poetry and criticism; he also tried, just when he was working on *The Waste Land,* to rewrite Ariel's song in full:

DIRGE

Full fathom five your Bleistein lies
Under the flatfish and the squids.
Grave's Disease in a dead jew's eyes!
When the crabs have eat the lids.
    Lower than the wharf rats dive
        Though he suffer a sea-change
        Still expensive rich and strange

That is lace that was his nose
    See upon his back he lies
(Bones peep through the ragged toes)
    With a stare of dull surprise
        Flood tide and ebb tide
        Roll him gently side to side
        See the lips unfold unfold
        From the teeth, gold in gold
Lobsters hourly keep close watch
Hark! now I hear them   scratch scratch scratch

(*The Waste Land Facsimile*, p. 121)

I think that, while this may not be a good poem, it is more than a burlesque or jape; it is an activation, so to speak, of certain potentials within "Full fathom five" itself. The horror of physical death is considerably transmuted, palliated, by Ariel's description of Alonso's state; but it is nevertheless latent, an emotional energy that is partly responsible for the drive to metamorphosis. Bleistein dissolves while Alonso petrifies, but this dissolution is a running wild of the same tensions that, concentrated, will make Alonso into submarine art. Eliot has simply pushed Ariel's song from one side of the lyric spectrum to the other, from the static image to the ceaseless flux out of which the image rises and into which it will sink. Here "Full fathom five" has been Coleridgized, taken apart into its primal constituents, made into a nonpoem; and indeed Coleridge in his play *Remorse* has a speech somewhat similar to Eliot's "Dirge," in which the protagonist imagines the body of a murdered man disintegrating into protozoa. It is as if Eliot had demonstrated that the music of Shakespeare's song was a refinement of a coarse jingle or folk song, something close to the roots of human anxieties about death. Eliot wrote of Donne and Webster that "Their words have often a network of tentacular roots reaching down to the deepest terrors and desires" (*Selected Essays*, p. 135); and in "Dirge" Eliot has derived these terrors or desires from their flowering in the words of Ariel.

The character of Bleistein, "Chicago Semite Viennese," drowning like Blake's Newton in the waters of materialism, seems as unlyrical as possible, but he is strangely associated with music in Eliot's imagination. In a poem written at about the same time as "Dirge," "Burbank with a Baedeker: Bleistein with a Cigar," Bleistein's

> lustreless protrusive eye
>   Stares from the protozoic slime
> At a perspective of Canaletto.

On one side of the image is the vanishing point of Canaletto's canalscape, the climax of civilization, and on the other side is Bleistein; indeed Canaletto is to this poem what Ariel is to "Dirge," a personification of exquisite art, to which Bleistein has the greatest possible unlikeness; with his eye like a lobster's or an amphibian's he regards this perfection from the greatest possible distance. Not only is Bleistein a squid in the midst of architectural and painterly glory, but he is surrounded by music as well, if the two halves of the poem are in close relation:

> Burbank crossed a little bridge
>   Descending at a small hotel;
> Princess Volupine arrived,
>   They were together, and he fell.
>
> Defunctive music under sea
>   Passed seaward with the passing bell
> Slowly: the God Hercules
>   Had left him, that had loved him well.

The last two lines are, of course, a paraphrase of a comment in *Antony and Cleopatra* (4.3. 16), after a company of soldiers hear mysterious music in the air and under the earth; they interpret this music as a sign of the presence of Hercules abandoning their leader Antony, as if Antony's strength were audibly dispersing around him. Soon Antony will be studying clouds, the rack that dislimns, in which shapes are as indistinct as water in water (4.14. 10–11); and he will tell his friend that "Here I am Antony; / Yet cannot hold this visible shape" (4.14. 13–14). The wonder of Eliot's allusiveness is that he manages to bring to bear on his text such a wealth of reverberations from his source; and I think that he appropriates from Shakespeare's play a whole body of references to dissipating music, dislimning pictures, the undoing of Antony's reputation and even his physical presence. Eliot's theme is the corruption of civilization, its retreat into the swamps from which it rose, and his emblem for this is the sinking of Venice. *Antony and Cleopatra* provided Eliot with vivid illustrations of nobility dissolving, dissolving with an almost kinesthetic immediateness; and so the tourist Burbank blurs out into the canals he came to inspect, and Canaletto's perspective yields place to Bleistein's as civilization resolves into the primal ooze. In the poetry Eliot wrote around 1920 there is frequently a strong feeling of the imminence of slime in all achieved forms, a vision of the protozoic close to the surface of the polished, the civil, the up-to-date; and these intuitions manifest themselves easily in the primary lyrical tension, between endless metamorphoses and the static image.

PROTEUS

Shortly before Eliot wrote "Dirge," James Joyce wrote the "Proteus" chapter of *Ulysses*, which takes almost exactly the same parodic theme:

> Five fathoms out there. Full fathom five thy father lies. At one he said. Found drowned. High water at Dublin bar. Driving before it a loose drift of rubble, fanshoals of fishes, silly shells. A corpse rising saltwhite from the undertow, bobbling landward, a pace a pace a porpoise. There he is. Hook it quick. Sunk though he be beneath the watery floor. We have him. Easy now.

> Bag of corpsegas sopping in foul brine. A quiver of minnows, fat of a spongy titbit, flash through the slits of his buttoned trouserfly. God becomes man becomes fish becomes barnacle goose becomes featherbed mountain. Dead breaths I living breathe, tread dead dust, devour a urinous offal from all dead. Hauled stark over the gunwale he breathes upward the stench of his green grave, his leprous nosehole snoring to the sun.
>
> A seachange this, brown eyes saltblue. Seadeath, mildest of all deaths known to man. Old Father Ocean. *Prix de Paris:* beware of imitations. Just you give it a fair trial. We enjoyed ourselves immensely. (*Ulysses*, p. 50)

Eliot's "Dirge" is one prolonged shudder, and this passage too dwells on the minute particulars of death by drowning, the growing public of what ought to be private, the full eversion of the human. Yet Joyce, like Shakespeare, suggests that the hideous lyric moment of endless flux is followed by a lyric moment of escape, a veering into beauty. In the strange catenary sentence that conflates Christ's incarnation with Proteus's impersonation of a corpse—"God becomes man becomes fish becomes barnacle goose becomes featherbed mountain"—we see that the breakdown of the human into a mire of tiny sea creatures leads at last to a certain etherealizing: the legend of the goose born out of barnacles, a legend well contrived for hungry monks who wished to eat goose during periods of fast when only fish was permitted, allows Joyce a shortcut for transforming fish upward in the food chain; and when the feathers of those geese are plucked into a featherbed mountain, we have at the end of the sentence, as at the beginning of it, something divine, a pillow fit for the gods, a movement out of carnal horror into the aerial. Though the corpse is picked at by minnows, Stephen develops a certain affection for "Seadeath, mildest of all deaths," as if the thought of the ceaseless mutation of one life into another were finally a source of comfort. Possibly the porpoise that the corpse seems to resemble, or that seems to nudge the corpse along, reminded him of the neo-Platonic story that the souls of the dead were conducted to the isles of the blessed on the backs of dolphins. Proteus, whose shape changes seem so sinister, is seen at last to be an agent of a sort of salvation, the Christ of the strictly secular world; and in the next paragraphs, when Stephen feels in his mouth a bad tooth that needs extraction and carefully lays a bit of dried snot on a rock as a kind of signature of his presence, it seems that he is exploring the possibility that he himself might be Proteus, a coenesthesia that encompasses all of existence from slime to rock to God. Stephen breathes dead breaths and eats urinous offal, and he knows that his own body is but another stage in the metamorphosis of corpse tissue. Earlier in the chapter (p. 40) he meditates on Occam's justification of Christ's physical omnipresence in every ceremony of the Eucharist. Every change, every inflection of the corporeal can be regarded, from a certain angle, as a transubstantiation, over which Proteus smilingly presides. When Stephen feels, under the sun's heat,

> I am caught in this burning scene. Pan's hour, the faunal noon. Among gumheavy serpentplants, milkoozing fruits, where on the tawny waters leaves lie wide. Pain is far. (p. 49)

he is at once Proteus seized by Menelaus and unseizable Pan lolling in Arcadia. When he says, "Come. I thirst," he is aping Christ for a moment. When he speaks, looking at the clouds forming over Dublin Bay, of the fall of Allbright Lucifer, "proud lightning of the intellect," we remember that in *A Portrait* Stephen took Lucifer's fall as a model for his own. When he calls himself, in a sour irony, "Toothless Kinch, the superman," the suggestion is made for an instant that what distinguishes the superman from the man is his very alterability, his Protean character. It is as if Stephen were granted a license to mimic every celestial or submarine presence, for to be Proteus is to be all the gods. The modality of the visible, of the audible, may be ineluctable, according to the refrain line of the chapter, but the perceiver is not tyrannized by the sensible world if he can incorporate into his body, by an act of empathy, the deep feeling of the internal organization of what he sees and hears; his imagination enables him to make experiments in identity comparable to any perceptual experiment. The man who is Proteus feels latent in himself the shape of whatever he beholds; and though for any mortal man the range of bodily plasticity is limited, such feelings nevertheless permit the lyrical hope that the body's degradation, disintegration, is not the end of us, but only an intermediate stage in our long metamorphosis into something better than we are. Proteus is always an ambiguous god, conducive to a delirium of identity, a shapeless incoherence. But he is nonetheless a god.

Proteus is for the purposes of this discussion a low avatar of Ariel, an Ariel slumming in the material world, helplessly mired in it and struggling to escape. In the domain of the lyrical, Proteus sinks and Ariel floats up. Ariel without Proteus is overkeen, inaudible music, too rarefied and angelic, hiding in a cowslip's bell or vanishing on the back of a bat; Proteus without Ariel galumphs cheerlessly through sodden self-transformations, never able to win the love of the helpless maiden or to break the clasp of a determined hero, always at a loss and too perplexed to discover the one right, proper shape. Proteus is sworn to speak the truth if he reverts to his own old man's body, but he is clearly in danger of losing all propriety and veridication in a helpless spasm of dissembling. Both Ariel and Proteus are magicians, and neither has anything to do with mimesis; they belong to the lyrical, and every lyric poem is a collaboration between them, in which Ariel seeks to move toward some unearthly, striking perfection and Proteus seeks to evade every finished form in favor of perpetual change. To some extent Proteus is the genius of lyrical prose and Ariel of lyrical poetry; but even in the quick outward-streaming prose of Joyce we feel hints of the presence of Ariel, in the suggestions of theophany, the allusions to resurrection in a line quoted from Milton's "Lycidas," the odd swerves into the beautiful, the glimpses of redemption from the wet inexorable monotonous changes of Proteus.

Of all great writers in English, Joyce probably is the most Protean: not only in the "Proteus" chapter of *Ulysses,* but in "Hades" (in which the envy of the drowned man reappears, p. 114), "Oxen of the Sun," "Circe," "Penelope," and all of *Finnegans Wake* is Proteus the informing spirit of the work; as Beckett remarks of *Finnegans Wake* in his essay "Dante . . . Bruno. Vico . . Joyce," Joyce's Purgatorio is circular and permits no escape (*Our Exagmination*, p. 21), makes no provision for any swing into transcendence, any final metamorphosis. The least Protean of our writers is perhaps Spenser, for whom Proteus seems an immitigable villain, willing to rescue the lovely and virtuous Florimell from an evil hermit only to attempt a further rape himself: he imprisons her in a sunless dungeon whose walls are waves until she will agree to become his lady (*Faerie Queene* 3.8). Proteus is important to *The Faerie Queene* not just as a character, but as a kind of plot force that infects the narrative with all manner of perplexities and false images; as soon as he enters the story the whole of book 3 becomes Protean in a sense: the incident of Proteus as a second beleaguerer, adapted from one of the most memorable episodes of Ariosto's *Orlando Furioso*, shows that Proteus embodies a principle of almost meaningless repetition, as he takes the place of an equally elderly, rapacious, and loathsome hermit. What value is it to substitute one such figure for another, except to make the plot skip a groove, like a phonograph needle on a defective record? In the very same canto a witch devises out of mercury, wax, silver sockets, golden wires, and pigments a false Florimell, so that, in the manner of Euripides' Helen, a troublesome eidolon will complicate and confuse the discourse while the real one languishes in jail, resisting all coarse enticements. It could be argued that these Protean shiftings provide a certain narrative impetus, but it also could be argued that such gnarled complexities are a sort of narrative disease, and that an excess of doubles and duplicity is starting to turn book 3 into a hall of mirrors, thin sea images from which the knights, trying heroically to overcome honest obstacles, monsters of flesh and blood, will be hard pressed to escape. To this extent Proteus, who is not terribly wicked or even especially noticeable in the catalog of Spenser's villains, is a more potent enemy than even Archimago. Duessa in disguise may be tricky, but she at least has weight and volume, stands for something real, evilly real, but the false Florimell will evaporate into thin air, for she is no one and means nothing. One might say that Proteus, though extremely attractive to a writer of fantastical romance, almost completely resists assimilation into an allegory and therefore threatens Spenser's whole project: Proteus has no denotative core, is simply random mutation given a proper name:

> To dreadfull shapes he did himself transforme,
> Now like a Gyant, now like to a feend,
> Then like a Centaure, then like to a storme,
> Raging within the waves: thereby he weend
> Her will to win unto his wished end.
>
> (3.8.41.1–5)

Proteus becomes ever less anthropoid, less meaningful, as he continues his self-transformations until he is nothing but the turbidity of water. He appears for the next, and last, time at the end of book 4, during the celebration of the marriage of two rivers, the Medway and the Thames:

> So both agreed, that this their bridale feast
> Should for the Gods in *Proteus* house be made;
> To which they all repayr'd, both most and least,
> As well which in the mightie Ocean trade,
> As that in rivers swim, or brookes doe wade.
>
> (4.11.9.1–5)

After this follows a long catalog of the world's rivers; but as Spenser constructs an immense gaudy pageant, blazoned with every telling particularity of each celebrated stream, Proteus grows to represent a contrary force, the principle of dissolution of significance, for all these interesting rivers will lose themselves in Proteus's house, the sea. The episode of Florimell's imprisonment by Proteus has a certain narrative charm, but the episode of her rescue (4.12) does not: the mother of her beloved Marinell entreats Neptune to command Proteus to release her, and Proteus is meekly obedient, as if Spenser finally found him an unwieldy, unsatisfying character, lacking in narrative force, too inconsistent and unreliable to be useful to a storyteller.

Proteus, then, is abandoned with little regret at the end of book 4; but in a sense he returns at the end of the whole *Faerie Queene*, and under another name he becomes the great antagonist of Spenser's whole creative work: Mutabilitie. This titaness overtly threatens to usurp the powers of the gods and to undermine every foundation of human dignity, virtue, and even identity:

> And men themselves doe change continually,
> From youth to eld, from eld to poverty,
> From good to bad, from bad to worst of all.
> Ne doe their bodies only flit and fly:
> But eeke their minds (which they immortall call)
> Still change and vary thoughts, as new occasions fall.
> (7.7.19.4–9)

Proteus was a menace because he could alter his shape as he chose; but Mutabilitie is infinitely more threatening because she can alter any shape in the universe as she chooses. Impelled by her, living things suffer a ceaseless pullulation and degradation, and the very elements themselves lose rank, decay from the simplicity of fire to the coarseness of earth (7.7.25); her final proof of her control is the fact of the precession of the earth's axis (7.7.55), and under her lash all axes wobble, all motion becomes erratic and ungoverned, all hierarchy and clear distinctions vanish into imperceptible graduations, all firm being blurs into a welter of appearances. Beneath her hand all things are clay, given temporary shape only so they may become misshapen, undone.

Such is the peril of Mutabilitie to gods and men; but secretly she is also a threat to Spenser's art. The allegorist postulates that the motions of the ethical and intellectual world and the motions of the sensible world run parallel, either because they are directed by a single common impulse or because they are interinforming. A good allegorist writes out of a desire to explore the properties of ethical and intellectual concepts by means of the narrative interactions of their hypostases, their physical representatives in his text, and he has the conviction that this manner of exploration is philosophically valid. In other words, he will take a narrative premise—for example, a jaded king who decides he will foil bad luck by finding Dame Fortune and proposing to wed her—and assume that something about human nature, and about the nature of fortune, can be discovered by seeing what happens in his story, that narrative craft can sharpen intellectual comprehension just as logical disquisition can. The allegorist, therefore, needs a certain confidence in the sensible world, confidence that the sorts of occasions human beings undergo—marriage, childbearing, death, hand-to-hand combat, rape—will, when applied to personified abstractions, be conducive to wisdom. Social interaction imposes boundaries upon the range of events possible to his prosopopoeias, but to the allegorist these limitations do not restrict him but open up new possibilities for displaying the family trees, the invariable antagonisms of Faith, Charity, Anarchy, Time, and so forth. The whole strategy of incarnating the abstract presupposes that fleshly relations are actually present in the intellectual world, that things above are as things below.

The doctrines of Mutabilitie's speech destroy these convenient assumptions. Unless something stands still, it cannot stand for anything; where all is tumescence and febrility and disintegration and mud, there is no possibility of symbolic representation; Mutabilitie herself, a flimsy arrogance, becomes the only allegorical character in her queasy cosmos. No wonder she appalls the other personages in book 7: she denies their right to exist; they grow unallegorical before her obtunding gaze. Spenser must find a way of contradicting her if *The Faerie Queene* is not to melt like the false Florimell into a breath of air and a few scattered trinkets; and he refutes her by making her refute herself. To demonstrate her mastery, Mutabilitie arranges a pageant of the months, a decelerating parade in which each month makes an ostentatious show of its attributes, its zodiacal sign:

> Next came fresh *April* full of lustyhed,
> And wanton as a Kid whose horne new buds:
> Upon a Bull he rode, the same which led
> *Europa* floting through th' *Argolic* fluds:
> His hornes were gilden all with golden studs
> And garnished with garlonds goodly dight . . .
> (7.7.33.1–6)

The sign of Taurus reminds Spenser of Jupiter's disguise as a bull, just as the sign of Aries in March reminds him of Jupiter's disguise as a ram when he wooed Helle. These splendid parade floats offer a subliminal reminder of Jupiter's erotic, all-inseminating power at just the moment when he seems in jeopardy of losing his authority to Mutabilitie; but more important, I think, the strutting forth of the months tends to dispute Mutabilitie's omnipotence by the very solidity and security of the emblems she waves forward. It is true that month succeeds month and the parade of time never halts, but it is also true that each month is unique, fully distinct, and retains every iconological virtue; the pageant's allegorical precision works against the all-blurring, all-demeaning spirit of Mutabilitie. Spenser's genius perhaps shows itself most characteristically in his allegorical processions, the pageants that give such savor to *The Faerie Queene.* In these pageants Spenser works toward an almost indiscriminate fullness of carefully incised allegorical particulars, the largest possible deck of cards; and though he repudiates Proteus, Mutabilitie, lest any figure be put in danger of representing something other than what it represents, this very drive toward repletion suggests that some faculty akin to Proteus is at work in his imagination. It may seem that Spenser cares about no servant but Ariel, who provides him with his absolute and completely determined figures, static images that have achieved an unequivocal meaning in the same way Alonso has achieved a final iconic form—Occasion with her hair growing over her forehead and bald behind (2.4.4), or the Blatant beast bellowing with a hundred tongues (5.12.41)—but there is also in his great poem a Protean sense that every new event alters, expands, refines our knowledge of whatever abstraction is denoted by a given character. In the last stanza of the last finished canto of *The Faerie Queene* Jupiter dismisses Mutabilitie by telling her that change is not, as she believes, a violation of the integrity of the changed thing; instead it is true of all things that "by their change their being do dilate" (7.7.58.5). In this line Ariel and Proteus collaborate, as they will in any considerable lyric achievement: every alteration of state ordained by Proteus, across the whole span of potentialities, brings the altered thing closer to the perfection desired by Ariel, its entelechy, the angel of the individual.

Chapter 2

THE BARD

IF the lyric mode has in it a certain appeal to the prehistoric, to some prelapsarian harmony prior to the divisions of the usual categories of things, then the writer of lyrics will tend to feel backward in his own sensibility toward a primal poet, toward a consciousness more synthetic and indiscriminate than his own, toward someone almost prehuman, whom I shall call the bard. If one looks far down into the roots of English poetry, one finds many stories of the magical powers ascribed to the *scop*, the Anglo-Saxon poet. Particularly among the Celtic strains of old Ireland and Wales, a myth has arisen that the very first poets attained an uncanny interpenetration with nature; here is a translation by Douglas Hyde of an ancient poem, which he believes the oldest surviving in Gaelic, attributed to Amergin, a Milesian colonist centuries before the birth of Christ:

THE MYSTERY

I am the wind which breathes upon the sea,
I am the wave of the ocean,
I am the murmur of the billows,
I am the ox of the seven combats,
I am the vulture upon the rocks,
I am a beam of the sun,
I am the fairest of plants,
I am a wild boar in valour,

I am a salmon in the water,
I am a lake in the plain,
I am a word of science,
I am the point of the lance of battle,
I am the God who created in the head the fire.
Who is it who throws light into the meeting on the
mountain?
Who announces the ages of the moon?
Who teaches the place where couches the sun?
(If not I)

The authenticity of this poem I am not prepared to vouch for; but it testifies to an ongoing appetite among modern men for an archaic vision of a poet exulting in his ability to deliquesce, to surpass his human shape and become animal or fish or elemental impulse or light or noise or word or god, to hold the cosmos together through sheer intellectual force. Other early poems reveal a similar metempsychotic delirium, for example, the "Welsh transmigration song of Taliesin" that Ernest Rhys quotes:

I was with my Lord in the highest sphere,
On the fall of Lucifer into the depths of hell
I have borne a banner before Alexander:
I know the names of the stars from north to south;
I have been in the galaxy at the throne of the Distributor:
I was in Canaan when Absalom was slain;
I conveyed the Divine Spirit to the level vale of Hebron;
I was in the court of Don before the birth of Gwdion.
(*Lyric Poetry*, p. 22)

Rhys also gives an Old English variant of Taliesin's song, called the Scald's or Scop's Tale:

Therefore can I sing + and tell a tale;
relate before many + in the mead-hall
how to me the noble folk + were wondrous kind . . .
I was with the Huns + and the Hreth Goths
with the Greeks I was and the Finns + and with Caesar.

The poet participates so fully in his poem that he becomes a foot soldier in the battles he sings of, a minor angel in the precincts of heaven, bearing Alexander's banner and assisting God in his theodicy. A modern equivalent of this can be seen in Ezra Pound's *Cantos,* in which the poet is ready to pitch in when Sigismondo Malatesta needs a hand (Canto 11) or to enlist as a musketeer in the rebellion under Tsehing (Canto 56). Taliesin is less primeval than Amergin in that the subject matter has now entered history, whereas Amergin seems untainted by the human; the drift from an untenably pure lyricality into the narrative mode has already begun. The degree of illumination, of triumphant fury, is lower in Taliesin than in Amergin, but the focus of the poetry is growing sharper, the content more significant; instead of brief glances from an eye that sees itself in all the things it sees, we have a body of articulate stories so vivid in the teller's mind that he dwells in an eternal narrative present. The bard is always a hypothetical ideal from which the real poet lapses and to which he sometimes aspires; no actual author is ever a bard, but insofar as he has intuitions of himself as not yet descended into particularity, not yet born, a naked impulsion not yet ingredient in matter, he can discover a bard inside himself. In general we may say that with each passing century English poets feel themselves increasingly estranged from the bard but become increasingly ingenious in their strategies for simulating the lost bard, for imitating the aggressively antidiscursive mental and verbal habits a bard would have had had a bard ever existed.

Most modern poets, and some not so modern, imagine that the bard is unhappy. Amergin and Taliesin marvel at the distendedness of their being; but there is another tradition according to which the bard is troubled by the monotony of the infinite, by the diffusion of identity required by a network of empathy maintained across the cosmos. The locus classicus of this sort of bard is Pythagoras, who, though more musician than poet, can be taken as the epitome of a purely lyrical visionary. In the great rhapsody that Ovid attributes to Pythagoras in the last book of the *Metamorphoses,* the philosopher exiled from Samos teaches

Numa about nature and the gods. What is remarkable about Pythagoras's long didactic speech is that the beds of the ocean rise and the mountains collapse, corpses are changed into little live animals that spawn and die, the she-bear licks a lump of inert matter into a cub and the phoenix is reborn from its own ashes, the hyena alters its sex and the chameleon eats air, and urine and coral petrify—all nature is caught in the circle of its immutable mutation—during the course of a diatribe against eating meat:

> And wee that of the world are part (considring how wee bee
> Not only flesh, but also fowles, which may with passage free
> Remove them intoo every kynd of beast both tame and wyld)
> Let live in saufty honestly with slaughter undefyld,
> The bodyes which perchaunce may have the spirits of our
> brothers,
> Our sisters, or our parents, or the spirits of sum others
> Alyed too us eyther by sum freendshippe or sum kin,
> Or at the least the soules of men abyding them within.
> And let us not *Thyëstes*lyke thus furnish up our boordes
> With bloodye bowells. Oh how leawd example he avoordes?
> How wickedly prepareth he himself too murther man
> That with a cruell knyfe dooth cut the throte of Calf, and can
> Unmovably give heering too the lowing of the dam,
> Or sticke the kid that wayleth lyke the little babe . . .
> (*Metamorphoses* 15.507–20, Golding's translation)

Pythagoras felt in his own body every wound suffered by an animal, for in his fabulous wisdom he remembered all the souls that he had been in previous lives; thus he dwelt in a world so tender, so surfeited with the human, that every calf and kid and bird mooed and baaed and twittered in a man's voice. To have the memories, the nervous system, of a Pythagoras is to live in perpetual anxiety, for pain is everywhere, even if it is only a swallow eating a bug, and all men who are not vegetarians are cannibals chewing on their own limbs. Here is the extreme of disillusionment, for rich sauces and noble hunting sport can in no way extenuate the immediate pang of teeth in a whole universe of victims. Golden-thighed Pythagoras, trying to catch what a star sang, trying to ascend out of the sodden corporeal into the crystalline spheres of superhuman music, is inevitably a misanthrope. Erasmus says in *In Praise of Folly* that Pythagoras had been philosopher, horse, fish, even sponge, and discovered like Gryllus that man was worst. Gryllus, of course, was that crewman of Odysseus who wished to remain a swine on Circe's island after Odysseus bargained for the disenchantment of his sailors. From Erasmus's version of Pythagoras, preferring the gamut of identities to any single shape, preferring the simplicities of inarticulate swelling and speed to man's debaucheries, it is not far to Shakespeare's Timon of Athens, who also sees mankind dizzily deconstructing into lower forms but resists the consolation that the body of a pig or an ass might be a notable improvement over a man's. We see, then, as we saw before, that the lyric afflatus that makes a mighty paean to the poet's intimacy with every other creature in the field of his comprehension can shift easily into a kind of magnified self-hatred, self-renunciation.

The bard who announces that he is all he beholds will become engrossed in his ingenious foreign shapes, contemptuous of the merely human, those who suffer from the delusion of private, exclusive potty little selves, Schopenhauer's *principium individuationis*. But every attempt to surpass or to render distended and absolute the commonplace self will result in a kind of selflessness; the perfectly personal is also the perfectly impersonal. The bard is consumed by the world he seeks to embrace—no wonder Pythagoras is horrified by carnivorousness, for he is in danger of being devoured by everything that has a mouth. There is a sense in which the bard is eaten up by each poem he writes: like Amergin he saturates his text in himself—"I am . . . I am . . . I am"—but he can attain no personal definition against this nature smeared black with his identity; he is as invisible as God in this creation that, he claims, expresses him in every line. The bard in his nervous Pythagorean version only makes explicit the tenuousness, the diffusion, the loss of being that threatens every bard, even the most exultant. The bard is always oppressed by his very wealth, an Alexander who grows feverish, dissipated, because he has no worlds left to conquer; and the Pythagorean is only the bard grown sick from overinclusion, glutted and cloyed, too sensitive to enjoy his immense resources of identity. The bard would like to be Ariel, working to sublimate all nature into a deathless aesthetic governed by the power of his imagination; but he is likely to decay into Proteus, vexed by strange lumpish swellings in his body, a mishmash of fetus and corpse. In Yeats's mythology of reincarnation, the overintellectual are succeeded by the overmoral, the rigid, who are in turn succeeded by the Hunchback, the Multiple Man, a deformed incoherent thing who feels that "A Roman Caesar is held down / Under this hump" ("The Saint and the Hunchback," lines 4–5), as well as Alexander and Alcibiades; he is endlessly disspirited by these potentialities lurking inside him, wishes to flay them out of himself with a whip. Yeats's Hunchback is the Pythagorean bard in the last spasm of self-hatred, unable to think or write or conquer or live, caught up in a helpless delirium in which he tries to suppress every fantasy of self so that he can be real, one.

Yeats's Hunchback is a sophistication of a figure important in his earlier poetry, the Druid. "Fergus and the Druid" (1892) sets out clearly the angst of the Pythagorean bard:

> *Fergus.* This whole day have I followed in the rocks,
> And you have changed and flowed from shape to shape,
> First as a raven on whose ancient wings
> Scarcely a feather lingered, then you seemed
> A weasel moving on from stone to stone,
> And now at last you wear a human shape,
> A thin grey man half lost in gathering night.

As Fergus explains how he chose to abandon the responsibility of his kingdom, cast away his crown, follow the Druid to his solitary haunts, the Druid keeps asking him what he wants, and finally he answers:

> *Fergus.* Be no more a king,
> But learn the dreaming wisdom that is yours.
> *Druid.* Look on my thin grey hair and hollow cheeks
> And on these hands that may not lift the sword,

This body trembling like a wind-blown reed.
No woman's loved me, no man sought my help.
Fergus. A king is but a foolish labourer
Who wastes his blood to be another's dream.

The Druid and Fergus are bound to each other by mutual envy. It seems as if the Druid's expertise in shape changing is a consequence of his human inadequacy, and indeed there is in Yeats's work a persistent theme of the poet as the most starved of men: in his essay "Discoveries" Yeats explains that in ancient times the blind man became a poet because he was deprived of every human excitement and satisfaction, and according to the famous description in "Ego Dominus Tuus" Keats pressed his nose to the sweet-shop window because he was famished for every delight that his poverty denied him. The Druid is not so much superhuman as subhuman, too battered and unreal, spectral, to get a kiss or lift a sword. He is outside the orbit of common life not because he disdains the human but because he is rejected by it; his residence in the domain of the imaginary, his transsentience with animals, his occult wisdom are all doubtful compensation for the vigorous life that is denied him. Fergus's reply to his discouragement suggests that the Druid is mistaken in believing there exists an especially meaty and splendid society that is above or below the province of magical images: a king finds himself involved not in thick reality but in a different kind of imaginative order, in which the king is not the controlling imagination but the controlled image, wasting himself "to be another's dream." Fergus wishes he could be a bard in the Amergin sense, in such a state of vaulting bliss that the whole of nature and society obeys his will and expresses his abiding presence; but he learns that he can aspire only to Druiddom, a state in which identity piddles out, blears into thin phantasmagoria, an intimacy with shadows:

Fergus. I see my life go drifting like a river
From change to change; I have been many things—
A green drop in the surge, a gleam of light
Upon a sword, a fir-tree on a hill,
An old slave grinding at a heavy quern,

A king sitting upon a chair of gold—
And all these things were wonderful and great;
But now I have grown nothing, knowing all.
Ah! Druid, Druid, how great webs of sorrow
Lay hidden in the small slate-coloured thing!

All key signature is lost in this excess of modulation. As a king Fergus had significance and responsibility, heft; as a Druid he is lost, dissolved in an acid of dreams. Yeats was obsessed with the feeling that the man with superior powers of imagination was ruined by his plasticity, his fecundity of invention; every triumph of metamorphosis was accompanied by an inevitable exclusion from the one thing most desired. This is why Proteus figures frequently in his work. The Druid of "Fergus and the Druid" can depict himself as a weasel or a raven or a drop of water or a slave or a king, but what he craves is to be no picture of a noble warrior but an actual one. The demon of book 2 of *The Wanderings of Oisin* (1889) also transforms himself into eel and fir tree and corpse in the course of his mighty combat with Oisin, but the struggle with an exceedingly plastic and irresolute monster, a dragon dreamily accommodating to Saint George's fantasies of an opponent, can come to no true and satisfying outcome, and so every four days Oisin and the demon repeat their epic battle. To play with images is to forgo life, to lose the grit and fierce embrace of the actual. Similarly, the wizard of "He Thinks of His Past Greatness When a Part of the Constellations of Heaven" (1898), an extremely resourceful shape changer, tries to accomplish with a thousand shadows the satisfaction that can come only from a solid thing:

I have drunk ale from the Country of the Young
And weep because I know all things now:
I have been a hazel-tree, and they hung
The Pilot Star and the Crooked Plough
Among my leaves in times out of mind:
I became a rush that horses tread:
I became a man, a hater of the wind,
Knowing one, out of all things, alone, that his head

> May not lie on the breast nor his lips on the hair
> Of the woman that he loves, until he dies.
> O beast of the wilderness, bird of the air,
> Must I endure your amorous cries?

As with Erasmus's Pythagoras, a certain revulsion against the human becomes the motive for a dizzying exploration of imaginative potentialities in oneself. Throughout the 1890s Yeats tried to impose discipline on his imagination through a series of exercises, conducted with the help of his astrologer uncle George Pollexfen, designed to show how the boundaries of each man's memory tend to blur out into a common racial memory, a storehouse of images; and he clearly felt the danger that these researches would lead to an irremediable diffusion of self. The poem cited above imitates the rhetoric of Amergin's "The Mystery" almost exactly but expresses the fear that grasping the sacred world-soul is strictly futile if it leads one away from human life, the precious unmysterious. When Yeats reviewed this period in his autobiography he called the chapter "Hodos Chameliontos," the Chameleon Road, because he felt that during the 1890s he had

> plunged without a clue into a labyrinth of images, into that labyrinth that we are warned against in those *Oracles* which antiquity has attributed to Zoroaster, but modern scholarship to some Alexandrian poet. "Stoop not down to the darkly splendid world wherein lieth continually a faithless depth and Hades wrapped in a cloud, delighting in unintelligible images."

The Druid has had such long acquaintance with unintelligible images that he has become one sheer human unintelligibility; and that is the fate that lies before every apprentice bard.

Amergin is a bard satisfied with his divinity; Yeats's Druid is a bard who would like to descend from the mountaintop and be a man; and the next stage on the long road from poetical panentity, nonentity, down to the human is the almost-bard, who has just ceased being a bard, just entered the commonplace, and now looks back with regret at what he has lost. This is the position in which we find the bard in Gray's "The Bard" (1757). Edward

I has just conquered Wales and has secured his rule by exterminating the bards as "exciters of the people to sedition" (Thomas Carte, *General History of England* [1750], 2:196); Gray imagines that one last bard, a ruined old man but still impressive, summons up his poetic powers to curse King Edward and to declaim a vision of England's future:

> On a rock, whose haughty brow
> Frowns o'er old Conway's foaming flood,
> Robed in the sable garb of woe,
> With haggard eyes the poet stood,
> (Loose his beard and hoary hair
> Streamed, like a meteor, to the troubled air)
> And, with a master's hand and prophet's fire,
> Struck the deep sorrows of his lyre.
> 'Hark, how each giant-oak and desert cave
> 'Sighs to the torrent's awful voice beneath!
> 'O'er thee, oh king! their hundred arms they wave,
> 'Revenge on thee in hoarser murmurs breathe;
> 'Vocal no more, since Cambria's fatal day,
> 'To high-born Hoel's harp or soft Llewellyn's lay.
>
> (lines 15–28)

Nature used to be subtly responsive to the felicities of the lyrists, as the trees made a choral accompaniment to noble or amorous music; but now Hoel and Llewellyn and all the rest are dead, and emotional variety has vanished from the landscape. Instead there is a single animating passion, the bard's fury; and it seems that the chasm of the Conway, the whole inner earth, has become a vast resonating cavity to amplify the song of the bard. The lyre itself, magnified by sympathetic vibrations in trees and caves, will eat up Edward. In the next stanzas the bard describes the corpses of his fellow poets, magically immune from violation by raven or eagle, and feels their souls joining his in the anthem of hatred he sings. As the bard grows complex with the ghosts of other bards, we see again the lack of individuality typical of the race: a bard is not a single creature but song itself given a provisional human identity, too thickly overlaid with harmonies derived from nature and society to seem a distinct person. Indeed, it is difficult for the bard to focus his attention on a particular man, even on the hated Edward I; instead, his gaze seems to drift away into a bright blur. When the bard—now a whole chorus of bards in one body—prophesies that a later Edward, the Black Prince, will die before his father, the whole sad race slides out of cognition, vanishes into the whirlpool:

> "Is the sable warrior fled?
> "Thy son is gone. He rests among the dead.
> "The swarm that in thy noon-tide beam were born?
> "Gone to salute the rising morn.
> "Fair laughs the morn and soft the zephyr blows,
> "While proudly riding o'er the azure realm
> "In gallant trim the gilded vessel goes;
> "Youth on the prow and Pleasure at the helm;
> "Regardless of the sweeping whirlwind's sway,
> "That, hushed in grim repose, expects his evening-prey.
> (lines 67–76)

The bard can glimpse certain incidents from the lives of the later kings of England but is for the most part content that father and son, King Queen Knave, the whole pack of cards, grow elided, collapse into a single allegorical pageant of doom. Just as earlier in the ode the trees seemed ready to strangle, the torrent to wash away King Edward and his men, so here too the bottom is about to fall from under the Saxon dynasties; Edward and the later kings have been assimilated against their will into a poem, in which the bard is author and the chief logic is poetic justice, clear retribution. The singularities, the particular vices and miseries, of subsequent kings founder, disappear in a general wreck; and similarly the particular bards, whose combined forces have made themselves an angry Poseidon taking vengeance on the English ship of state—Taliessin is among them—vanish into light:

> 'Stay, oh stay! nor thus forlorn
> 'Leave me unblessed, unpitied, here to mourn:
> 'In yon bright track, that fires the western skies,
> 'They melt, they vanish from my eyes.

'But oh! what solemn scenes on Snowdon's height
'Descending slow their glittering skirts unroll?
'Visions of glory, spare my aching sight.
(lines 101–7)

"Solemn scenes" is a theatrical term, and it is beginning to appear that English history is a well-made play, in which the turmoils and wanton slaughters of the Saxon kings reach a peripety and are replaced by the magnanimities of the Tudor line, thought to be of the old Briton strain. From this happy end imposed on history in the theater of the bard's vision, he next turns his attention to a real Elizabethan playwright, Shakespeare:

'The verse adorn again
'Fierce war and faithful love,
'And truth severe, by fairy fiction dressed.
'In buskined measures move
'Pale Grief and pleasing Pain,
'With Horror, tyrant of the throbbing breast.
(lines 125–30)

The bard is composing the career of Edward I and his successors as if he were writing a new cycle of history plays: the Horror of the slaying of the bards turns out to be a pleasing Pain, for Edward has been annulled, absorbed into a large context in which his acts can be seen to have no lasting meaning—his whole line is displayed as a temporary aberration in the general splendor of Britain:

'Fond impious man, think'st thou yon sanguine cloud,
'Raised by thy breath, has quenched the orb of day?
(lines 135–36)

And the final movement to Shakespeare and Milton confirms that the powers of the bard are not ended with the suicide of the last bard of old Wales, this outlingerer of his time: there is a single lyric potency that may assume the nearly random instrument of Taliessin or Shakespeare or the present bard. The individual is superseded by the majesty of the lyric order, which compels events to move according to music, making of history a grand opera. But though the bard sees that the forms of significant action appear and disperse according to a rhythm, he has nevertheless, in his cursing and in his dying, entered into history, the discursive; and time and prose, having intruded into the passionate inconsequence of music, will continue to be the enemies of bardic lyricality.

THE DEATH OF FANCY

When Gray's bard throws himself over the cliff, we may feel at least some small relief that poetical genius has not perished with him: Shakespeare and Milton will be—have been—poets equal or superior to the bard. If these two are the only great poets subsequent to the age of the bards, however, there is cause for some alarm; the bard was the remnant of a whole community of resourceful magicians, whereas the spirit of making seems in later times granted only to one in a million. Edward I has almost succeeded in sweeping the earth bare of poets. A modern poet, then, must indulge in a calculated archaism, must dress himself in the vatic weeds of an extinct race if he is to exercise any of the old powers. Shakespeare has Portia sing, in *The Merchant of Venice* (3.2.70), a little song with a secret clue to Bassanio about the proper casket to choose, and in this song she tells of the birth and death of fancy—"Let us all ring fancy's knell." This sums up the next movement in the falling away from the bard: since we live in a time when all the bards are long exterminated, let us celebrate what we can never be. Such a celebration usually has the clandestine hope that a sort of minor bardhood will descend upon the man who can most artfully lament the death of imagination.

Gray himself had some confidence in his ability to join the ranks of bards. In his "The Progress of Poesy" (1754, 1757)—another Pindaric ode, written just before "The Bard"—Gray traces the roots of poetry back not into the Celtic twilight of "The Bard," but into Greek antiquity. There it is clear that poetry is a river:

> Awake, Aeolian lyre, awake,
> And give to rapture all thy trembling strings.

From Helicon's harmonious springs
A thousand rills their mazy progress take;
The laughing flowers, that round them blow,
Drink life and fragrance as they flow.
Now the rich stream of music winds along,
Deep, majestic, smooth, and strong,
Through verdant vales and Ceres' golden reign:
Now rolling down the steep amain,
Headlong, impetuous, see it pour:
The rocks and nodding groves rebellow to the roar.
(lines 1–12)

Gray's comment on this stanza is of interest:

> The subject and simile, as usual with Pindar, are united. The various sources of poetry, which gives life and lustre to all it touches, are here described; its quiet majestic progress enriching every subject (otherwise dry and barren) with a pomp of diction and a luxuriant harmony of numbers; and its more rapid and irresistible course, when swoln and hurried away by the conflict of tumultuous passions.

It is as if nature consists of desiccated forms made substantial, plump, by the action of poetry. The title of the poem leads us to believe we are going to hear about poesy, but the tenor is soon lost in the roar and rush of the vehicle—as Gray says, subject and simile are one—as if the tendency of poetry to amalgamate or unite things is so great that it cannot in itself be isolated. Poetry remains impalpable and invisible, a weightless humidity or phlogiston that invigorates the external world. Gray compares it to a stream, but one might say it is the impulsion that makes the stream fast and sparkling, conducive to new growth, wet. Of the poet he has as yet said almost nothing—Gray himself has a vision of the sacred mountain of the Muses, a mountain that seems depopulated—as if in prehistory poetry existed independent of any man, a random creativity flowing through things. The bard is so immanent in the landscape, in the metaphorical stream, that he has not yet attained any human shape.

In the following stanzas the disembodied passions start to

attach themselves first to Jove, who is pacified by the music, then to Venus, whose venereal dances grow frisky and light-minded, at last to "Man's feeble race" (line 42), which the Muse consoles for its pitiful lot. The Muses have still not needed any particular human instrument to achieve music, as if music and poetry, little discriminated from each other, were simply a part of the atmosphere in ancient times, a free-floating inspiration. When we first hear of a human poet we are already out of Greece, almost in the intemperate climate of "The Bard":

> In climes beyond the solar road,
> Where shaggy forms o'er ice-built mountains roam,
> The Muse has broke the twilight-gloom
> To cheer the shivering native's dull abode.
> And oft, beneath the odorous shade
> Of Chile's boundless forests laid,
> She deigns to hear the savage youth repeat
> In loose numbers wildly sweet
> Their feather-cinctured chiefs and dusky loves.
> (lines 54–62)

Here we have a further development of the poem's basic metaphor, that poetry is water. In savage prelife men live on icebergs; as poetry civilizes there is a great thaw, an outrush of feeling. The Orpheus of South America, the feather-cinctured chief, the wild loose numbers, look forward to the Bard, whose electrified hair streams out like a meteor; the poet connects and energizes, pulls all men together with the tractile thread of his passion made musical. When Gray proceeds to Shakespeare, he adds another tributary to the theme of the wateriness of poetry, as Cybele gives the young Bard of Avon a pencil, to adorn his representations of nature, and some golden keys:

> Thine too these golden keys, immortal boy!
> This can unlock the gates of joy;
> Of horror that and thrilling fears,
> Or ope the sacred source of sympathetic tears.
> (lines 91–94)

Gray's use of Cybele in this stanza, like his use of Ceres at the beginning of the poem, suggests that the poet is imbued with deep control of natural rhythms, almost himself a Chthonian deity. He governs the flow of tears, for there is internal hydraulic pressure as well as the external course of the stream of poetry; indeed, Gray seems to conceive modern poetry as more psychological, sympathetic, conducive to the community of suffering mankind than the poetry that delighted Jove and Venus. Gray's idea of poetry is almost exactly that of Auden, who writes in "In Memory of W. B. Yeats" (1939) of the "seas of pity" that lie "Locked and frozen in each eye"—the glacier is a favorite metaphor for unexpressed solitary emotion—and who declares that the river of Yeats's poetry will connect the "ranches of isolation," will be a "healing fountain" in the "deserts of the heart." Auden goes one step further than Gray in indicating that the poet is himself water—Yeats in death has become his poems, become his admirers, turned from a silly fellow who believed in spooks into a true bard, a dynamic in nature—but Gray comes close to this implication in his treatment of poetry as a force latent in the cosmos, trying to flow through any aperture that presents itself. Gray's picture of Shakespeare is encouraging, but perhaps the most salient feature of the Progress of Poesy is that it is a retrogression: the fields of earth, even the sacred mountain, are left desolate, disenchanted, as the sad Muses abandon a Greece spoiled by modern tyranny (line 77); and Shakespeare, Milton, Dryden seem to have used up the poetical impulse of England:

> Hark, his hands the lyre explore!
> Bright-eyed Fancy hovering o'er
> Scatters from her pictured urn
> Thoughts that breathe and words that burn.
> But ah! 'tis heard no more———
>
> (lines 107–11)

If Fancy is not dead, she is at least a missing person. Gray is painfully aware of his inadequacy compared with his model Pindar; but if he cannot be a new Theban eagle, if he cannot fly at a high altitude, he does believe he can get off the ground, "mount and keep his distant way" (line 121). It seems we can trust Gray to husband his dribbles of fancy, retain a certain efficacy as a poet; we must look elsewhere for a genuinely extinct fancy, Imagination Dead Imagine. Such an example is not far; if Gray's contemporary William Cowper believed himself damned, another contemporary believed that he had no imagination, that no imagination was left in his world: William Collins.

Collins was, unfortunately, a minor poet who saw little use in any endeavor except the few supreme acts of imagination given to a race; to be less than Spenser or Shakespeare was to be nothing at all. His most powerful and original poem, the "Ode on the Poetical Character" (1746), is one of the first poems in English to make great poetry of the poet's confession of poetical inadequacy; much later this theme would give the young Ezra Pound material for his most impressive work, including "Near Perigord" and *Hugh Selwyn Mauberley.* Before Collins's gaze was always a vision of a poet who could create worlds and populate them, a solitary all-competent godhead; but he knew that he, Collins, could be no more than a pretender to the title:

As once, if not with light regard
I read aright that gifted bard,
(Him whose school above the rest
His loveliest Elfin Queen has blessed)
One, only one, unrivalled fair
Might hope the magic girdle wear,
The wish of each love-darting eye;
Lo! to each other nymph in turn applied,
 As if, in air unseen, some hovering hand,
Some chaste and angel-friend to virgin-fame,
 With whispered spell had burst the starting band,
It left unblest her loathed, dishonoured side;
 Happier hopeless fair, if never
 Her baffled hand with vain endeavour
Had touched that fatal zone to her denied!
Young Fancy thus, to me divinest name,
 To whom, prepared and bathed in heaven,

> The cest of amplest power is given,
> To few the godlike gift assigns
> To gird their blest prophetic loins,
> And gaze her visions wild, and feel unmixed her flame!
> (lines 1–21)

In the second stanza Collins describes how Fancy wooed God at the beginning of time, when he was making the heaven and the earth, how God set her on a throne and appointed her a sort of demiurge, continuing the creative act, illustrating, impassioning the land. She is eager to find new candidates for inspiration, but they are lacking; Collins imagines the presentation of aspirants for the title of poet as a variant of the competition for Florimell's lost girdle in *The Faerie Queene*: there the False Florimell won the contest but could not fasten the girdle (4.5.16). Collins, by comparing himself to the False Florimell, suggests ominously that he too is a substanceless image, confect of ice and wax, not a human being but a counterfeit; it is as if, failing to be a bard, he is scarcely fit to live. Himself a wraith, Collins haunts the locales in which genuine poets dwelt; in the epode he imagines Eden taking shape in Milton's mind:

> High on some cliff to Heaven up-piled,
> Of rude access, of prospect wild,
> Where, tangled round the jealous steep,
> Strange shades o'erbrow the valleys deep,
> And holy genii guard the rock,
> Its glooms embrown, its springs unlock,
> While on its rich ambitious head,
> An Eden, like his own, lies spread;
> I view that oak, the fancied glades among,
> By which as Milton lay, his evening ear,
> From many a cloud that dropped ethereal dew,
> Nigh sphered in heaven its native strains could hear:
> On which that ancient trump he reached was hung;
> Thither oft his glory greeting,
> From Waller's myrtle shades retreating,
> With many a vow from hope's aspiring tongue,

My trembling feet his guiding steps pursue:
In vain—such bliss to one alone
Of all the sons of soul was known,
And Heaven and Fancy, kindred powers,
Have now o'erturned the inspiring bowers,
Or curtained close such scenes from every future view.
(lines 55–76)

Roger Lonsdale, in his edition of Gray, Collins, and Goldsmith, has pointed out that the oak tree has Druidical and oracular associations; Collins seems to be imitating every stance, every stride of the great man, as if to fool the eye of Fancy into taking him for Milton, but he remains unoracular, not a bard. In the strophe Collins was like the False Florimell; now he is like Satan trying to climb the hill of Eden, forever outcast no matter how he insinuates himself into the scene. He who would be Fancy's most ardent prophet instead seems to desecrate the domain of her highest triumphs; he has almost become an antibard, making pedestrian and cold whatever he approaches, the Midas touch in reverse. It is this sublimated desperation that gives the poem its peculiar savor. In "An Ode on the Popular Superstitions of the Highlands of Scotland," Collins considers how much Shakespeare drew from the implausible dreams of the folktales when he wrote *Macbeth*, how lies can be transfigured into the matter of art (lines 176, 191); and Collins imagines how Fancy will lead him over the Scottish landscape to "the faded bower, / Where Jonson sat in Drummond's shade" (lines 211–12). Again there is the hopeless feeling that where genius once operated, where a bard sat and saturated the ground and the trees with his transforming power, some residue, some echo of heavenly music should still inhere. One of Collins's earlier works was a little song:

When howling winds and beating rain
In tempests shake the sylvan cell,
Or midst the chase on every plain,
The tender thought on thee shall dwell.
(lines 17–20)

The full title of this is "A Song from Shakespeare's Cymbeline / Sung by Guiderius and Arviragus over Fidele, Supposed to Be Dead." That is, the song is an anachronistic sequel to "Fear no more the heat o' th' sun," and according to Earl Wasserman this is one of the first of the eighteenth-century imitations of Shakespeare. It is softer, more indistinct, less solemn and peremptory than "Fear no more," but it is so similar to it in theme and style that it is hard to guess why Collins would have written it, invited such a comparison, unless one supposes that he wished to efface himself utterly, to become a colorless novelty through which dead genius could again shine. Collins may have thought that his best hope of lasting fame was to become a parasite feeding on more successful poets; failing that, he made himself a shrine to the missing bard. And possibly he ventured upon a still further imitation of the bard's delirium, his lyric omnipotence, when, like other poets in the bard-haunted later eighteenth century, he went mad and was carried off to an asylum.

FANCY'S RESURRECTION

During this period of English poetry there arose a general myth, that the lyric energies that had once infused the whole world through the medium of the bard had withdrawn, elevated themselves, grown incorporeal and ungraspable. Fancy survived but had turned her back on mankind. Gray celebrated the moment at which the imagination had made her furious retreat from the human world, Collins searched for a faint iridescence that might linger in modern times; but it was their great successor Blake who described most fully this state of irrelation between the bard and the present world. In his youthful *Poetical Sketches* Blake imagined the Muses as still ubiquitous, still lovely and potent, but scornful of men:

Whether on chrystal rocks ye rove,
  Beneath the bosom of the sea
Wand'ring in many a coral grove,
  Fair Nine, forsaking Poetry!

How have you left the antient love
    That bards of old enjoy'd in you!
The languid strings do scarcely move!
    The sound is forc'd, the notes are few!
        ("To the Muses," lines 9–16)

This strangulation, this aesthetic paralysis, is the consequence of the blindness of poets to the genii loci, to the Muses, to the earth's connective tissue. Opposed to this loss of the music of things is another poem from this collection:

Lo! to the vault
    Of paved heaven,
With sorrow fraught
    My notes are driven:
They strike the ear of night,
    Make weep the eye of day;
They make mad the roaring winds,
    And with tempests play.
        ("Mad Song," lines 9–16)

In the next stanza the lunatic poet compares himself to "a fiend in a cloud" and turns away from the East—Blake mentions in "To the Muses" that melody has vanished from the East, from Greece, the seat of the old lyric afflatus—because the light "doth seize my brain / With frantic pain." There is a bard, and there is a world of settled, comfortable, attractive forms; but the bard lacks a world, slinks off into a phantasmagoria of darkness and incoherent energies, a night responsive to his stormy will but not especially real, while the world persists in its plump prettiness, its green corners and coral groves, and resists being made into poetry. For Gray the bard is an ideal of a poet as vehement, effective, clairvoyant as one could wish, but Gray has limited confidence in his existence; Blake, on the other hand, believes in the bard but has little faith in the sensible world that seems to resist him. In the "Introduction" to *Songs of Experience* Blake exhorts the reader to hear the voice of a Bard, all-seeing, intimate with Christ in the Garden of Eden:

O Earth O Earth return!
Arise from out the dewy grass . . .
Turn away no more:
Why wilt thou turn away
The starry floor
The watry shore
Is giv'n thee till the break of day.
(lines 9–10, 16–20)

Earth is asked to supersede her boundedness, the prison of shore and sky imposed on her by God the Father, the overrational gubernator eventually called Urizen. The bard, then, represents a kind of urgency to transgress all restriction, to cross the frontiers impressed upon experience by the straightedge and compass of the false creator. The bard works to annul category. But against this stirring speech Earth replies, in the next poem, "Earth's Answer," that she is too heavy, too enchained, too petrified to rise to the bard's challenge without some assistance. Whereas Gray's Bard sought to blight a world that was murderous to poets, Blake's seeks to animate, to make dance, a world lumpish, passively resistant to any transformation. How much Blake owes to Gray can be seen in some of the watercolors he made for Gray's "The Bard": in one of them, illustrating the lines about the giant oaks and the desert cave sighing to the torrent beneath, the trees waving their hundred arms vengefully over Edward—as if the trees were themselves Druid magicians casting as vicars the spell the Bard is seeking to cast—Blake drew a mighty Michelangelesque nude: the Bard has a beard streaming down like a river, a massive oak wreath, complete with acorns, seemingly growing branches from itself as supplementary arms for the Bard, a big drooping moustache shaped like imbricated oak leaves. The whole effect indicates that the Bard, like Baucis and Philemon, is himself turning into an oak; Gray's vague suggestions of the Bard's interpenetration with nature, his magic playing like an electrical field over tree and torrent and his own body, have been literalized into a powerful figure not much discriminated from the natural world. The head of another wreathed bard is tucked in his armpit, like Eve in God's cloak in Michelangelo's *The Creation of Adam*, and another bardic face is visible in the river beneath. These must represent the dead bards who have joined their voices into his, but since their faces look exactly like that of the main Bard, it seems that there is one and only one Bard, reflected from every natural form, as if the oaks and the streams were only clandestine aspects of his being.

> For I tell you
> Beneath this powerful tree, my whole soul's fluid
> Oozes away from me as a sacrifice steam
> At the knife of a Druid. . . .
> I tell you my blood runs out on the floor of this oak,
> Gout upon gout.
>
> Above me springs the blood-born mistletoe
> In the shady smoke.
>
> (lines 9–12, 15–18)

This is, of course, no eighteenth-century poet describing the death of the last bard, passing out into vegetative reality, dispelling himself into shadowy interanimation, but a more recent poet, D. H. Lawrence, writing in "Under the Oak" of how, caught outdoors with a woman and full of sexual mystery, he feels himself turning into a Druid by sacrificing his modern self to his archaic being. The theme of the death of the last bard here passes effortlessly into the theme of the modern poet wishing to enhance his bardlike qualities, to find the extinct bard inside himself. I think the reason there has been an enduring fascination with the death of the bard is that the moment in which bardic energies disperse, depart from the earth, will, if studied carefully enough, yield the secret of regaining these energies. Only a poet who wished to become a bard would scrutinize the bard's death so closely. Blake in *A Descriptive Catalogue* offers for sale the painting of Gray's Bard and congratulates himself for making a minutely accurate depiction of a spirit, something visible only to the immortal eye, not to "the mortal perishing organ of sight" (p. 37). The next painting he describes is of King Arthur's last battle, "in which only

Three Britons escaped, these were the Strongest Man, the Beautifullest Man, and the Ugliest Man":

> The Strong man represents the human sublime. The Beautiful man represents the human pathetic, which was in the wars of Eden divided into male and female. The Ugly man represents the human reason. They were originally one man, who was fourfold; he was self-divided. . . . in the reign of that British Prince, who lived in the fifth century, there were remains of those naked Heroes, in the Welch Mountains; they are there now, Gray saw them in the person of his bard on Snowdon; there they dwell in naked simplicity; happy is he who can see and converse with them above the shadows of generation and death.

To Blake, Arthur and Albion and Gray's Bard are but different names for the One Man, naked and all embracing, Pan before his divisions into male and female, feeling and mind, perceiving eye and perceived nature. Blake was the first poet to make a precise mythology about the processes of differentiation through which lyric inarticulateness enters time and space; but I believe that poets before and after him have written preeminently lyrical poetry under the assumption that the Bard was a recuperable role. The passage just cited is a version of the story of the Four Zoas, written for the uninitiated in words of one syllable, but similar to the penultimate plate of Blake's masterpiece *Jerusalem:*

> And every Man stood Fourfold. . . .
> South stood the Nerves of the Eye. East in Rivers of bliss the Nerves of the
> Expansive Nostrils West, flowd the Parent Sense the Tongue. North stood
> The labyrinthine Ear. Circumscribing & Circumcising the excrementitious
> Husk & Covering into Vacuum evaporating revealing the lineaments of Man
> Driving outward the Body of Death in an Eternal Death & Resurrection. . . .

The Four Living Creatures Chariots of Humanity Divine . . .
. . . conversed together in Visionary forms dramatic which bright
Redounded from their Tongues in thunderous majesty, in Visions
In new Expanses, creative exemplars of Memory and of Intellect
Creating Space, Creating Time according to the wonders Divine
Of Human Imagination. . . .

(98.12, 16–20, 24, 28–32)

I have alleged that the writer of lyrics struggles against his medium, because the words he uses cannot be musical notes; here we see expressed the faith that the reunited One Man, to some extent derived from Gray's Bard, will be able to speak—his speech can only be directed at himself, one hemisphere of the brain talking to another, because there exists nothing but him—in words that are themselves "Visionary forms dramatic": things, but things in a state of preexistence. The gist of this conversation seems to be an almost contentless creativity, a speech that is continually ramifying into time and space, a created world, without ever getting there, without becoming heavy and oppressed, delimited by reason's stiff categories and the pulp of the sensuous body. Here the dream of the bard reaches a climax; later poets will develop a more sophisticated vocabulary, unvocabulary, to describe this prehistoric or posthistoric zone of bright omnicomprehension, but no poet will achieve a fuller image of the bard's eerie prehensile grasp of his world.

LYRIC IRONY

The bard, as defined above, is a hypothetical limit to the convergence of the poet and the poem: as the poem approaches the condition of music, a pure outward streaming of passion, or simply Mutability, an audible principle of change without any particular set of changed things, so the poet becomes a mere vehicle of passion or of metamorphosis, absolute and unearthly. Song and singer reach out to the unity that Yeats posited in his famous line from "Among School Children": "How can we know the dancer from the dance?" The period from about 1750 to 1830 was a time when English poets were preeminently ambitious, eager to explore the extent to which they could approximate the bard; but there has always been another strain of English lyric poetry, whose practitioners accepted cannily the impossibility of ever becoming bards and sought to use the resources of the bardic high imagination without committing themselves to the pretense of barddom. The poet of this sort of lyric does not attempt the complete engagement of himself with his poetry, does not identify himself with the sensible world his poems record. He becomes too heavy for his lyrics and allows himself to precipitate out of his poems as a concrete persona. Of course the bard can be regarded as a persona of sorts, an unusually preposterous and delusory one, since no one has ever met a bard and few can fully credit his existence, even in the prehistoric past. But to speak of the bard as a persona is a critical error, I believe—it is to mistake an attractive technical device, inextricable from the lyric mode, for a conscious self-characterization by the poet. As soon as poets become notably self-conscious about the personae they assume, the bard is dead, for he can thrive only as long as no one inquires into his psychology, his motivations, his character traits.

There are a few poems in English where we can actually observe, as a serious matter, the fall of the poet out of the poem. Foremost among these is Shelley's *Epipsychidion* (1821), in which the poet seems finally to achieve a full translation of himself and his beloved into fire:

> Spirit within two frames, oh! wherefore two?
> One passion in twin-hearts, which grows and grew,
> Till like two meteors of expanding flame,
> Those spheres instinct with it become the same,
> Touch, mingle, are transfigured; ever still
> Burning, yet ever inconsumable . . .
> One Heaven, one Hell, one immortality,

And one annihilation. Woe is me!
The winged words on which my soul would pierce
Into the height of Love's rare Universe,
Are chains of lead around its flight of fire—
I pant, I sink, I tremble, I expire!
(lines 574–79, 586–91)

This vision, which included in one passage (lines 345–83) a compelling dance of the planets in which Shelley and his wife and his mistresses were imagined as earth, moon, comet, and sun, reaches an amazing zenith as even the heavenly bodies incorporealize into sheer light. Here the poet is lost in the subject matter of his poem: he and Emily have alike grown denatured, musical. But the tremendous lyric pressure required for this fusion cannot be sustained, and the leaden festoons of vowels and consonants pull down to earth this twin-lobed human sublimity: the expression destroys the thing expressed. If "the deep truth is imageless" (*Prometheus Unbound* 2.4.116), then every image is a lie, a violation, and the heavy verbality of poetry drags it into the mud. It is interesting that the passage cited above grows increasingly rhetorical, oratorical, exclamatory (One Heaven, one Hell, one immortality. . . . Woe is me!). The words start to call attention to their own nature, and the repetitions that were supposed to be incantatory sound instead like something out of an old handbook of rhetoric. The bard's own verbal devices have turned against him, and he falls to earth, the words of his text clattering around his ankles, poet and poem hostile to each other, both estranged from vision.

The sudden awareness of the discrepancy between the poet as bard and the poet as fallible man results in what may be called lyric irony. In the *Epipsychidion* this irony approaches a tragic intensity; but in most poems in which this phenomenon can be seen it is a species of wit. I suspect that the grace of many of the highfalutin lyrics in English is due to lyric irony, the consciousness of the audience that the poet is not the loud-spouting rhapsode who is the ostensible speaker of the poem, but instead is a fairly ordinary fellow who is putting on a show. But since we have no account of the circumstances in which most of our famous traditional lyrics were declaimed, or presented to their intended audience, we must infer from what we know of the milieus of poets' lives how seriously they might have wished us to take their conceits, their posturings. Yet some considerable lyrics record inside themselves the act of deflation by which the bard fizzles into a commonplace emoter. We can understand, I believe, exactly how this process works in Chaucer's "To Rosemounde":

Nas never pyk walwed in galauntyne
As I in love am walwed and ywounde,
For which ful ofte I of myself devyne
That I am trewe Tristam the secounde.
My love may not refreyde nor affounde;
I brenne ay in an amorous plesaunce.
Do what you lyst, I wyl your thral be founde,
Thogh ye to me ne do no daliaunce.
(lines 17–24)

At the beginning of this poem the reader might credit the emotions expressed, the traditional conceits of the ruby cheeks and the barrel of tears, as plausible elements in a poem designed to woo the cruel fair. Now it is true that in such a poem it is a useful strategy for the poet to dramatize his dejection concerning his beloved's coyness; but to present himself as a fish slopped over with a heavy sauce is to go too far. When he intimates that he thinks of himself as a second Tristram, he is doing what love poets usually do, what Shelley did in the *Epipsychidion*, transporting himself and his beloved into a legendary realm, evacuated of all human complexity, where love is absolute and immobile; but this self-inflation, coming quickly after the pike in galantine, can only have the effect of comedy. The only proper response in the audience is, Look at this fool who is comparing himself to Sir Tristram. It has been suggested that "Poperyng," the birthplace of Sir Thopas in the gayest and most deadpan of the Canterbury Tales, is a clue to the reader to take the whole tale as puppetry; and similarly "To Rosemounde" makes of courtly love a kind of Punch and Judy show in which "Chaucer" is only a stooge manipulated by the real poet, laughing up his sleeve. Ezra Pound was fond of claiming that Sextus Propertius, or indeed any poet he liked, was a prototype of Laforgue; but the claims of Chaucer in this poem, where the poet erects a dummy in order to engage in a parody of self-excoriation, are better than those of many poets. This lyric irony is not necessarily a repudiation of the role of the bard, for the poet retains, hidden behind his text, an extreme freedom, a lack of definition, an imagination shackled by no restraint; he has simply made a sophisticated recognition that the poet *as he appears in the poem* may look stupid if he arrogates to himself bardic privileges, and so he dramatizes himself in the most unbardlike manner possible.

Any sort of lyric that is designed to be penetrated, that manifests beneath its artful and conventional surface some historical situation, is to an extent ironical. Pastoral poetry is a fruitful example, for in it we almost invariably find some dressing up of modern folk in the guise of shepherds and nymphs, some fussing with wigs and rustic weeds: indeed the pastoral may be defined as the sort of poetry in which historical personages try to enact an archetype, try to see themselves reconstituted under the aspect of the prehistoric, the lyrical. When Samuel Johnson objected to the frigid artificialities of the pastoral conventions of Milton's "Lycidas," he was displaying a standard of propriety according to which lyrics should not be ironical: to Johnson, Milton's decision to speak of himself and Edward King as shepherds was ludicrous, insincere, for Johnson had no relish for the complicated aesthetic effects obtainable from the deliberate diminution of persona, from the working out of human suffering within the confines of a toy landscape full of decorous dolls. Of course it is rare that pastoral poetry will overtly show its ironical character by unmasking its actors, by dissolving the scene from smooth, bucolic prelife to the urgencies of the present, by passing directly from the lyrical to the mimetic; but this does happen at times, usually when love is the issue at stake, for the love poet wishes his mistress to fall in love not with the persona of his poem, who is but an agreeable phantom, but with the actual man who wrote it. For this reason he will try to excite her interest in him with a lyric theater in which Astrophel moons over Stella, or some such contriving of timeless personages, then try to deflect her excitement from the poem to the poet with a sudden immanence of his own face, as colossal as that of the puppeteer who rises at the end of his performance, dwarfing not only the puppets but the whole stage. This requires a collapse of the lyrical.

I cannot tell from the text whether "To Rosemounde" is the kind of poem in which the author is attempting this trick; Chaucer is so exceedingly witty and evasive that any number of situations might have motivated the poem. But I am fairly confident that Ben Jonson's "A Celebration of Charis" is just what I have been describing, a poem in which the author is attempting to endear himself to his lady through a strategy of calculated stoops from lyrical flights. Jonson claims in it that Charis belongs to an order of reality in which dwell Venus and Cupid and a whole pretty pantheon. Wherever he turns his gaze he sees a ballet or masque of the gods; the one creature exiled from this world of lyrical figments is alas the poet, Ben Jonson. He is confident that poets have access to deity; but "Poëts, though devine are men" (1.5), and he is over fifty years old, likely to invite derision if he makes a spectacle of his wooing (1.1–4). He keeps trying to introduce himself into the imaginary realm of love's divinities, to mythify and depersonalize himself into fit company for Cupid and Charis, but the lyrist can never turn lyrical, and he makes a pitiful display of himself by his efforts. In the first episode of the poem he sees Charis, runs after Cupid, uncovers Cupid's eyes, and frantically instructs him to shoot his dart at Charis. But Cupid is himself amazed at the sight of her and feebly runs away without helping Ben; so Ben picks up the bow that Cupid has dropped and, fumbling, tries to shoot Charis himself:

> But she threw
> Such a Lightning (as I drew)
> At my face, that tooke my sight,
> And my motion from me quite;
> So that there, I stood a stone,
> Mock'd of all: and call'd of one
> (Which with griefe and wrath I heard)

Cupids Statue with a Beard,
Or else one that plaid his Ape,
In a *Hercules*-his shape.
(2.23–32)

Try as he will to find the right costume, to smear on the right makeup, he cannot successfully play the role of Cupid; belly and black hair keep pooching out of the corset. In the province of the lyric all must be dainty and ethereal, with playful *putti* making arithmetical experiments with the permutations of lovers; but Ben remains thick, sweating, corpulent, grounded. The poet is unable to participate in his poem, which remains weightless, gay, inconsequent while he struggles to fly into the *tra-la* by flapping his heavy arms. He makes himself appear ridiculous, but this ridiculousness is far more charming than the spectacle of a fifty-year-old man writing a poem in which he presents himself as the romantic lead; by keeping an amusing tension between his gross self and the fully lyrical domain of Charis and the gods, Jonson comes as close as he dare to presenting himself as a plausible object of affection, his very excess of self-deprecation inviting the referent of "Charis" to say, Come, you're not so bad as all that. His sexual urgency, his somewhat unplayful feelings of grief and wrath, also seem to resist any sublimation into the lyrical and keep him stranded in reality; but at the same time they make him appear credible, sincere, a man of flesh and blood trapped in an opera, unable to sing. Later in the poem Ben attempts an aria, a high lyric in which are ascribed to Charis a dove-drawn chariot, hair bright as the morning star, all the classical attributes of Venus:

Have you seene but a bright Lillie grow,
    Before rude hands have touch'd it?
Ha' you mark'd but the fall o' the Snow
    Before the soyle hath smutch'd it?
Ha' you felt the wooll of Bever?
    Or Swans Downe ever?
Or have smelt o' the bud o' the Brier?
    Or the Nard in the fire?

Or have tasted the bag of the Bee?
O so white! O so soft! O so sweet is she!
(4.21–30)

Here we find ourselves at a crossroads in which the ahistorical nature of English lyric poetry asserts itself, for Ezra Pound, caught in a detention camp at Pisa, with little more than Confucius, the Bible, and *The Pocket Book of Verse* to consult, alluded to these lines of Jonson's at the climax of Canto 74:

This liquid is certainly a
property of the mind
nec accidens est but an element
in the mind's make-up
est agens and functions dust to a fountain pan otherwise
Hast 'ou seen the rose in the steel dust
(or swansdown ever?)
so light is the urging, so ordered the dark petals of iron
we who have passed over Lethe.
(74/449)

This passage comes after a description of a ball dancing on a fountain's jet; formed water and the formed iron filings around a magnet are metaphors for the constructive powers in the mind, in the cosmos, that impose design upon the random. There is a sense in which the purpose behind the Cantos is epical, but there is another sense in which it is lyrical, for Pound is seeking to translate the sodden, heavy world around him into a domain of continual metamorphoses into beauty—it is this process of revision that he calls, in a famous letter to his father, the "bust thru from quotidien into 'divine or permanent world.' " Like Ben Jonson in "A Celebration of Charis," Pound strives to find pagan gods—not at work in the pleasant vicinity of a beautiful woman, but in the sad locus of his confinement—strives to elevate into aboriginal or African mythology the Negro prisoners surrounding him (74/426–27), strives to see the outlines of a del Cossa fresco in the immediate scene (77/473). The Pisan camp is a perfect test of his belief, for if the gods ordain here a magnet's rose, some visible design, they must do so everywhere. Also like Ben Jonson, Pound keeps falling out of his poem, turning into a squat dull presence everywhere impeding the bursting through into the divine. At one point in Canto 78, Pound interrupts his endless lamentation of extinct restaurants to speculate, "one might do worse than open a pub on Lake Garda" (78/480); and this intrusion of a postwar Pound who might, if not hanged as a traitor, keep a local pub suggests an inglorious end to the earnest poet attempting to sustain a vision of an earthly paradise in the midst of ruin. Self-flagellation is an enduring theme of the Pisan Cantos:

> J'ai eu pitié des autres
> probablement pas assez, and at moments that suited my own
> convenience
> Le paradis n'est pas artificiel
> l'enfer non plus.
>
> (76/460)

> The ant's a centaur in his dragon world.
> Pull down thy vanity, it is not man
> Made courage, or made order, or made grace. . . .
> Thou art a beaten dog beneath the hail,
> A swollen magpie in a fitful sun,
> Half black half white
> Not knowing wing from tail . . .
> Rathe to destroy, niggard in charity,
> Pull down thy vanity,
> I say pull down.
>
> (81/521)

Pound can see a universe of divine presences, of shapes forming themselves in ether, like a crystal funnel of air above an altar (90/608), or like the gods who image themselves in air and then unimage themselves again (25/119), or like the musical notes that hang still before his eyes:

> . . . the waves taking form as crystal,
> notes as facets of air,

and the mind there, before them, moving,
so that notes needed not move.

(25/119)

The danger is that through uncharitableness, through irritability, Pound may be excluded from this ubiquitous antiworld, this feast, this deliquescence into music. What is in Ben Jonson a sophisticated ploy at once to compliment a woman and smilingly to admit his own inadequacy to his conjured world of perfected feeling, is in Pound a serious fear that he will remain in a sensible hell while paradise stretches round him on all sides, a Tantalus more tortured than the original.

LYRICAL ETHICS

From one perspective it seems that the lyric mode is amoral. The archetype Proteus, who passes from one shape to another at random, in whom all shape is but a long dissembling of identity, suggests that at the heart of the lyric there is continual prevarication. The great poem in English to demonstrate the unethicality of the lyric is Donne's "The Progress of the Soul" (1601), which traces back to the Garden of Eden one particular soul, originally that of the apple of the tree of the knowledge of good and evil, and follows this soul through an unedifying succession of avatars, as mandrake and sparrow and fishlet and wolf and ape. The Progress of the Soul is such a garbled and spastic movement that it might well deserve Molly Bloom's name for it, Metempike-hoses. Donne is not interested in the mature condition of most of these avatars, indeed he usually kills them off before they leave the embryo, a continual thwarting of expectation; what interests Donne is the first division of the zygote, the primal shaping force exerted by the soul:

Out crept a sparrow, this soul's moving inn,
On whose raw arms stiff feathers now begin,
As children's teeth through gums, to break with pain;

His flesh is jelly yet, and his bones threads,
All a new downy mantle overspreads;
(19.181–85)

This is the primary lyric fascination, the fascination with the indeterminate; the protozoon has the energy of every beast latent within it, and the poet has attained the point where teeth are as likely to erupt as feathers, the quick of metamorphosis. Donne did not complete the poem, but the last lines show the amorality of his "sullen writ," the vision of Proteus:

There's nothing simply good, nor ill alone,
Of every quality comparison
    The only measure is, and judge, opinion.
(52.518–20)

The absolute standard vanishes into the real fortuitousness of the soul's progress; it is no accident that it is the soul of the apple that suffers these jerks of metempsychosis, for the knowledge of good and evil is torn apart by these oblivious passages into the random, and the soul dwindles from an ethically responsible abstraction of identity to a naked animating spark, indifferent to the acts of its provisional vehicle.

From another perspective, however, there is an ethic in the lyrical mode. Many of the metamorphoses in Ovid display the workings of a kind of justice, which offers the consolation of a shape change to those who have endured, or are about to endure, grievous wrong, such as Philomela and Daphne. There is another sort of morality in the lyric mode too, though it is given its simplest expression not in any English poem but in Rilke's "Archaic Torso of Apollo," in which the poet imagines how the statue's missing head must have gazed down at its body, a glance that made incandescent the breast and the loins:

Or else this stone would not stand so intact
beneath the shoulders' through-seen cataract
and would not glisten like a wild beast's skin;
and would not keep from all its contours giving

light like a star: for there's no place therein
that does not see you. You must change your living.
(Leishman's translation, lines 9–14)

To the sinned against the lyric mode says, You may change your life; to the sinner, to the ordinary man, the lyric mode says, You must change your life. Transfiguration is not only a gift; sometimes it is an ethical imperative. Before Rilke's poem there was a small tradition of admonitory statues; in the Don Juan story, for example, the statue of the man Don Juan murdered comes back to terrify him, to offer him salvation, at last to damn him. Da Ponte, the librettist of Mozart's *Don Giovanni*, handles this episode especially well: during the banquet, in which Don Giovanni shows himself as a raving sensualist, deaf to Elvira's imprecations against her seducer, his henchman Leporello compares his heart to a stone:

Cold must that man be,
Heartless as marble,
Who without pity
Mocks her cry.

It is as if the petrification of the villain summons up the dead Commendatore, the Stone Guest, who is a superior sort of stone:

Lep. Ah . . . O God . . . Keep him away . . .
He . . . the statue . . . of marble . . . who nodded.
I could see him in the moonlight . . .
I could hear each marble shoe.
Ta. Ta. Ta. Ta.
(Auden-Kallman translation)

The change from man to statue suggests a purity, a simplicity, an implacability impossible to a merely organic creature; the marble is streamlined into moral perfection, and it loudly or silently compels the spectator to imitate it. The statue represents not apathy or heartlessness but naked form not quite ingredient in matter, the soul freed from its mortal encumbrance. Similarly, Ariel's vision of King Alonso turned to coral and pearls is designed to chasten, to evoke sacred awe; it helps to direct Ferdinand in the direction of proper action. In the case of Pound, the poet is obsessed with broken statues:

> There died a myriad,
> And of the best, among them,
> For an old bitch gone in the teeth,
> For a botched civilization . . .
> For two gross of broken statues,
> For a few thousand battered books.
> (*Hugh Selwyn Mauberley* 5)
>
> the huntress in broken plaster keeps watch no longer
> (Canto 76/473)

The broken statue is an image that has lost both moral and aesthetic authority, that can no longer force the spectator to change his life. The authority of statues is an ancient theme: behind these statues are the little idols so beloved of Wilde ("The Decay of Lying") and Yeats (*The King's Threshold*), which Greek brides used to hang on their bridal beds in order to make their newly conceived children resemble gods, as if the ocular pressure could shape the fetus in the womb. The man who is in the process of subliming himself will look to a statue for guidance; and that Ben Jonson, in "A Celebration of Charis" (2.30), changes into an ugly statue only shows that something has gone wrong in the process of self-transfiguration, as if a magician tried to change himself into a bird and wound up a man with feathers instead of hair.

As we descend out of the rigor, the lyrical austerity that Rilke and the English aesthetes espoused, we find that with poets of a certain temperament the untransfigured can hold great charm. It may be, as Auden says in "In Praise of Limestone," that when he imagines the blessed he sees statues in Elysium, marbles in a marble landscape, but opposed to such a vision he gives another command, the antilyrical imperative: "find sun's luxury enough" ("1929," 2); "Find the mortal world enough" ("Lullaby"); "God bless this green world temporal" ("Lauds"). Ben Jonson is another poet of a relaxed and easy disposition, a poet particularly intrigued by the collapse of the world of lyrical artifice, not only when the apprentice Cupid freezes into obese stolidity, but also at the end of "A Celebration of Charis" where, after Charis has offered a fanciful description of her ideal suitor, divergent from Ben Jonson in every conceivable way, another lady takes exception to these stringent requirements, declaring that she does not care for her lover's mind, et cetera: "What you please, you parts may call, / 'Tis one good part I'ld lie withall" (10.7–8). This deflation of Charis's fantasy is exactly parallel to Ben's deflation of his own coy, twittery dreams of Cupid and Venus, though it would be unchivalrous for Ben in propria persona to accomplish this himself. Sexual earthiness reasserts itself, and the lyric mode leaves behind only a faint film of grace over the proceedings.

The great master of lyric deflation, however, is the later Yeats. In his earlier work he sought assiduously to become a statue or, as he put it, to attain his antiself. The antiself was defined as the exact opposite of everything one naturally was, the complement of identity; to move toward achieving it was to find creative power, fluency, nonchalance, as Yeats explained in "Ego Dominus Tuus." The antiself is the bard in twentieth-century guise; the eighteenth-century poets knew that their condition was as unlike the bard's as they could imagine, but it was left to Yeats to define the bard as what he was not. What one is not is a broad region, including oceans, forests, and mountains, so the antiself is not only an artificial construct, a translation of oneself into unnature, a Byzantine icon with empty eyes, but also a Druidical attunement with the cosmos, an entry into the whirlwind. In the last part of Yeats's career, however, the antiself starts to become increasingly indistinguishable from the self, and the bard becomes not a specter of unearthly disengagement, self-appeasing or self-affrighting, but a grubby old man:

"A young man in the dark am I,
But a wild old man in the light,
That can make a cat laugh, or
Can touch by mother wit
Things hid in their marrow-bones
From time long passed away,
Hid from all those warty lads

That by their bodies lay.
("The Wild Old Wicked Man," 1937)

Ben Jonson tried to seduce by erecting a fantasy of old gods and goddesses, all of whom were celebrating Charis, including her in their mythological pageant. The Wild Old Wicked Man alleges that he has poetical power but seems to tell no story, make no cat laugh. The bald assertion of bardhood has replaced the exercise of a bard's powers; he dramatizes his decrepitude instead of sweeping away his intended woman with a fit of supernatural eloquence—though this dramatization is itself eloquent. He has fallen into squalor, seems exiled from every mystery, a burned-out case, capable of transforming nothing and no one, expert only in one part; yet even in this state of extreme degradation he displays something lyrical, makes a touching song of his unsonglike condition. The lyric muse can leave the bard battered and destitute, brainless, but she never, it seems, abandons him utterly. Yeats knew that muses were fickle, sexy creatures who liked to put on airs: "Muses resemble women who creep out at night and give themselves to unknown sailors and return to talk of Chinese porcelain" (*A Vision*, p. 24); yet he did not scorn even the most stale and withered muse, like Crazy Jane, or the mad old woman who keeps the till in "The Circus Animals' Desertion." In a recent poem, by Donald Justice, we see the drama of bard and muse stripped down to its barest:

THE TELEPHONE NUMBER OF THE MUSE

Sleepily, the muse to me: "Let us be friends.
Good friends but only friends. You understand."
And yawned. And kissed, for the last time, my ear.
Who earlier, weeping at my touch, had whispered:
"I loved you once." and: "No, I don't love him.
Not after everything he did." Later,
Rebuttoning her nightgown with my help:
"Sorry, I just have no desire, it seems."
Sighing: "For you, I mean." Long silence. Then:
"You always were so serious." At which

I smiled, darkly. And that was how I came
To sleep beside, not with her; without dreams.

I call her up sometimes, long distance now.
And she still knows my voice, but I can hear,
Beyond the music of her phonograph,
The laughter of the young men with their keys.

I have the number written down somewhere.

"You always were so serious" is the same charge laid on the ineffectual poet by the woman in T. S. Eliot's "Conversation Galante" and, in a slightly different form, in its model, Laforgue's "Autre Complainte de Lord Pierrot." The muse, at least the lyric muse, is frivolous; if she is seized with an ethical fit she will usually teach by means of wonder, of unearthly delight, like Ariel, who is almost a male muse. Here she has descended about as far as she can into corporeality; she seems almost indistinguishable from a jilting girl friend, and we know her a muse only from a few traits—her imperturbability, her facetiousness, her inconstancy, and the dreamlessness of the sleep slept by the poet who lacks her favor. If some poets see how far they can go in the direction of the bard, other poets see how far they can go in the opposite direction; but though Justice's poet, sunk into sour, mundane reminiscence, is at an infinite remove from the delirium of Gray's Bard, both are lamenting the loss of imagination from human life. But even the poet at the extreme of the unlyrical can, if he is a poet at all, recapture something of the bard's fevers; the telephone number is written down somewhere. No poem can be completely lyrical, but it may also be true that no poem can be completely unlyrical. The bard's diffuse and horrid face is dormant inside even the most casual, the most debonair, of poets.

Chapter 3

NATURA LYRICA

THE bard, in such various guises as Gray's Bard and Yeats's Wild Old Wicked Man, may profitably be depicted as an old man; but it was one of the achievements of Romantic poetry to show that the bard could as well be a baby. The poets of the nineteenth and twentieth centuries have proved that the aborigine, the caveman, could be lithe, young, beautiful. It is true that Yeats conceived his Druids as ancient, beicicled with wisdom, but in contrast we have D. H. Lawrence offering a sinuous and light-footed vision of the Neanderthal, too graceful and ferocious to be human (*St. Mawr*, p. 50). The proper domain of the lyrical is, from one vantage, the prehistoric; so it is not surprising that poets would find the ideal lyric subject to be an infant touching with wonder an infantile world.

Lyrical nature, then, is nature newborn or embryonic, not yet congealed into particular forms. Of the great lyric poets in English, two have been conspicuously interested in academic philosophy, Shelley and T. S. Eliot; and both have shown a certain fascination with nature in the egg, not yet hatched into an articulate world. Shelley's fragmentary essay "On Life" contains the following passage:

> Let us recollect our sensations as children . . . we less habitually distinguished all that we saw and felt from ourselves.

> They seemed as it were to constitute one mass. There are some persons who in this respect are always children. Those who are subject to the state called reverie, feel as if their nature were resolved into the surrounding universe or as if the surrounding universe were resolved into their being.

Yeats quoted this passage with great approval in his essay on Shelley's philosophy, commenting that Shelley confused his unique experience as a poet with the common experience of all, and that Shelley "must have expected to receive thoughts and images from beyond his own mind . . . for he believed inspiration a kind of death" (*Essays and Introductions*, pp. 80–81). Some poets seek lyricality in death, others in the unborn; in either case it is sought in an exceedingly mingled condition, a zone of being in which poet and nature are little discriminated from each other, whether ashes or ashes, dust or dust. The nature that is most accommodating to what Shelley calls reverie, the nature that carries in its lumpish toils the traces of the poet's being, is lyrical nature.

In Eliot's philosophy, a far more systematic matter than Shelley's, the infantilism of all mental and physical objects is diligently investigated. We have had occasion before to note in Eliot's work that emotional protoplasm, feeling before it has attained any precise definition, is both a horror and the locus of the poetical. In his dissertation, *Knowledge and Experience in the Philosophy of F. H. Bradley* (1916), Eliot asserts that the perceiver and his perceived world ramify out of a unitary state of indefiniteness that he calls, following Bradley, *immediate experience*—that is, experience so immediate that no one has ever experienced it, for there was as yet nothing to be felt and no one to feel, only a blank agitation, a potent zero seeking to realize itself in a huge, deceptively hefty and inert, uncontradictory world, and a complacent, deceptively knowledgeable and self-sufficient spectator of that world. This philosophy supposes that poet and nature are born from the same womb and that careful inspection discloses their fraternity, their geminatedness: feelings, Eliot claims, are just as public and objectively valid as furniture, as we assume when we declare that we know an intimate friend's feelings better than he does himself. Similarly, objects—chairs, anvils, vases, trees—despite their homely appearance of persistence, their discreet unchangeability, nevertheless are inherently subjective, everywhere provocative of illusion, as proved by the stick that seems to bend when its image is refracted by water: "It is only in social behaviour . . . that feelings and things are torn apart. And after this separation they leave dim and drifting edges, and tend to coalesce" (p. 25). Presocial perception, therefore, is concerned with juvenile objects, objects still wet from the amniotic fluid out of which perceiver and perceived alike were born. The lyric mode posits a world of such objects, half-intelligible and half-intelligent, Claes-Oldenberg-soft, humid with feeling.

Eliot tends to fudge the issue of temporality. Exactly when was it that immediate experience took place, if none of my present experiences is immediate? Yesterday my sensory apparatus was very much as it is today. Eliot's metaphors for suggesting immediate experience appeal to the womb, or to the aborigine, or to mollusks and tunicates, but when pressed he denies that immediate experience took place in any of them: "turning our attention to lower levels of being . . . we find . . . a general impoverishment. . . . No stage can be so low as to be mere feeling; and on the other hand man surely feels more than the animal" (p. 18). Yet despite this declaration Eliot remains fascinated by the sea anemone's digestive system (p. 44), by the concept of truth in the world of the jellyfish (p. 166). If a jellyfish's experiences are no more immediate than mine, there is still something about a jellyfish's truths through which we can intuit some of the attributes of immediate experience: if I were a transparent bag of water I would resemble a finite center, the hollow sphere in which, according to Bradley, self and world are virtual. Immediate experience, being prior to clocks, to any knowledge of time, is not to be found on a chronological scale, whether that of my personal life or that of the eons; it resides in its own continual present, a hovering formlessness constantly resolving itself into a psychology and a sensible universe. In this sense I and my world are newborn every instant, and if I am attentive enough I will be able to feel inside me, around me, this indwelling infantility that parallels my life.

Poets have always postulated a nature not like our nature, but parallel to it and better, in danger of falling into heaviness and decay: a *natura lyrica.* The vision of Eden is clearly of this sort; and one of the extraordinary presentations of this lyrical nature is in the description of the Garden of Adonis in *The Faerie Queene,* where old Genius

> letteth in, he letteth out to wend,
> All that to come into the world desire;
> A thousand thousand naked babes attend
> About him day and night, which doe require,
> That he with fleshly weedes would them attire:
> Such as him list, such as eternall fate
> Ordained hath, he clothes with sinfull mire,
> And sendeth forth to live in mortall state,
> Till they againe return backe by the hinder gate.
>
> After that they againe returned beene,
> They in that Gardin planted be againe;
> And grow afresh, as they had never seene
> Fleshly corruption, nor mortall paine.
> Some thousand yeares so doen they there remaine;
> And then of him are clad with other hew,
> Or sent into the chaungefull world againe;
> Till thither they returne, where first they grew:
> So like a wheele around they runne from old to new. . . .
>
> Infinite shapes of creatures there are bred,
> And uncouth formes, which none yet ever knew,
> And every sort is in a sundry bed
> Set by itselfe, and ranckt in comely rew:
> Some fit for reasonable soules t' indew,
> Some made for beasts, some made for birds to weare,
> And all the fruitfull spawne of fishes hew
> In endless rancks along enraunged were,
> That seem'd the *Ocean* could not containe them there.
>
> (3.6.32–33, 35)

Here is the universe in utero. We are told that the Garden of Adonis has walls of iron and gold, and a hoary attendant, and fecund soil, but other than those details and the upwelling Chaos that provides new substance for the teeming forms, the Garden is empty, an indistinct amenability in which there swell the thousand thousand babes. Here all animals are vegetables, but seem also to resemble tiny human children, for no boundary lines yet obtain among animal, vegetable, and human; all things are slowly discriminating themselves out of loam and humus, slowly descending into real nature. What has long exasperated many students of Spenser is that the Garden of Adonis both is and is not the lower world. Spenser seems to say that the Garden is a great womb for the lower world's generation, but also that some of these babes never leave the Garden at all, go about their business, grow old, and die without ever leaving these precincts consecrated as a nursery for another, more keenly suffering place. Furthermore, as Spenser elaborates his vision, he populates it with an agent who, one would think, ought to work his mischief only in lower nature, Time:

> Great enimy to it, and to all the rest,
> That in the *Gardin of Adonis* springs,
> Is wicked *Time,* who with his scyth addrest,
> Does mow the flowring herbes and goodly things,
> And all their glory to the ground downe flings,
> Where they doe wither, and are fowly mard:
> He flyes about, and with his flaggy wings
> Beates downe both leaves and buds without regard,
> Ne ever pittie may relent his malice hard.
>
> (3.6.39)

Why would Spenser permit this infection of his Garden, where all the vegetable souls of things should seemingly be pretemporal, immune from time? Why should this antimasque of generation be forced into becoming a high analogue of the whole reincarnative cycle? The answer lies, I think, in the fact that poets wish to discover in our present world the world that is not quite born, the world prior to established categories, the world in which metaphor and simile are not figures but truths, the lyrical world. A vision of Eden is more attractive if it exists not in 4004 B.C., but at all times and places. The Garden of Adonis is an Eden that specifically obeys this condition of immediacy, what Kafka meant when he said it is "possible that not only could we live continuously in Paradise, but that we are continuously there in actual fact, no matter whether we know it here or not" (*The Great Wall of China*, p. 174); what Yeats meant when he asked

> Is Eden far away, or do you hide
> From human thought, as hares and mice and coneys
> That run before the reaping-hook and lie
> In the last ridge of the barley? Do our woods
> And winds and ponds cover more quiet woods,
> More shining winds, more star-glimmering ponds?
> (Introductory poem to *The Shadowy Waters*)

Spenser labors to make the Garden of Adonis converge with the nature we experience, where Time is as potent a force as Genius, so that we may feel more sharply how close it is to us, how dominant its productions are in our lives. The Garden of Adonis is a place of simultaneous incipience and perfection, in which "There is continuall spring, and harvest there / Continuall, both meeting at one time" (3.6.42.1–2); and in this temporal confusion we behold a model of our state simplified into a tense reconciliation of opposites. The Garden of Adonis is Eden, lost, delectable, infinitely removed, yet at the same time a preworld always hovering above our world, always falling into the panoply of natural affairs; it is at once unfallen and wretched with our wretchedness, and therefore the ideal locus of poetry.

In the Garden of Adonis we see lyrical nature not only isolated in itself, but defined in relation to lower nature: it is a perpetual becoming in which nothing attains full being until it enters the unlyrical world of the solid and the stolid; it is a condition of generating, but whatever is generated must leave and take up residence elsewhere. The lyricality of the Garden can also be seen in the fact that it is at once a place and a person:

And sooth it seemes they say: for he may not
For ever die, and ever buried bee
In balefull night, where all things are forgot;
All be he subject to mortalitie,
Yet is eterne in mutabilitie,
And by succession made perpetuall,
Transformed oft, and chaunged diverselie:
For him the Father of all formes they call;
Therefore needs mote he live, that living gives to all.
(3.6.47)

If the Garden is an abstraction of natural life, Adonis is an abstraction of the Garden, a benign but unimaginable personification of Altering, in which no deviation may disturb his high conclusiveness. In Adonis, as in his garden, there slumber the forms of all creatable things.

The canto on the Garden of Adonis is a bubble in the text of *The Faerie Queene*; ostensibly it accounts for the origin of Belphoebe and Amoret, but it would be a mere digression if it were not an epitome of the whole, an attempt by the author to make explicit the conditions of his art, for the Garden operates under rules only slightly more extreme than those that govern the poem in general, where a vast, seemingly endless swell of characters are spawned and strut and disappear, obscurely alluding to a "lower world," Elizabethan England. Adonis is, at last, the imagination, both a faculty and a locale, from which forms keep proliferating until they populate a cosmos, and in which time and suffering exist but work in an unusually picturesque, smooth, and expert fashion. If we consider Adonis and his garden not as an episode in an interminable epic, but as an allegory of a poet and his imagination, relative to a less imaginary world, we have the basic drama of the Romantic nature poem.

Wordsworth's landscapes are at once deeply, tremulously felt and little particularized; and I believe they are best understood as new versions of the Garden of Adonis, places in which arise in endless profusion prenatural forms, forms intense but not quite explicit, forms still saturated with the presence of their father,

Wordsworth-Adonis. The lakes, the mountains, the thorn trees are startling, dewy fresh, because they are still infantile; the umbilical cord between them and the imagination is not yet severed. This is made clear in book 2 of *The Prelude,* in the course of a remarkable meditation in which Wordsworth thinks of the baby he once was and experiences a vertigo of regression:

> No outcast he, bewildered and depressed;
> Along his infant veins are interfused
> The gravitation and the filial bond
> Of Nature that connect him with the world.
> (2.261–64; all citations are from the 1805 text)

Wordsworth sees his poetical career as a swaddling and a coddling of the infant in himself, as if he were ceaselessly pregnant with his own fetus:

> From early days,
> Beginning not long after that first time
> In which, a babe, by intercourse of touch
> I held mute dialogues with my mother's heart,
> I have endeavoured to display the means
> Whereby the infant sensibility,
> Great birthright of our being, was in me
> Augmented and sustained.
> (2.280–87)

The axolotl is a larval form of the tiger salamander that never matures but grows fat and inarticulate, becomes capable of reproducing itself without the discomfort of adulthood; it is a useful emblem for certain Romantic poets, not as they really were but as they would have wished to be. I believe that this extreme neoteny seeks a vision of its surrounding universe as inchoate, as unperformable, as itself. As Wordsworth says in the Prospectus to *The Excursion,* no one is surprised to hear that the mind is fitted to the world, but he will proclaim, in addition, how exquisitely "The external World is fitted to the Mind" (line 68). A study of Wordsworth's vision of the external world in its quickest, most exalted states shows that it sometimes plays the role of mother to the fetal poet, at other times is itself unborn, reticent.

Wordsworth seems to be often exasperated in his attempts to find an imagery appropriate for prenature, nature in the womb. He often turns with awe to clouds, yet clouds suggest murkiness, obscurity, oppressiveness, all qualities unsuitable for suggesting what nature was before it was fully *there*; still, he likes to compare the Imagination to a cloud, as if it were the faculty that could behold the subliminal cloudiness in solid things:

> Imagination!—lifting up itself
> Before the eye and progress of my song
> Like an unfathered vapour, here that power,
> In all the might of its endowments, came
> Athwart me. I was lost as in a cloud,
> Halted without a struggle to break through,
> And now, recovering, to my soul I say
> "I recognise thy glory."
>
> (6.525–32)

Just-born nature, like the babe of the Immortality Ode, comes trailing clouds of glory. This passage comes just after Wordsworth's account of his crossing Simplon Pass without knowing it, a preteristic disappointment soothed by the realization that in all natural scenes what is important is not what is, but what is about to be. The sharp contours, the minute divisions of the landscape, distract the spectator from its actual incipience, its unfinishedness, its slow moving into significance; Wordsworth's preferred vistas usually contain a suggestion of something unrealized, indeed unrealizable on a sensible earth. Therefore, as the poet ponders this sudden steam bath of Imagination in which he is plunged, the chosen details of the Alpine landscape start to readjust themselves under the aspect of this higher diffuseness; whereas he previously noticed the helpful peasant, the stony channel of the stream (lines 513–16), now he speaks of "woods decaying, never to be decayed" (line 557)—Tennyson remembered this line in "Tithonus"—of "Winds thwarting winds" (line 560), of "Black drizzling crags" (line 563):

The unfettered clouds and region of the heavens,
Tumult and peace, the darkness and the light,
Were all like workings of one mind, the features
Of the same face, blossoms upon one tree,
Characters of the great apocalypse,
The types and symbols of eternity,
Of first, and last, and midst, and without end.
(lines 566–72)

The landscape smears, grows fuzzy and turbid, *pointilliste*; and as the forests and the crags undo themselves, become incoherent and spattered, they simultaneously grow alphabetlike, legible; the breakdown of clear shape leads to a gain in meaningfulness. In a manuscript of 1807 Wordsworth inserted lines about

Huge fragments of primaeval mountain spread
In powerless ruin, blocks as huge aloft
Impending, nor permitted yet to fall.

—lines suggesting that what is interesting in the landscape is what is impending in it, an overhanging of something about to fall, the force of revelation. The mountain shatters into a ruin in order that the shattering energy may be displayed, may take precedence over any fixed form. In this way the locus of the imagination becomes upheaval and explosion, decay, degradation, aerial swirls and spurts, as the imagination seeks external images imbued with something of its own character. Elsewhere in this passage Wordsworth speaks of infinitude as our true home, "something evermore about to be" (line 542), and the subject of the poem changes from a homely description of an Alpine trek to a description of the infinitude lurking within the Alpine scene. The poet's all-regressing eye has traced the mountains back to their juvenile forms, to their geological infancy.

The proper language for infinitude is the oxymoron, in which the categories of the finite are most outrageously defied. The thrust of Wordsworth's imagination in the Simplon Pass episode is to roll up the Alpine backdrop into unity, even though that unity is full of contradiction, "Tumult and peace, the darkness and the light" (line 567). The mind that can hold together these tense oppositions has duplicated in itself the creative mind that thought the mountains into being; it can feel in itself the plastic energies exerted by God. Coleridge, in his lecture on *Romeo and Juliet* (*Lecture VII*, 1811–12), defended Romeo's use of oxymoron—"Misshapen chaos of well-seeming forms! / Feather of lead, bright smoke, cold fire, sick health!" (1.1.185–86); Coleridge observed that here we have

> an effort of the mind, when it would describe what it cannot satisfy itself with the description of, to reconcile opposites and qualify contradiction, leaving a middle state of mind more strictly appropriate to the imagination than any other, when it is, as it were, hovering between images. As soon as it is fixed on one image, it becomes understanding; but while it is unfixed and wavering between them, attaching itself permanently to none, it is imagination. Such is the fine description of Death in Milton:—
>
> The other shape,
> If shape it might be call'd, that shape had none
> Distinguishable in member, joint, or limb,
> Or substance might be call'd, that shadow seem'd,
> For each seem'd either: black it stood as night;
> Fierce as ten furies, terrible as hell,
> And shook a dreadful dart: what seem'd his head
> The likeness of a kingly crown had on.
>
> *Paradise Lost*, Book II
>
> The grandest efforts of poetry are where the imagination is called forth, not to produce a distinct form, but a strong working of the mind, still offering what is still repelled, and again creating what is again rejected; the result being what the poet wishes to impress, namely, the substitution of a sublime feeling of the unimaginable for a mere image.

This might be an exact statement of the recipe Wordsworth followed for recasting the natural scene after the great venting of imaginative vapors in the Simplon Pass episode. The landscape is systematically disassembled in the poet's uncreating spasm of imagination, dematerialized until the spectator sees no particular image, only the "workings of one mind" (6.568), what Coleridge calls the "strong working of the mind." Nature reduced to its embryo is not an immanence of distinct forms, but a hovering of images that refuse to descend; the details of the landscape are repelled, rejected, as soon as they alight on provisional images—hedgerows, hardly hedgerows—because the imagination is greedy, insists on keeping its images in the domain of the metamorphosable. This shiftiness of natural detail is one of the predominant features of Wordsworth's poetry, for example, in "The Green Linnet":

> My dazzled sight he oft deceives,
> A Brother of the dancing leaves;
> Then flits, and from the cottage eaves
> Pours forth his song in gushes;
> As if by that exulting strain
> He mocked and treated with disdain
> The voiceless Form he chose to feign,
> While fluttering in the bushes.
> (lines 33–40)

The bird that camouflages itself as a leaf is unusually close to that intense center, that womb of creation, in which birds and leaves are not yet differentiated. Coleridge cites this stanza in chapter 22 of the *Biographia Literaria* as an example of the fourth excellence of Wordsworth's poetry, "the perfect truth of nature in his images and descriptions, as taken immediately from nature, and proving a long and genial intimacy with the very spirit which gives the physiognomic expression to all the works of nature." Wordsworth has little concern with nature expressed, blatant; he turns inward from the expression to what is expressed, from the vernal wood to the impulse within it. In fetal nature he finds birdleaves, leafbirds, things not yet resolved into full entity.

In the famous definition of imagination in *Biographia Literaria* 13, Coleridge says that the imagination "dissolves, diffuses, dissipates, in order to re-create; or where this process is rendered impossible, yet still at all events it struggles to idealize and to unify."

In the poetry of Wordsworth and Coleridge, the re-creation is often less evident than the dissolution; one might almost believe that the imagination were more fully engaged in the act of unmaking than in the act of making, indeed that dissolution were itself re-creation. Coleridge goes on to claim that the imagination is "*vital*, even as all objects (*as* objects) are essentially fixed and dead"; if this is the case, then a poet's newly minted objects, his re-creations, are in danger of being stiff, inert, stillborn, unless they show traces of the indeterminate, the dissolute. I have said that Wordsworth keeps searching for a higher nebulousness in natural forms, though he does not wish to allege that the perceived world is a cloud. A more satisfying emblem for the relation between juvenile nature and mature nature is a cloud that is continually resolving into a definite world, as Wordsworth suggests in a long simile in *The Prelude*, originally written as a commentary on the Simplon Pass episode, about a spelunker who has just entered a cave and

> sees, or thinks
> He sees, erelong, the roof above his head,
> Which instantly unsettles and recedes—
> Substance and shadow, light and darkness, all
> Commingled, making up a canopy
> Of shapes, and forms, and tendencies to shape,
> That shift and vanish, change and interchange
> Like spectres—ferment quiet and sublime,
> Which, after a short space, works less and less
> Till, every effort, every motion gone,
> The scene before him lies in perfect view
> Exposed, and lifeless as a written book.
>
> (8.716–27)

I take it this is a model for every exercise of imagination: the excitement lies in the focusing, in the accommodation of the inner eye: the previous chaos, with its blobs and blurs, is unspeakable and a bore; the subsequent cavescape is a conventional illustration from a tourist's handbook, and a bore; but the passage from one state to the other provides the keenest delight. The imagination is covetous of its images, and every settled picture it offers is at once an expression and a betrayal; the imagination much prefers a state of giddy half-creation in which images "shift and vanish, change and interchange," in which the art of choice is not painting but music, an unstable dynamic. The cave of this passage suggests that the poet has entered subnature, another version of prenature, the domain of the imagination. Although Wordsworth is disappointed with the visible reality of the cave, it soon undergoes a remarkable resorption into the fantastical:

> But let him pause and look again,
> And a new quickening shall succeed, at first
> Beginning timidly, then creeping fast
> Through all which he beholds: the senseless mass,
> In its projections, wrinkles, cavities,
> Through all its surface, with all colours streaming,
> Like a magician's airy pageant, parts,
> Unites, embodying everywhere some pressure
> Or image, recognised or new, some type
> Or picture of the world—forests and lakes,
> Ships, rivers, towers, the warrior clad in mail,
> The prancing steed, the pilgrim with his staff,
> The mitred bishop and the thronèd king—
> A spectacle to which there is no end.
>
> (8.728–41)

We are almost, it seems, travelers on the Hodos Chameliontos, the road of unintelligible images, so quickly does image succeed image in a puzzling welter; yet we are not back to the chaos with which we started. The world that springs out of the cave walls is full and feverish, vivid, hyperactive, but it does not appear to be the genuine re-creation that the imagination performs; instead, it is merely the work of fancy, that faculty that "has no other counters to play with, but fixities and definites . . . a mode of Memory emancipated from the order of time and space" (Coleridge, *Biographia Literaria* 13). Earlier in book 8, Wordsworth described how his book learning provided him with material on which his "wilfulness of fancy and conceit" (line 521) could operate: and thus a certain significant feature in the landscape, probably only a black rock, could be transformed into "a burnished shield" or "An entrance now into some magic cave" (lines 573, 576)—could be absorbed into old-fashioned romance. Wordsworth calls such phenomena the shapes "Of wilful fancy grafted upon feelings / Of the imagination" (lines 584–85). The warriors, bishops, kings, and prancing steeds with which the poet populates his cave seem equally fancy-ful, as if the boy who saw an entrance to fairyland in a black rock had managed to enter it, to climb down into the locus of moonshine. I believe this is the kind of re-creation typically found in Wordsworth's poetry: after Imagination has dissolved the sensible world, just at the point when it ought to utter *I am* and become the god of a new creation, it suddenly stops, shakes its head, looks around helplessly; and another, less gifted demiurge, Fancy, steps forward, attempts to make the cosmic effort, offers its slightly awkward and mechanical new world as if it were the genuine article. The Imagination is almost the Anarch of Pope's *Dunciad* 4, whose uncreating word utters a false apocalypse; it is confident in its powers of dissolution, hesitant in creation. When at the climax of *The Prelude*, on Mount Snowdon, nature and the imagination unite in a single cloud that is at once opaque and transparent, massy, substantial, and yet everywhere permeable—Wordsworth's best emblem for prenature, lyrical nature, nature sublime and shapable according to the mind's plastic stress—it is significant that it is night and the poet can see nothing. In the looming and embroiled darkness, in the great giddy billowing of an imagination that can suck up the wide earth's majesty into a sea of mist (13.50), any finite image would be an intrusion. The imagination, engrossed in the lightness and the speed of its own workings, can find its perfection only in the undoing of images.

The fancy, with its machine-tooled likenesses, its waxy solderings, its rigidly applied principles of conjoining, is an adolescent or adult faculty; the imagination is always avid of novelty and metamorphosis, always a child. Even Wordsworth wishes to grow up, and, though he would have objected to the claim, he in many ways prefers fancy to imagination as his career evolves. Keats's famous denunciation of the egotistical sublime in Wordsworth is not as felicitous as it seems, for as Wordsworth grows more egotistical he grows less sublime. To Coleridge in *Biographia Literaria* 2, it is clear that the genius, living most of his life in "the ideal world," must lack "the sensation of *self*"; and I believe Wordsworth's poetry tends to demonstrate this. The fascination with the impulsive imagination is, as Eliot's philosophy as well as Coleridge's suggests, a fascination with a state both prenatural and pre-egotistical. The ideally imaginative sensibility is in one sense childish, fetal, and in another sense wholly extraterrestrial, as a passage in *The Prelude* suggests: Wordsworth discusses the infiltration of "human-heartedness" into the emotions he feels for natural objects formerly loved as an "Angel, if he were to dwell on earth, / Might love in individual happiness" (4.237–38). The dawning of common sympathy, the growing clamor of the still, sad music of humanity, interferes with the old glad immediacy with which Sirius, Jupiter, the Pleiades formerly shone, when Wordsworth was angelic, almost a heavenly body himself. In a long simile Wordsworth compares this falling off of love to a langorous man bending over the side of a slow boat, who

> Sees many beauteous sights—weeds, fishes, flowers,
> Grots, pebbles, roots of trees—and fancies more,
> Yet oft is perplexed, and cannot part
> The shadow from the substance, rocks and sky,
> Mountains and clouds, from that which is indeed
> The region, and the things which there abide
> In their true dwelling; now is crossed by gleam
> Of his own image, by a sunbeam now,
> And motions that are sent he knows not whence,
> Impediments that make his task more sweet;
>
> (4.252–61)

This simile, like the related simile of the cave in book 8, may be a general statement of the predicament of the Romantic poet: he is originally impersonal, an angel in spontaneous rapport with the cosmos, but his face slowly takes shape, becomes a thick mask everywhere interfering with his vision until he can see only himself and nothing of what is around him. As the bard descends into history, grows self-conscious, a vivid personality, he is destined to be estranged from the world on which his imagination operates; both man and nature become sharply delineated, cold, withdrawn into their separate beings. To an adult, there is no such thing as Imagination, and the light once attributed to it becomes the glimmering of Fancy, a romantic and literary unreality, what he calls in the "Elegiac Stanzas Suggested by a Picture of Peele Castle" "The light that never was, on sea or land" (line 15).

THE ORDINARY SUBLIME

The tendency of the poetry and criticism of Wordsworth and Coleridge is to extend the domain of the sublime from an emotion appropriate to certain rare and exalted experiences to a general heightening of the pitch of every mean, paltry, or grand event of life. To the eighteenth century the sublime was a shock, a vertigo, a reeling over the abyss; to the nineteenth century it is a nimbus, an aura that might infuse even pedestrian things, a tincture of indeterminacy latent in every determinate form. A few citations from earlier authors will show what I mean:

> the Sublime therefore must be Marvellous, and Surprising. It must strike vehemently upon the Mind, and Fill, and Captivate it irresistibly. (Jonathan Richardson, *The Connoisseur*, 1719)
>
> Our Imagination loves to be filled with an Object, or to graspe at any thing that is too big for its Capacity. (Addison, *Spectator*, no. 412, 3:540, 1712)
>
> The passion caused by the great and sublime in *nature*, when those causes operate most powerfully, is Astonishment; and astonishment is that state of the soul, in which all its motions are suspended, with some degree of horror. In this case the mind is so entirely filled with its object, that it cannot entertain any other, nor by consequence reason on that object which employs it. (Burke, *A Philosophical Enquiry*, 2:1, 1759)

> Longinus maintains that a high degree of sublimity is utterly inconsistent with accuracy of imagination; and that Authors of the most elevated genius, at the same time that they are capable of rising to the greatest excellencies, are likewise most apt to commit trivial faults. (William Duff, *An Essay on Original Genius*, 1767)
>
> Longinus observes that the effect of the sublime is *to lift up the soul; to exalt it into ecstasy; so that, participating, as it were, of the splendors of the divinity, it becomes filled with joy and exultation; as if it had itself conceived the lofty sentiments which it heard.* (Richard Payne Knight, *Analytical Inquiry into the Principles of Taste*, 1805)

In these observations there are certain common themes: sublimity is something like an epileptic fit; it is a state in which captious precision of detail is lost in smeary genius. It represents, paradoxically, a perfection of mental activity—for to a man undergoing a seizure of sublimity the whole sensible world looks as if it were created by himself—and also a complete paralysis of mental activity, a blastedness, a boggling. Some modern psychologists believe that the catatonic cannot move a muscle not because his brain is stupefied, but because the conduction of electricity through the nerves of his brain is so rapid and urgent that it defies any activation of particular motor nerves. The speculative physiology of the old theorists of the sublime fits this exactly and suggests that prolonged sublimity is catatonia.

Wordsworth, in a fragmentary essay "The Sublime and the Beautiful," noted this paradox and distinguished two species of the sublime, which one might call overstrain versus abasement:

> Power awakens the sublime either when it rouses us to a sympathetic energy & calls upon the mind to grasp at something towards which it can make approaches but which it is incapable of attaining—yet so that it participates force which is acting upon it; or, 2dly, by producing a humiliation or prostration of the mind before some external agency which it presumes not to make an effort to participate, but is absorbed in the contemplation of the

> might in the external power, &, as far as it has any consciousness of itself, its grandeur subsists in the naked fact of being conscious of external Power at once awful & immeasurable; so that, in both cases, the head & the front of the sensation is intense unity. (*Prose Works* 2:354)

Either the imagination is flooded with the energies released by its failure to swallow the elephant, or Mont Blanc, so that the mind loses itself in an objectless delirium, or the imagination so fully dejects itself before an overpowering image that the mind loses all sense of its identity. Both states are conducive to unity, in the first case because all knowledge of the external world vanishes in the mind's spasm of energy, in the second case because the mind vanishes before the puissance of the external world. Though Wordsworth does not use the words, the first is the sublimity of exaltation, the second is the sublimity of terror.

T. S. Eliot says, adding a third member to the set of sublime emotions, that the poet is able "to see beneath both beauty and ugliness; to see the boredom, and the horror, and the glory" (*The Use of Poetry*, p. 106). To some extent Eliot's doctrine of immediate experience is a late sophistication of these notions of the sublime: Eliot assumes that behind every finite act of perception there is a state of "annihilation and utter night" (*Knowledge and Experience*, p. 31) in which world and mind alike swoon, yield, coalesce. Eliot simply extends sublimity until it covers the whole realm of perception, for he claims that every object and every sentiment has inside itself a kernel of the sublime. All feeling that is not "A toothache, or a violent passion," all feeling that has "never succeeded in invading our minds to such an extent as completely to fill it" (*Knowledge and Experience*, p. 23)—this is almost the language of Burke—is half-objectified, articulate, moving toward definition or, as Burke might say, dwindling out of sublimity.

Wordsworth's poetry goes far toward integrating sublimity with other, more matter-of-fact experiences. Although in his essay on the sublime he keeps much of the old habit of reserving the term for heaven and hell, extreme paroxysms of the imagination, he nonetheless suggests that sublimity is part of the usual rhythm of human perception:

> as we advance in life, we can escape upon the invitation of our more placid & gentle nature from those obtrusive qualities in an object sublime in its general character; which qualities, at an earlier age, precluded imperiously the perception of beauty which that object if contemplated under another relation would have been capable of imparting. (*Prose Works* 2:349)

Many previous commentators had considered the teaser of the object that had mixed in it sublime and beautiful features; but Wordsworth is the first known to me who considers that the sublime is likely to decay effortlessly into the beautiful as a man's advancing years blunt the fever of oversharp perceptions. Not only does sublimity tend to grow plump and comfortable, habituate itself into beauty, but it also may arise in retrospect, when we contemplate a landscape or the "Cistine Chapel," something decided by Baedeker and all authorities to be sublime, but which only disappointed us, left us unstricken by violent feeling, when first we saw it (*Prose Works*, 2:358–60). A sensitive man proceeding about his daily activities will naturally find sublime feelings rising and ebbing in him; sublimity is a feature of common life, not something vertiginous and spectacular, overwhelming, rare. Before the Romantic movement everyone treasured the choice feeling one got when staring down a ravine full of eagles; but with the Romantics such shivers began to seize people who only looked at a flower:

> To see a World in a Grain of Sand
> And a Heaven in a Wild Flower
> Hold Infinity in the palm of your hand
> And Eternity in an hour
> (Blake, "Auguries of Innocence," lines 1–4)

> the least of things
> Seemed infinite; and there his spirit shaped
> Her prospects, nor did he believe,—he *saw*.

What wonder if his being thus became
Sublime and comprehensive! . . .

    what good is given to men,
More solid than the gilded clouds of heaven?
What joy more lasting than a vernal flower?
(Wordsworth, *The Excursion*, 1.230–34, 3.437–39)

I hold you here, root and all, in my hand,
Little flower—but *if* I could understand
What you are, root and all, and all in all,
I should know what God and man is.
(Tennyson, " 'Flower in the Crannied Wall,' " lines 3–6)

Sublimity, then, becomes not a brain sensation caused by the excessive stress in the nerves of the eye as they try to take in something too large for comfort, the horizon of the ocean, the turbid night, the infinitely receding colonnade of the Gothic cathedral—this was Burke's explanation—but instead a sense of the diffuseness dormant in every created thing, a pensive decompression of form. Both Burke (*A Philosophical Enquiry* 2.3) and Coleridge (*Lecture VII*, 1811–12, cited above) quote with great approval Milton's description of Death, a shapeless shape and a shadowy substance, as the epitome of the sublime; but whereas to Burke Milton's Death is an example of the appropriateness of obscurity in describing sublime entities, to Coleridge Milton's Death leads to a general recommendation of imagelessness in art; as though it would be a good thing if every epic and drama and panegyric and little exclamation of feeling appealed to a higher and more vivid indeterminacy. Sublimity is at last a kind of exercise of the eye, a willed unfocusing, or a focusing on a spiritual penumbra, a tremulousness in the circumambient ether. By the twentieth century James Joyce has taken this sort of sublime perception into the city, the one place previously excluded as hopelessly mundane, and in *Stephen Hero* has renamed it the epiphany, that is, an adjustment of the focus of the spiritual eye, which transfigures even the most banal and squalid object, a street clock or the spectacle of a vulgar flirtation. Later, in *Ulysses,* in a scene in "Oxen of the Sun" where Leopold Bloom is thinking of Mrs. Purefoy's newborn child and of his own lack of progeny, Joyce produces a meditation that spirals dizzily through the cycles of generation to the beginning and end of time, to the desolation and futility of all living things:

> Huuh! Hark! Huuh! . . . Elk and yak, the bulls of Bashan and of Babylon, mammoth and mastodon, they come trooping to the sunken sea, *Lacus Mortis.* Ominous, revengeful zodiacal host! They moan, passing upon the clouds, horned and capricorned, the trumpeted with the tusked, the lionmaned the giantantlered, snouter and crawler, rodent, ruminant and pachyderm, all their moving moaning multitude, murderers of the sun. . . . And the equine portent grows again, magnified in the deserted heavens, nay to heaven's own magnitude, till it looms, vast, over the house of Virgo. And, lo, wonder of metempsychosis, it is she, the everlasting bride, harbinger of the daystar, the bride, ever virgin. It is she, Martha, thou lost one, Millicent . . . coifed with a veil of what do you call it gossamer! It floats, it flows about her starborn flesh . . . winding, coiling, simply swirling, writhing in the skies a mysterious writing till after a myriad metamorphoses of symbol it blazes, Alpha, a ruby and triangled sign upon the forehead of Taurus. (p. 414)

This terminal symbol, this celestial apocalypse, is of course only the red triangle on the label of a bottle of ale. The deflation of Bloom's vast blurred, slightly inebriate thought into the trademark on the ale bears many technical resemblances to the styles of sublimity in Romantic and Symbolist poetry; but it is here a joke, for the millennial ominousness—Astraea, in the matronly form of Mrs. Purefoy, has descended from the sky to announce a new age—exuberates in extreme disproportion to the bottle into which it collapses, a spent genie. We trust heaven in a wildflower, but not in Bass ale. If Ariel is the playful spirit of lyricality, he is clearly the genius of this passage, for the frisky metamorphoses and metempsychoses here described—even fallen into the tar pit, even cooked on a spit, the oxen of the sun keeping mooing and snuffling—suggest that we are in an Eden where nothing serious can happen. In this passage Joyce proves that sublimity can embrace its own parody without diminution of aesthetic force. Coleridge's doctrine that the imagination is most potent when it is hovering between images, refusing to descend, is a doctrine that passes easily into a recommendation for a certain gingerliness, even frivolity, in the imagination's treatment of its images; if the image is random and insignificant, why should it not be a succession of toy extinct animals, or the label on a bottle of ale? As the idea of the sublime becomes more inclusive, disperses into a modality for all perception, it becomes increasingly identical to what I call the lyrical. The extension of the emotional range of the sublime to include first subtle shades of moodiness, and finally the smirking, the boring, the hilarious, makes it increasingly similar to the lyrical, where the singer can sing of any feeling as long as that feeling is resolved into music, elevated out of the usual prose of things.

LIMBO

I have claimed that in Romantic and modern literature the sublime, which always had altitude, was granted breadth as well; and I shall claim that it also came to attain a certain depth. Traditionally the word "sublime" has been derived from an expression meaning "above the threshold," in which "sub" undergoes an odd change from its usual meaning of "below." It has been opposed to the bathetic, that is, the deep; but there arises a kind of sublimity that is genuinely below the threshold yet in no way bathetic, in which is explored the emotion of contentlessness. In many striking passages in nineteenth- and twentieth-century literature we see a style of sublimity that oscillates wildly from high to low, as if it were a single psychosis with manic and depressive phases. The high, or manic, phase searches for a perfect rhetoric for the bard, now praised not only as the master of nature but as a personification of nature, as if the Great Imagination of nature itself, the cloud bank out of which Mount Snowdon congeals, were a plausible vocation for a human being. The most attractive rhetorical forms for this aspiration to pannatural subjectivity turned out to be *I become all that I behold* and *I am the actor and the acted-upon:*

Are not the mountains, waves, and skies, a part
Of me and of my soul, as I of them?
(Byron, *Childe Harold's Pilgrimage* 3.75, 1813)

For all are Men in Eternity. Rivers Mountains Cities Villages,
All are Human & when you enter into their Bosoms you walk
In Heavens & Earths; as in your own Bosom you bear your
Heaven
And Earth, & all you behold, tho it appears Without it is
Within
(Blake, *Jerusalem*, 71:15–18, c. 1815)

So that my soul beholding in her pride
All these, from room to room did pass;
And all things that she saw, she multiplied,
A manyfacèd glass;

And, being both the sower and the seed,
Remaining in herself became
All that she saw, Madonna, Ganymede,
Or the Asiatic dame—
(Tennyson, "The Palace of Art," deleted stanzas, 1832)

I am a part of all that I have met;
(Tennyson, "Ulysses," 1833)

There was a child went forth every day,
And the first object he look'd upon, that object he became . . .
The early lilacs became part of this child,
And grass and white and red morning-glories, and white and
red clover, and the song of the phoebe-bird . . .
(Whitman, "There Was a Child Went Forth," 1855)

When me they fly, I am the wings;
I am the doubter and the doubt,
And I the hymn the Brahmin sings.
(Emerson, "Brahma," 1856)

I the grain and the furrow,
  The plow-cloven clod,
And the plowshare drawn thorough,
  The germ and the sod,
The deed and the doer, the seed and the sower, the dust
  which is God. . . .
These too have their part in me,
  As I too in these;
      (Swinburne, "Hertha," lines 36–40, 141–42, 1871)

The first of these passages merely finds Byron dramatizing an unusually excited state of mind, striking a typical posture, playing the role of the Bard; the last is ostensibly spoken not by a man but by a deity who *is* the earth, who *is* the world-ash-tree, who feels rising in her sap the secrets of sea and land. As the century progresses the tantalizing rhetoric seeks a more adequate persona, one worthy of speaking it. Yet throughout this time there is a countertheme, according to which this subliming, this vaporizing of nature into psychology is oddly morbid, distorted, fatal. Coleridge, who can speak eloquently of the superiority of the unimagined to any possible image, who is infatuated by the indefinite, could in another mood write this poem:

The sole true Something–This! In Limbo's Den
It frightens Ghosts, as here ghosts frighten men.
Thence cross'd unseiz'd–and shall some fated hour
Be pulverized by Demogorgon's power,
And given as poison to annihilate souls–
Even now it shrinks them–they shrink in as Moles
(Nature's mute monks, live mandrakes of the ground)
Creep back from Light–then listen for its sound;–
See but to dread, and dread they know not why–
The natural alien of their negative eye.

'Tis a strange place, this Limbo!–not a Place,
Yet name it so;–where Time and weary Space
Fettered from fright, with night-mare sense of fleeing,
Strive for their last crepuscular half-being;–

Lank Space, and scytheless Time with branny hands
Barren and soundless as the measuring sands,
Not mark'd by flit of Shades,—unmeaning they
As moonlight on the dial of the day!

("Limbo," lines 1–18, 1817)

Coleridge seems to be trying to outdo Milton's Death, to manufacture objects, half-objects, still more resistant to shape; indeed the effect of presenting the unmade, the unmakable, is even stronger here than in *Paradise Lost*, for whereas Milton describes Death from his usual calm, quasi-divine vantage point, Coleridge describes Limbo as if his own eye, his own thought processes, were as degenerate as the thing he describes; the whole poem is composed in an exceedingly nervous, jerky fashion, as if the poet's grasp of his subject were shaky, reeling, clonic. Longinus says of the sublime that the contemplator feels he has created what he contemplates, and so it is not surprising that Limbo infects the observer with its own garbledness. If this were a drawing and not a poem—in his lecture on *Romeo and Juliet* Coleridge uses Milton's Death to prove the superiority of words to pictures—we would note that the pencil scarcely touched the paper yet made demented zigzags, smudges, scrawls. Limbo is the kingdom of the unimaginable, and it cannot tolerate any image. What is the Something that frightens ghosts as elsewhere ghosts frighten men? Coleridge does not say—the poem is full of expressions that lack antecedents—but if I read it correctly it does not matter, for any solid, determinate thing is a torment, a poison, to the fully confounded denizens of Limbo. Limbo is an antiworld, a shapelessness parallel to our own shapeliness, a place in which the critical categories of our universe, time and space, shrivel and despair, grow dim; here Eternity crucifies Time. In the middle section Coleridge's gaze turns from Limbo back to earth and sees, instead of the eye-aching imagelessness of the beginning of the poem, an elaborate and detailed image, which looks like Human Time, an Old Man:

But that is lovely—looks like Human Time,—
An Old Man with a steady look sublime,
That stops his earthly task to watch the skies;

But he is blind – a Statue hath such eyes;
Yet having moonward turn'd his face by chance,
Gazes the orb with moon-like countenance,
With scant white hairs, with foretop bald and high,
He gazes still, – his eyeless face all eye; –
As 'twere an organ full of silent sight,
His whole face seemeth to rejoice in light!
Lip touching lip, all moveless, bust and limb –
He seems to gaze at that which seems to gaze on him!
(lines 19–30)

Coleridge specifically says that this "sweet sight" is not in Limbo, and it is hard to see exactly what relation exists between Limbo and this highly developed description of Human Time. It may suggest that the mere existence of Limbo debilitates the earth we know; once one becomes cognizant of the prevailing categorilessness that underlies our cosmos, then our time, our space grow discredited, vitiate. In Limbo there is no time, though there is movement, a flitting of specters – a movement that does not calibrate itself into any distinct chronology but remains as meaningless "As moonlight on the dial of the day." In the passage cited above, this simile for the temporal absurdity of Limbo is expanded into a model for terrestrial time: the sundial is personified into a blind Old Man, Father Time, who gazes at the moon as if he could obtain from it a true reading of the hour, but it is only a feeble charade: the moon looks like an eye, and the Old Man's whole blind face looks like an eye, but instead of mutual visibility we have only its parody, a mutual random ignorance. Human Time has grown half-witted, dumb, through a kind of contagion from Limbo. A device common in the work of poets wishing to express a happier vision of sublimity is panpsychism, the attribution of a soul to every inanimate object, so that the universe consists of a congeries of tensely sensitive beings regarding each other; this is the tendency of the lovely passage of Eliot's "Burnt Norton" that speaks of roses that "Had the look of flowers that are looked at." Coleridge's "He seems to gaze at that which seems to gaze on him" seems almost like a kind of malevolent foreparody of Eliot's line; and Coleridge seems intent on putting out every natural and human eye in order to create a vision of a blind, gummy, gelatinous nonworld, in which vague half-things keep getting absorbed into a still vaguer pulp. When this is accomplished the poet can then display our world under the aspect of a negative sublime.

The persistence in Coleridge's poetry of the image of the blind, fatuous eye beholding the moon is remarkable. In "Dejection: An Ode" (1802) the poet dramatizes himself looking out at a peculiarly empty evening sky, cloudless, starless, but with a crescent moon: he knows that all of it is beautiful, but "I see, not feel, how beautiful they are" (line 38); he is conscious too that he gazes at this lovely vacuity "with how blank an eye!" (line 30). If this engrossing anesthesia, this mutual vacancy, were elaborated into a cosmos, it would be Limbo. On a few occasions Coleridge set out deliberately to write a bad poem; three specimens are printed in a note at the end of the first chapter of the *Biographia Literaria*, and the first of them, "which had for its object to excite a good-natured laugh at the spirit of *doleful egotism*, and at the recurrence of favourite phrases," displays another recurrence of this favorite image:

> Pensive at eve, on the *hard* world I mused,
> And *my poor* heart was sad; so at the *Moon*
> I gazed, and sighed, and sighed; for ah how soon
> Eve saddens into night! mine eyes perused
> With tearful vacancy the *dampy* grass
> That wept and glitter'd in the *paly* ray:
> And I *did pause me* on my lonely way
> And *mused me* on the *wretched ones* that pass
> O'er the bleak heath of sorrow. But alas!
> Most of *myself* I thought! . . .

Again there is the vacancy, the slushiness, the involution, the willful unreality; but here we see that the general metaphysical infection of Limbo has spread to the domain of the aesthetic and that good art, like every other good thing, is perplexed and ruined by the contagion of the indeterminate. This galumphingly stupid sonnet, even more than the poem "Limbo," shows the collapse of Coleridge's program for an art made sublime by its disdain for any finite image. Limbo, as a place of interest in Coleridge's baffled and amazed imagination, expires in a damp fizzle; but toward the end of his life Coleridge extricated himself from this bog of speculation long enough to record a vision not of purgatory but of hell:

> Sole Positive of Night!
> Antipathist of Light!
> Fate's only essence! primal scorpion rod–
> The one permitted opposite of God!–
> Condensèd blackness and abysmal storm
> Compacted to one sceptre
> Arms the Grasp enorm–
> The Intercepter–
> The Substance that still casts the shadow Death!–
> ("Ne Plus Ultra," lines 1–9, c. 1826)

The last of these lines clearly alludes to Milton's Death; and here at last Coleridge treats Milton's Death with something of Milton's confidence, his ferocity, his free yet taut lyric energy. Indeed, if there is any passage in English poetry in which the Unimaginable seems to leave some aerial trace of its vehemence, its whirling indefiniteness, it is this passage; here if anywhere the superiority of the imagination that hovers and does not descend is made manifest.

It would be of some interest, I think, to compile a history of the theme of Limbo in poetry. In general, descriptions of Limbo carry a certain feeling for the demonic sublime, but usually not with any of Coleridge's sense of real horror; instead there is a lightness, a facetiousness, as if the poet did not choose to take seriously the sad puddle of self and world often found in its precincts. Milton's figure of Death has grandeur, superbity, but when Milton comes to depict other states of indeterminacy he tends to make them appear trivial. Satan in Chaos is not at his most glorious, as he

O'er bog or steep, through strait, rough, dense, or rare,
With head, hands, wings, or feet pursues his way,
And swims or sinks, or wades, or creeps, or flies:
(*Paradise Lost* 2.948–50)

Milton's Limbo is made of still thinner gruel:

then might ye see
Cowls, Hoods and Habits with thir wearers tost
And flutter'd into Rags, then Reliques, Beads,
Indulgences, Dispenses, Pardons, Bulls,
The sport of Winds: all these upwhirl'd aloft
Fly o'er the backside of the World far off
Into a *Limbo* large and broad, since call'd
The Paradise of Fools . . .
(3.489–96)

As in Chaucer's *House of Fame*, the vast outpouring of earthly folly, whispered, insinuated, blared from every rooftop, leaves a high, dim residue; too insubstantial, too lacking in gravity to sink, this clerical inanity rises into an upper analogue of terrestrial confusion, now expressly a whirlwind, a gibberish. Limbo here is a parody of the Last Judgment, as if the clergymen were too fatuous and airheaded to have souls, and therefore only their clothes and their pieces of paper fly up into the heavens.

Milton's Limbo seems to be remembered in many passages in T. S. Eliot's poetry, from the little wet swirl of withered leaves in the first of the "Preludes" to the "Men and bits of paper, whirled by the cold wind / That blows before and after time" in "Burnt Norton" 3. Eliot always seems to conceive the sensuous world as Limbo—as he put it in a canceled passage from the third part of *The Waste Land*, in London men neither think nor feel—but Eliot's one near-explicit description of Limbo is *The Hollow Men*:

We are the hollow men
We are the stuffed men
Leaning together
Headpiece filled with straw. Alas!
Our dried voices, when

We whisper together
Are quiet and meaningless
As wind in dry grass
Or rats' feet over broken glass
In our dry cellar

Shape without form, shade without colour,
Paralysed force, gesture without motion;

Those who have crossed
With direct eyes, to death's other Kingdom
Remember us—if at all—not as lost
Violent souls, but only
As the hollow men . . .

There are two places discussed in this poem: the first is called death's dream kingdom, and it is where the hollow men are found, a muffled, blubbery Limbo; the second is called death's other Kingdom, and it is the domain of the actual. The eyes in death's other Kingdom serve exactly the same function in this poem that "Something" serves in Coleridge's "Limbo": from the intolerable light the hollow men shrink in terror, put on "deliberate disguises / Rat's coat, crowskin, crossed staves" in the hope that a scarecrow can shoo off whatever agency demands that they become real. Their state of chosen meaninglessness is not especially pleasant, but, like the burrows in which the denizens of the Waste Land spend their winter, it offers a certain security, even a certain comfort. The discourse of this choric song is not so resolutely imageless as that of Coleridge's poem; but such images as can be found here are fleeting, scattered, skittery, like the broken glass and the rats that scuttle over it; when we hear of "stone images . . . Under the twinkle of a fading star," the locale seems almost infinitely removed from the world of our experience, as if Easter Island statues were erected on the planet Pluto; and when the hollow men call their residence "This broken jaw of our lost kingdoms" and note that "There are no eyes here," we suspect that this domain is only blindness and defective speech magnified into a private droopy, inward-turned, willfully unreal world. Limbo in Eliot's poetry is often a state in which one is chewed in a fractured mouth: in "Hysteria" the narrator is inhaled in a spasm of a woman's laughter, "bruised by the ripple of unseen muscles," and in *Ash-Wednesday* the stair that the poet climbs looks like "an old man's mouth drivelling, beyond repair, / Or the toothed gullet of an agèd shark." It is the punishment that Dante meted out to Brutus and Judas in the bottom of hell; but in *The Hollow Men* the role of Satan's cud is oddly meditative, painless, ruminant, a refuge from the difficulties of maintaining a human identity.

The Hollow Men can be construed as a criticism of the philosophy expounded in Eliot's dissertation, a philosophy the poet is beginning to abandon. The metaphysics that Eliot developed from Bradley is unusual in that it makes little provision for discriminating the real from the unreal; Eliot admits we are all in the habit of making such determinations, but he claims such "practical" operations of the mind have no metaphysical significance; to Eliot even such a chimerical locution as "a round square" denotes something as real as anything can be, because "there is no reality to which it should correspond and does not" (*Knowledge and Experience*, p. 55). This strange philosophical disability, what some would call a disease of metaphysics, arises from Eliot's notions of the relation between the ideal and the real. Nothing is either exclusively ideal or exclusively real, for the ideal and the real are two moments in the history of any object, any feeling: "Reality is simply that which is intended and the ideal is that which intends" (p. 36). The chair I sit on could not be real if there were no idea that pointed to it; nor could the chimera be ideal if it did not terminate in some reality. The poetical consequence of such belief is a certain complacency, a resting content in what most of us would call unreality. Why should one descend into the commonplace, the delimited, if one can remain hovering in the imaginary without any loss of prestige?

There is a passage in *Knowledge and Experience* in which Eliot seems to anticipate something of the predicament of the Hollow Men:

> When the poet [E. B. Browning, in *Sonnets from the Portuguese* 26] says
>
> *I lived with shadows for my company*

> she is announcing at once the defect and the superiority of the world she lived in. The defect, in that it was vaguer, less of an idea, than the world of others; the superiority, in that the shadows pointed toward a reality, which, if it had been realized, would have been in some respects, [a] higher type of reality than the ordinary world. (pp. 55–56)

The world of the Hollow Men is of course in no sense superior to our world; but this passage suggests the quality of its defectiveness quite nicely. It is not only unreal but unideal as well; it has not been thought out correctly, not been *felt out* correctly, and persists simply as a limp muzziness of half-thoughts and half-feelings. Here nature has collapsed into a kind of black hole. If, as Eliot says, "The cruder and vaguer, or more limited, is somehow contained and explained in the wider and more precise" (p. 167), then the Limbo of this poem is a preworld, what our world looks like to people whose faculties of mind and feeling are blunted, paralyzed; indeed, its infantile and autistic qualities are shown clearly in the nursery-rhyme parodies, in the whimper that supersedes the bang.

> *Here we go round the prickly pear*
> *At five o'clock in the morning.*
>
> Between the idea
> And the reality
> Between the motion
> And the act
> Falls the Shadow
> *For Thine is the Kingdom*

I suspect that, in Eliot's scheme, these fragments of a prayer are utterly futile, for the defect of the Hollow Men lies not in the stars but in themselves. They are guilty of metaphysical sloth and suffer from a false philosophy that trusts that despite their accedia some benevolent god might decide to make them real, to create them; but since they remain wretched, jejune, uncreated, they imagine that a malign external force—the Shadow—frustrates their hope, is responsible for their failure to exist. The disease, however, is inside them; it lies in their willful evasiveness, their refusal to think, to feel, to pray, to *act*. In 1933, some eight years after he wrote *The Hollow Men*, Eliot decided, after years of painful indecision, to mail from America a deed of separation from his mentally ill wife Vivienne. According to Robert Sencourt, as he dropped the letter into the mailbox he quoted the following lines from Shakespeare's *Julius Caesar* (*T. S. Eliot: A Memoir*, p. 151):

Between the acting of a dreadful thing
And the first motion, all the interim is
Like a phantasma, or a hideous dream.

This passage is clearly the type for the chant rhythms in the last part of *The Hollow Men*. "The Love Song of J. Alfred Prufrock," *The Waste Land* 5, *The Hollow Men* all are cautionary fables about the paralysis of the will, a condition that not only debilitates the sufferer but reduces him to unbeing. As human agency withers and vanishes, nature also loses its pith, blurs, contracts to a few broken rocks and cacti on the otherwise featureless plain of the sublime.

The last of the anthropologists of Limbo we shall study in this brief cultural history is W. H. Auden:

LIMBO CULTURE

The tribes of Limbo, travellers report,
On first encounter seem much like ourselves;
They keep their houses practically clean,
Their watches round about a standard time,
They serve you almost appetising meals;
But no one says he saw a Limbo child.

The language spoken by the tribes of Limbo
Has many words far subtler than our own
To indicate how much, how little, something
Is pretty closely or not quite the case,
But none you could translate by *Yes* or *No*,
Nor do its pronouns distinguish between Persons.

In tales related by the tribes of Limbo,
Dragon and Knight set to with fang and sword
But miss their rival always by a hair's-breadth,

Old Crone and Stripling pass a crucial point,
She seconds early and He seconds late,
A magic purse mistakes the legal tender:

"And so," runs their concluding formula,
"Prince and Princess are nearly married still."
Why this concern, so marked in Limbo culture,
This love for inexactness? Could it be
A Limbo tribesman only loves himself?
For that, we know, cannot be done exactly.

Auden's Limbo seems a far easier, less sinister place than Milton's or Coleridge's or Eliot's—slightly crackpot and dithery, inconclusive, but devoid of metaphysical terror. And yet it shares certain features with the other Limbos: the hour of day is uncertain, not absurdly random as in the case of Coleridge's moonlit sundial, but nevertheless a symptom of insecurity; and, though no one either whimpers or sets off bombs, there is a pervasive childishness, a gliding away from touch, a burbling off into incoherence—no wonder the traveler can find no official children there, for the residents seem presexual, incapable of synchronizing themselves sufficiently for coitus. As in the other Limbos, Auden supposes that the denizens dwell in a state of chosen unmeaning: their fairy tales are dreary things indeed, bereft of action or incident, in which the standard legendary personages stamp about in bewildered isolation, in which events almost manage to happen but never do, in which every arrow misses its target. These tales are the paltry scripture of a world as hollow as that of *The Hollow Men*, a Potemkin village elaborated into a civilization, a culture that looks just like any suburbia but mysteriously fails to constitute itself properly, to attain relations among its parts. It is eerie because it verges closely upon the world we know, and yet is nonsensical—how can a couple be *nearly* married?—incompetent, as if it were a diorama of our culture devised by extraterrestrial beings who had a few snapshots, a child's storybook, but no notion of the reference or significance of our cultural artifacts. It is the world of the *not quite right*, which disturbs through infinitesimal inaccuracies. Like Eliot's Limbo, it offers the unpleasant possibility that our secular domain may itself be infected with some small subliminal wrongness that deranges, vitiates, the lives we choose to lead. If self-love is the typical condition of those who dwell in Limbo, it is plausible that Limbo is simply the world around us.

"Limbo Culture" is part of a mythology concerning the approximate and the exact, heaven, purgatory, and hell. We should not assume from this poem that Auden is intolerant of ambiguity, eager for certitude; in fact, if approximation is Limbo, exactness is hell:

> *All exact science is dominated by the idea of approximation.* (Bertrand Russell.) If so, then infernal science differs from human science in that it lacks the notion of approximation: it believes its laws to be exact. (*The Dyer's Hand*, p. 273)

As Auden goes on to explain, the devil is a kind of hellish sociologist who believes that "*all men are the same*" and are governed by invariable laws of conduct, which he, the devil, tries to verify: "What to us is a temptation is to him an experiment: he is trying to confirm a hypothesis about human behavior" (p. 274). Almost all of Auden's villains are accurate quantifiers. Caesar, according to *For the Time Being* (*The Summons* 3), is great because he has conquered the Kingdom of Infinite Number: "Last night it was Rule-of-Thumb, to-night it is To-a-T; / Instead of Quite-a-lot, there is Exactly-so-many." What is vile about this secular precision is that it tends to depersonalize. Once Auden imagined a telephone directory for heaven, in which each man, each grain of sand, each electron in the universe was precious, personal, worthy of its own proper name; opposed to this is the blank catalog of hell, a mere string of numbers, for those in hell "do not *have* numbers, they *are* numbers" (*The Dyer's Hand*, p. 274). The gaze of the devil, of Caesar, attempts to reduce human complexity to the simplicity of physics and therefore attempts to unrealize the sensible world:

> *The Two Chimerical Worlds*
> 1) The magical polytheistic nature created by the aesthetic illusion which would regard the world of masses as if it

> were a world of faces. The aesthetic religion says prayers to the Dynamo.
> 2) The mechanized history created by the scientific illusion which would regard the world of faces as if it were a world of masses. The scientific religion treats the Virgin as a statistic. (*The Dyer's Hand*, p. 62)

Hell is the second of these two chimerical worlds. The first is, according to Caliban's speech in *The Sea and the Mirror*, the continuous phantasmagoria set into play when Ariel's power grows absolute, a state of overmeaningful giddiness in which everything is sacred and all gods are false:

> All the phenomena of an empirically ordinary world are given. Extended objects appear to which events happen—old men catch dreadful coughs, little girls get their arms twisted, flames run whooping through the woods . . . but these are merely elements in an allegorical landscape to which mathematical measurement and phenomenological analysis have no relevance. . . . there are as many faiths as there are searchers, and clues can be found behind every clock, under every stone, and in every hollow tree to support them all.
>
> Again, other selves undoubtedly exist, but though everyone's pocket is bulging with birth certificates, insurance policies, passports and letters of credit, there is no way of proving whether they are genuine or planted or forged. . . . Everything, in short, suggests Mind but, surrounded by an infinite extension of the adolescent difficulty, a rising of the subjective and subjunctive to ever steeper, stormier heights, the panting frozen expressive gift has collapsed under the strain of its communicative anxiety, and contributes nothing by way of meaning but a series of staccato barks or a delirious gush of glossolalia. (*Collected Poems*, p. 338)

The imagination here exuberates in a condition of complete liberation from any need for fidelity to fact, for numerical accuracy; this delirium is the antithesis of the scientist's inhuman scrupulosity—though every delirium, as the word suggests, presupposes a furrow out of which it runs. Amid this wilderness, these images that yet fresh images beget, there is no room for even an approximation to the world as we know it. Where, then, is Limbo, on the scale between aerial fantasy and hellish exactitude? Limbo is the disconcerting place obtained by taking Ariel's negligence and ignorance, his blithe disregard for fact, and stripping him of every shimmer of imagination. Limbo is a world abandoned both by Ariel and by B. F. Skinner; it combines the worst features of both chimerical worlds, for it is both pedestrian and unsteady, banal and fuzzy. To this extent it is fair to say that it is the most chimerical world of all.

The revulsion against Limbo, against this stunted and inane version of the sublime, is partly a warning against the lyrical mode itself. In Eliot's *The Hollow Men*, as in its ancestor Tennyson's "The Lotos-Eaters," the verbal texture keeps approximating the songlike, the jingly, a dim, diffuse submersion of speech into a choral ode in which meaning is veiled, not fully developed into the articulate, the discursive. Auden's "Limbo Culture" is not especially musical, but the favorite art of the Ariel of *The Sea and the Mirror* is opera, probably the grand nonsensical bel canto of Bellini; and where Ariel is paramount, glossolalia abounds and words start to lengthen, elide, stretch into minims and semibreves. The criticism that "Limbo Culture" makes of Limbo is similar to a criticism Auden makes of music. The residents of Limbo speak a jumbled, helplessly oblique sublanguage, in which full assent or denial is impossible and the pronouns do not "distinguish between Persons"; despite the fact that Auden was perhaps fonder of music and more knowledgeable about it than any other great English poet, he realizes that music can make no personal discriminations:

> In verbal speech one can say *I love you.* Music can, I believe, express the equivalent of *I love,* but it is incapable of saying whom or what I love, you, God, or the decimal system. . . . Music, one might say, is always intransitive and in the first person. (*Secondary Worlds*, p. 91)

Music may be able, as Auden says in "The Composer," to pour out forgiveness like wine, or at least to be an analogue for the forgiveness of sin, but it is in some degree defective in that it, like science, can be no respecter of human uniqueness. The poet who strives for lyricality at the expense of all else, like the Ariel-besotted fellow in *The Sea and the Mirror*, hoists himself into Limbo, perhaps a more coruscating and tingly place than that of "Limbo Culture," but Limbo nonetheless. Lyricality demands more fascination with the unintelligible and prehuman than those who damn Limbo are willing to allow.

THE LYRICAL ASPECT OF SATIRE

Wordsworthian nature and Limbo are the two serious versions, one benign, the other malignant, of *natura lyrica*, the physical world in its prephysiognomic and juvenile phase. But no age is ever so unlyrical in sensibility that lyrical nature is entirely absent; instead it is demoted to a subterranean domain of metaphor and striking figure, to reappear for certain special effects. Lyrical nature becomes a kind of fever or jazz, not often manifest, reserved for the presentation of sickliness or strange-mindedness. The first half of the eighteenth century is generally, and I think correctly, considered one of the least lyrical periods in English literature; and in that span, devoted to clarity and the explicit, the whole lyrical tendency becomes deformed, suspect. Ariel still on occasion presides, but he is regarded as a spirit of disease; and embryonic nature, nature unformed and metamorphosable, can still be found, but chiefly as a locus for derision.

I cannot quite resist the temptation to specify the precise moment when lyricality shifts from Miltonic sublimity to Augustan ridiculousness: it is the date, in 1677, of the publication of Dryden's "The Authors Apology for Heroique Poetry; and Poetique License," the preface to *The State of Innocence*, an opera based loosely on Milton's *Paradise Lost*. In his preface Dryden is eager to defend Milton's, and his own, boldness by means of citations from Longinus's *On the Sublime:* better faulty excellence, antiquity suggests, than polished mediocrity. In the course of this charming polemic Dryden declares that "imaging is, in itself, the very height and life of poetry" (*Literary Criticism of John Dryden*, ed. Arthur C. Kirsch, p. 110), but he does not mean by imaging the cold, exact representation of natural forms: he means instead the vivid, rousing depiction of immaterialities, centaurs and chimeras, purely fanciful beings, the bringing into entity of transcendental objects. This, to Dryden, is the sublime mode of the imagination: to make an image of something hitherto imageless. He is too modest to assert that he has made a genuine image anywhere in his present opera, but, he says, if there is an image to be found it is in the following passage:

> Seraph and cherub, careless of their charge,
> And wanton, in full ease now live at large:
> Unguarded leave the passes of the sky,
> And all dissolved in hallelujahs lie.
>
> I have heard (says one of them [Dryden's critics]) of anchovies dissolved in sauce; but never of an angel in hallelujahs. A mighty witticism (if you will pardon a new word!) but there is some difference between a laugher and a critic. . . . Mr. Cowley lies as open too in many places:
>
> Where their vast courts the mother waters keep, etc.
>
> For if the mass of waters be the mothers, then their daughters, the little streams, are bound, in all good manners, to make courtesy to them, and ask them blessing. How easy 'tis to turn into ridicule the best descriptions, when once a man is in the humour of laughing till he wheezes at his own dull jest! But an image which is strongly and beautifully set before the eyes of the reader will still be poetry when the merry fit is over: and last when the other is forgotten. (pp. 111–12)

It is noteworthy that the image Dryden chose to commend is an image of deliquescing, of losing form—an image caught in the act of undoing itself. It is of the same class of imaginariness as Milton's Death, a substantial insubstantiality, which Burke eighty years later would take as the very type of the sublime. The jape of Dryden's critic, comparing the angels to anchovies, shows how fatuous this sort of sublimity sounds when subjected to an obtuse literalization; and Dryden himself clearly understands just how this species of hilarity operates, how the simple mechanical elaboration of a figure coarsens it, hardens it, removes any aura of the celestial, the uncanny. Dryden himself is a transitional sensibility, but his anonymous critic is all Augustan; and in the next generation the sublime is largely relegated to anchovies, to all the doubtful hardware and accouterments of civil life. But in order to describe the lyrical element of Augustan poetry I shall first have to propose a little theory of satire.

I believe that satirical poetry is governed by two somewhat opposing tendencies, which may be called the analogical and the excrementitious. What can I do if I wish to deride someone? I can call him an ape, or I can call him a turd. These choices may not seem so far removed from each other, but in fact my choice will have important consequences if I choose to write a poem. If I call my victim an ape—or a weasel, or a woodlouse, or a professor of literature, or any derogatory name in a world of definite things—I am immediately granted a universe of discourse upon which my imagination can operate, a place full of gorillas, baboons, marmosets, bananas, watering holes, zoological data about odd sexual behavior, a large and detailed hierarchy of phenomena that I can use to make an explicit analogy between the world of my victim and the world of the ape. This is a basic strategy for writing a satirical poem; and indeed many of the notable satires in English literature show a remarkable fascination, on the technical level and on the level of imagery, with detailed analogies of human life:

hast thou seen,
O Sun, in all thy journey, vanity,
Such as swells the bladder of our Court? I
Think he which made your waxen garden and
Transported it from Italy to stand
With us, at London, flouts our Presence, for
Just such gay painted things, which no sap, nor

Taste have in them, ours are; and natural
Some of the stocks are, their fruits, bastard all.
(Donne, "Satyre IV," lines 166–74, c. 1598)

This waxen garden, so helpful for derision of the court, will serve as a paradigm for the whole analogical mode of satire: the satirist erects a scale model of the scene he wishes to mock, fills it with toy men with wind-up keys in their backs, a city made of toothpicks, a locomotive too small to carry a matchbox, and claims that the larger world is exactly like his diminutive and shriveled caricature.

If I call my victim a turd, the possibilities for extending my satirical fantasy suddenly become limited. To some extent I can evoke a bathroom scene or perhaps the interior of the intestinal tract, or, like Ben Jonson in "On the Famous Voyage," take a journey down a sewer; but in reality there is little I can do to elaborate my invective beyond calling him a turd again, in a louder voice. I do not have a detailed realm of analogy to which I can appeal; one turd is very much like another—although Swift, in the passage from "An Examination of Certain Abuses, Corruptions and Enormities in the City of Dublin, 1732" where he claims to be able to distinguish Irish turds from English ones by consistency, texture, and terminal curl, labors as best he can to impose analogy upon the excrementitious. Waste products are featureless, formless, the vanishing point of all experience; therefore they are the satirical equivalent of the sublime, and excrementality becomes the lyrical vein in satire, as opposed to the strict similitudes and logical ramifications of the analogical vein.

To some extent the analogical mode tends to decay into the excrementitious. The satirist, once he has shoved the court down an analogical level into the world of apes, can explore this lower analogue to his heart's content; but eventually he is likely to feel the temptation to push it down a further level, to that of marionettes or vermin; if he surrenders to this temptation he may wish to descend still further; but this strategy can be taken only so far, for hell, as Dante understood, is an inverted cone, and the scope of imaginative action shrinks the further one descends into it. Excrement, then, is for the satirist the limit of descent and the limit of contraction; it is the place where all the bright, biting resemblances of the satirist's art grow blurred, turbid, blunt. It is no wonder Donne's satires are full of wax gardens, puppets dancing on organ pipes, and many other trivializing analogies for his victims and their habits and locales; but what is interesting is his feeling of alarm at having set in motion satirical energies that he cannot quite control and that may end as badly for him as for his victims:

> Who wastes in meat, in clothes, in horse, he notes:
> Who loves whores, who boys, and who goats.
> I more amaz'd than Circe's prisoners, when
> They felt themselves turn beasts, felt myself then
> Becoming traitor, and methought I saw
> One of our Giant Statutes ope his jaw
> To suck me in, for hearing him.
>
> ("Satyre IV," lines 127–33)

Under the spell of satirical contagion, Donne pretends to worry that his victim's loathsomeness will turn the satirist himself into a swine; and such a charm of metamorphosis can terminate only in mastication, digestion, excretion. To speak the language of satire tends to reduce the satirist's own speech to excrement; it was Swift, of course, who discovered most of the fun of this logic, but Donne anticipates:

> But he is worst, who (beggarly) doth chaw
> Others' wits' fruits, and in his ravenous maw
> Rankly digested, doth those things outspew,
> As his own things; and they are his own, 'tis true,
> For if one eat my meat, though it be known
> The meat was mine, the excrement is his own:
> But these do me no harm . . .
>
> ("Satyre II," lines 25–31)

Satire as a whole is a kind of digesting machine, which renders increasingly misshapen versions of its object—first ape, then pig, then curd of ass's milk, then feces. And it is so zealous for meat that it will chew up the satirist himself and everything he says before it will stop. Satire introduces a disquieting element of instability into the outer world, and for this it requires the collaboration of Proteus in his most malevolent aspect, everywhere breaking up articulated forms into increasingly primitive and abject declensions of being. If it is possible to take the wax garden passage of Donne's fourth satire as a model of analogical satire, one might look to a passage of Pope for a model of excrementitious satire:

Let Courtly Wits to Wits afford supply,
As Hog to Hog in Huts of *Westphaly*;
If one, thro' Nature's Bounty or his Lord's,
Has what the frugal, dirty soil affords,
From him the next receives it, thick or thin,
As pure a Mess almost as it came in;
The blessed Benefit, not there confin'd,
Drops to the third who nuzzles close behind;
From tail to mouth, they feed, and they carouse;
The last, full fairly gives it to the *House*.
Fr. This filthy Simile, this beastly Line,
Quite turns my stomach—*P*. So does Flatt'ry mine;
("Epilogue to the Satires: Dialogue II," lines 171–82)

I imagine that Donne's passage about the thieves who chew his wit is the germ of this, for Pope "translated" Donne's second and fourth satires from Donne's hunchbacked, clumping, hyperenjambed, almost meterless rhymed decasyllables into the agreeable clockwork minuet of Augustan couplets. This passage, with its chain of excrement growing ever more excrementitious with each subsequent digestion, will serve as a model for the tendency in satire to keep slipping down the greased Chain of Being into increasingly fouler and more indistinct forms.

In the works of Pope there is another kind of satirical sublimity, which corresponds more exactly to Wordsworthian prenature. Excrementality is postnatural, overnatural; it is the pit into which created forms degenerate. But there is in Pope something else, a pit out of which created forms arise, or do not quite arise. The first book of *The Dunciad* (1728) begins with the theogony of Dulness, "Daughter of Chaos and eternal Night" (1.10), and few passages of Pope are more intriguing than his description of preverbal chaos:

> Here she beholds the Chaos dark and deep,
> Where nameless somethings in their causes sleep,
> 'Till genial Jacob, or a warm Third-day
> Call forth each mass, a poem or a play.
> How Hints, like spawn, scarce quick in embryo lie,
> How new-born Nonsense first is taught to cry,
> Maggots half-form'd, in rhyme exactly meet,
> And learn to crawl upon poetic feet.
> Here one poor Word a hundred clenches makes,
> And ductile dulness new meanders takes;
> There motley Images her fancy strike,
> Figures ill'pair'd, and Similes unlike. . . .
> Here gay Description Ægypt glads with showers;
> Or gives to Zembla fruits, to Barca flowers;
> Glittering with ice here hoary hills are seen,
> There painted vallies of eternal green,
> On cold December fragrant chaplets blow,
> And heavy harvests nod beneath the snow.
>
> (1.53–64, 71–76)

Any satirist can use excrement to demean his object; it is, as far as I know, Pope's invention to leap backward from the residue of the organic to its conception, to besmear his object with amniotic fluid. Dulness is less the mistress of decay than the mistress of the fetal, of people and words that continually pullulate without having got themselves born; she is a kind of womb in which her chosen bawl like so many big imbecile babies. In Pope's gnostic mythology she is the demiurge of a botched creation, of an antiworld that displays its uterine slime, its essential shapelessness, at every turn; nothing can attain the acuity of finished form under her anesthetic gaze. When she (or her vice-dullards on earth) tries to utter the creative Word, it stutters, quibbles, will not let itself be pronounced; and so there flows forth a provisional, misbegotten nature in which sea and dry land, winter and summer, attempt a wretched coexistence at the same place, same time. If I am right in believing that Pope echoes, at the end of the cited passage, Titania's speech in *A Midsummer Night's Dream* (2.1.106–14), in which hoary-headed frosts fall on the rose and an odorous chaplet of summer buds is set on old Hiems's thin and icy crown, then we have a fine example of the relation between this satirical strategy and the idea of lyricality: in Shakespeare the vision of nature is airy and unsettled, tentative, wispy, beautiful, and in Pope the tune is the same, but coarsened, flatulent, transposed into the bass register. To the Augustan sensibility the lyrical is hard to distinguish from the incompetent.

A great many passages in *The Dunciad*, particularly in the third book, appeal to the metaphysical origin of things, to nameless things sleeping in their causes, as if Pope's Dulness is the First Cause of a universe in which no cause has quite descended into an effect. Thus we see Bavius, the master of Lethe, rehearsing to Settle the long history of his "transmigrating soul" (3.41) through its endless avatars of Boeotians and Dutchmen, and we are told of the Hyperborean land that is the birthplace of arctic rivers (3.80), and we are offered a theatrical skit in which "a new world, to Nature's laws unknown, breaks out refulgent, with a heav'n of its own" (3.237–38):

> The forests dance, the rivers upward rise,
> Whales sport in woods, and dolphins in the skies,
> And last, to give the whole creation grace,
> Lo! one vast Egg produces human race.
>
> (3.241–44)

The second of these lines alludes to a famous passage in Horace's *Ars Poetica:*

> His Muse professing height, and greatnesse, swells;
> Downe close by the shore, this other creeping steales,
> Being over-safe, and fearing of the flaw:
> So he that varying still affects to draw
> One thing prodigiously, paints in the woods
> A Dolphin and a Boare amidst the floods.
>
> (Jonson's translation, lines 39–44)

Horace here denounces several varieties of poets, including the apprentice Longinian who, seeking great elevation of subject, ends in bombast, and the poet who seeks a cheap amazement by means of impossible juxtapositions. This last too may be a species of false sublime, the only kind of sublimity comfortable to the Horatian, Augustan, sensibility, too acutely aware of the thinness of the line between genius and madness. It is a sensibility that lacks a taste for the uncreated, the inspissate, and feels no fascination for the egg out of which both whale and pig are hatched, for the mutability of homologues, the wings latent in the dolphin's fins. Dulness is the principle that rejects categories and blurs distinctions, that reduces created things to a primal seethe; given a bath and a change of clothes, she is Wordsworth's Nature. When at the end of *The Dunciad* the Anarch's uncreating word makes "The sick'ning Stars fade off th' aethereal plain" (3.342) and all the disciplines of knowledge fold themselves together and collapse into Truth's "old cavern" (3.347), the stage is set for Shelley's Demogorgon, who lies coiled at the bottom of the world, exceedingly content with what appears so fearful here, the dark imagelessness of truth.

Pope's imagination continually uses the infantile, the inchoate, the epicene as elements in the description of satirical objects. Some believe that Pope's most devastating satirical passage is the denunciation of Sporus in the "Epistle to Dr. Arbuthnot":

> Eternal Smiles his Emptiness betray,
> As shallow streams run dimpling all the way.
> Whether in florid Impotence he speaks,
> And, as the Prompter breathes, the Puppet squeaks;
> Or at the Ear of *Eve*, familiar Toad,
> Half Froth, half Venom, spits himself abroad . . .
> His Wit all see-saw between *that* and *this*,
> Now high, now low, now Master up, now Miss,
> And he himself one vile Antithesis.
>
> (lines 315–20, 323–25)

Here Sporus is depicted as an infernal amphibian, a jumble of mismatched parts, at once fetal and overrefined, hermaphroditic, too impotent to ascend into unmixed being; like Milton's Death he is nonentity embodied, like Mr. Knott in Beckett's novel *Watt* a human oxymoron. He has dwindled to a mosquito, almost regressed into the incorporeal, become a malign ghost flitting around a human ear. He is extremely lyrical. Just how easily the technique used to annihilate this poor victim can be twisted into delicacy, grace, ethereal loveliness—in short, all that is usually meant by lyricality—can be observed in another poem of Pope's:

> Nothing so true as what you once let fall,
> "Most Women have no Characters at all."
> Matter too soft a lasting mark to bear,
> And best distinguish'd by black, brown, or fair.
> (lines 1–4)
>
> And yet, believe me, good as well as ill,
> Woman's at best a Contradiction still.
> Heav'n, when it strives to polish all it can
> Its last best work, but forms a softer Man;
> Picks from each sex, to make its Fav'rite blest,
> Your love of Pleasure, our desire of Rest,
> Blends, in exception to all gen'ral rules,
> Your Taste of Follies, with our Scorn of Fools,
> Reserve with Frankness, Art with Truth ally'd,
> Courage with Softness, Modesty with Pride,
> Fix'd Principles, with Fancy ever new;
> Shakes all together, and produces—You.
> (lines 269–80)

Pope's compliments are all the more piquant for verging so closely upon insult. The "Epistle to a Lady," the second of the *Moral Essays*, begins with an assertion that seems to make all women obedient subjects of the goddess Dulness: they are inert matter, clay too liquid to hold any shape, mere womby dough. Yet when Pope begins to examine women he does not find inanition, spongy vacancy, but instead discovers a vivacity so fleeting that it cannot settle into any definition; instead of characterlessness he finds a superabundance of character, confused by inconsistency, feminine featheriness. Technically the passage in which Pope attempts to describe the charm of his correspondent is identical to the description of Sporus: both present a human contradiction, an unintelligible being that spans the whole gamut of sensibility; but of course the lady is pure iridescence, an angel of irresolution, while Sporus is monstrous, a sick fatuity.

In Pope's poetry every solid image stands precariously—"Plac'd on this isthmus of a middle state" (*An Essay on Man* 2.3)—between two formlessnesses, chaos and excrement, the unbegun and the terminal pulp. Those natural and human images that Pope admires, such as the half-tame landscape gardens of the "Epistle to Burlington" or the Man of Ross in the "Epistle to Bathurst," have attained by labor a condition of security, high definition; while the objects of Pope's satire are those who carry in themselves the traces of something jejune or fecal, some stain of the uncreated or the already rotten. Yet the "Epistle to a Lady" shows that Pope could use lyrical devices for purposes not wholly satirical; and there is a passage in *An Essay on Man* that shows a hint of the *natura lyrica* the Romantic poets would later extol:

> Why has not Man a microscopic eye?
> For this plain reason, Man is not a Fly.
> Say what the use, were finer optics giv'n,
> T' inspect a mite, not comprehend the heav'n?
> Or touch, if tremblingly alive all o'er,
> To smart and agonize at ev'ry pore?
> Or quick effluvia darting thro' the brain,
> Die of a rose in aromatic pain?
> If nature thunder'd in his op'ning ears,
> And stunn'd him with the music of the spheres,
> How would he wish that Heav'n had left him still
> The whisp'ring Zephyr, and the purling rill?
> (1.193–204)

If Dulness is the great enemy in *The Dunciad*, here it seems that her companion goddess Acumination is equally fearsome; between the too blunt and the too sharp there is little to choose. The deafening loudness of the music of the spheres is an ancient hypothesis; but Pope has gone far beyond tradition in imagining the intolerability of the sensuous world, the continual stab it would give to those beings whose eyes and ears and skin were sufficiently acute. This feeling for the hypervivacity of things is almost like Blake's, except that Pope praises his creator for endowing him with properly enfeebled senses, whereas Blake kept straining his eyesight, lovingly postulating the world as it would appear to men whose eyes rotated 360 degrees and whose nostrils were not bent down to veil the sense of smell. But whenever Pope becomes jumpy, rapid, oversensitive, neuralgic, unbalanced—and he is so in many of his best-known passages—he exhibits a tendency toward the lyrical.

THE DEATH OF NATURE

Jorge Luis Borges has said that, while it is easy to understand and even credit the philosophy of Berkeley, it is almost impossible, in the course of day-to-day life, to think strictly within its limits. Similarly, it is difficult to maintain a strictly lyrical vision of reality, to feel that the outer world is a continuous phantasmagoria, to understand that solid things, in Eliot's words, have dim and drifting edges. The history of poetry is a long approaching toward and falling from this sort of understanding, and in every generation one can find those who, with a kind of relief or even triumph, abandon the struggle for full lyricality. The first sign of this motion toward the prosaic is the relegation of poetry to a secondary world, the restriction of the scope of the poet's action to a deliberately artificial and unreal domain. When Peacock says, in *The Four Ages of Poetry* (1820), that we know that "there are no Dryads in Hyde-park nor Naiads in the Regent's-canal" (p. 15), he suggests that the world of poetry and the world of modern science are hopelessly divergent and that poets had better learn to cope with the defectiveness of their mythologies as best as they can. When the ability to sustain the lyrical mode starts to flag, a fissure develops between nature and unnature, and poets abandon the former to physicists, agronomists, and painters of the *plein-air* school. This can be understood, in some cases, as a strategy of desperation, designed to preserve and exalt the lyrical mode against the incursions of those who seek to ridicule it.

If any contemporary of Peacock had the wit and the zeal to restore the dryads to Hyde Park, it was Shelley. It is well known that Shelley wrote *The Defence of Poetry* (1821), one of the supreme manifestos of lyricality, as a rebuttal to the thesis of Peacock, who claimed, or pretended to claim, that poets were at heart mere snuffling panegyrists long since outgrown by modern civilization. But Shelley had in Philip Sidney a more powerful antagonist than Peacock, despite the seeming agreement of purpose between the two great poets. Sidney announces, in perhaps the best-known passage in *An Apology for Poetry* (1595), that the poet outdoes nature; but to outdo nature is also to be estranged from it:

> Only the poet . . . doth grow in effect another nature, in making things either better than nature bringeth forth, or quite anew, forms such as never were in nature, as the Heroes, Demigods, Cyclops, Chimeras, Furies, and such like; so as he goeth hand in hand with nature, not enclosed within the narrow warrant of her gifts, but freely ranging only within the zodiac of his own wit.
>
> Nature never set forth the earth in so rich a tapestry as divers poets have done, neither with pleasant rivers, fruitful trees, sweet smelling flowers, nor whatsoever else may make the too much loved earth more lovely. Her world is brazen, the poets only deliver a golden. (pp. 14–15)

The true successor of Sidney is not Shelley but Oscar Wilde:

> Facts will be regarded as discreditable, Truth will be found mourning over her fetters, and Romance, with her temper of wonder, will return to the land. The very aspect of the world will change to our startled eyes. Out of the sea will rise Behemoth and Leviathan. . . . Dragons will wander the waste places, and the phoenix will soar from her nest of fire into the air. We shall lay our hands upon the basilisk, and see the jewel in the toad's head. Champing his gilded oats, the Hippogriff will stand in our stalls, and over our

> heads will float the Blue Bird of happiness. . . . But before this comes to pass we must cultivate the lost art of Lying. (*Complete Works*, p. 991)

In this catalog from "The Decay of Lying" (1891) the imaginary beasts keep growing more intimately ridiculous as Wilde conceives a Derby Day of hippogriffs, a new preciousness in common toads. Shelley had confidence in the imagination's power to transform and regenerate the outer world; to Wilde the outer world is boring, pedestrian, but omnipotent, and the imagination must retreat into the antiworld of deliberate prevarication. Wilde and Sidney have a common antagonist, whom Sidney calls the historian and Wilde the artist of Realism; both are truth tellers wretchedly saddled with the obligation of being factual, draft horses left far behind by Pegasus's friskings in the purely fantastical. As a rule of thumb, it may be said that the defender of poetry who dotes on imaginary animals, like Wilde, Sidney, and the Dryden of the preface to *The State of Innocence*, has surrendered much of the poet's domain; to take pride in the hippogriff is to concede the banality of the horse.

If sensible nature is unlyrical, unfit for poetry—as it certainly was for Wilde, who begins "The Decay of Lying" with a tirade against even the tamest, most self-effacing landscape, full of gnats, slime, uncooked birds—then poets will attempt to create a new, adequately lyrical nature, laden with every splendor but alas only weakly real. This attempt leads to the manufacture of the aesthetic refuge, an asylum with a most distinguished history.

One of the first fully elaborated refuges for art in English literature is Michael Drayton's *The Muses Elizium* (1630); indeed, it is an archetype for the whole subsequent development of the theme:

> There Daysyes damaske every place
> Nor once their beauties lose,
> That when proud *Phoebus* hides his face
> Themselves they scorn to close.
> The Pansy and the Violet here,
> As seeming to descend,

Both from one Root, a very payre,
For sweetnesse yet contend,

And pointing to a Pinke to tell
Which beares it, it is loath,
To judge it; but replyes, for smell
That it excells them both,

Wherewith displeasde they hang their heads
So angry soone they grow
And from their odoriferous beds
Their sweets at it they throw.

The winter here a Summer is . . .
("The Description of Elizium," lines 21–37)

The absence of seasonal change, the abundance of blossom, the panpsychism, the thorough conduciveness to joy, all of these are the usual qualities of the Blessed Isles; but what is remarkable in this poem is the coquettishness, the overrefinement of the flowers. I suggested earlier that the mingling of the primal and the sophisticated is a feature of the lyric mode, and here we have that carried to extraordinary lengths. As Drayton begins his immense poem with a description of a (so far) humanless landscape, the landscape itself, in compensation for the absent mankind, adopts every human trait, grows playfully supercivilized. The little odor contest of the pansy, the violet, and the pink prefigures the flyting of Doron and Dorilus in the third nymphal (thus Drayton denominates the divisions of his poem), so that it seems that every human deed is simply an actualization of forces latent in the landscape, that men simply reenact the ongoing drama of the flowers and the streams. Here we see the motto of the aesthetic refuge: Nature itself is art. The flowers vie without rancor for perfection of fragrance; if they are capable of anger, it is an anger that expresses itself as a new loveliness of smell, for all expression here is channeled into a general pressure toward the beautiful. The variety of human emotion exists and is embodied in the landscape, but it is entirely decorative; Drayton is careful to avoid any suggestion of the oversymmetrical and the consequent sterility, monotony, by introducing a wanton playfulness, even fickleness, into the elements of his heavenscape. Thus the brooks, bedecked with lilies, refuse to be confined to their banks, as if they strayed

> Faire *Flora* in her state to viewe
> Which through those Lillies looks,
> Or as those Lillies leand to shew
> Their beauties to the brooks.
> (lines 61–64)

These flowers have the look of flowers that are looked at. The brook has eyes and struggles to approach the lilies; the lilies have eyes, such deep eyes that the spirit of spring shines through them, and are so proud of their beauty that they preen before the brook. Each element in the landscape is seized with this sublime interanimation, this delicate outgroping of beauty toward a further beauty, under the aspect of a courtly flouncy flirtatiousness.

As the poem continues, the shepherds and nymphs spark and woo and sing songs and suffer disappointment and give away lambs and trade herbal remedies and stage merry festivals and generally go about their rural lives with an unusually rich and robust harmlessness; some of their duties they neglect, but never the command that urges universal grace. In the later nymphals, however, the pastoral boundaries, which demand a certain lithe coolness of tone and the exclusion of immitigable pain, start to become oddly distended; the whole focus of the poem begins to lose sharpness. In the seventh nymphal a proclamation is read, banning Venus and Cupid from the precincts of Elysium. It is true that the blind archer is vexatious, but exile is a harsh penalty, and Elysium seems more frigid, inhospitable, unacceptable for his absence. The eighth nymphal celebrates the wedding of a nymph and a fairy; at the beginning one of the maids is puzzled by the disproportion in scale between the nymph and the "dwarfish Fayry Elfe" and is quickly reassured that no undue miscegenation is taking place; but we may wonder whether an Elysium in which Queen Mab and Venus seem to compete for power is not suffering from a certain mythological shapelessness. In the tenth, and last, nymphal, an event unprecedented in Elysian history occurs: a satyr invades their innocuous land, and the nymphs flee in horror from this intrusion of ugliness. When he tells his story, the denizens of Elysium become more sympathetic: he was driven out of his forest home by the shortsighted human race, who cut down all the trees for firewood and will have to suffer for their folly when they find themselves on a spoiled, bare earth with nothing left to burn. The kind Elysians are happy to give the satyr shelter until the collapse of the human economy, when the forests will be fit for goat feet once again. With this invitation the whole poem ends, but I do not feel confident that the state of Elysium can tolerate a large influx of refugees.

I believe that Drayton, like most inventors of an aesthetic refuge, cannot solve its basic dilemma: either the residents of the refuge become helpless aesthetes, constricted and trivialized by their child's life of singing and piping, dancing and disporting, competing in charitable gestures, or they attempt to expand the limits of the refuge to include, in gingerly fashion, first winter, then old age, then unrequitable love, then misshapenness, then chronic disease, then death, until the refuge is not a refuge at all but a scale model of our ordinary life.

Either the refuge has foot-thick walls, in which case its dwellers perish from nutritive deficiency or apnea, or its walls are too flimsy and cripples, bacteria, come pouring in. The finest example in English poetry of the first sort of aesthetic refuge is Tennyson's "The Palace of Art" (1832), in which the Soul has reduced all of history, culture, mythology, work of intellect to a gaudy series of frescoes, statues, and stained-glass windows, as if these high matters did not refer to a solidly determinate world—where men inquire into reality and try to ameliorate pain—but were instead subjects of shivery private delectation. By pounding life into this bright cortical film the Soul hopes to unrealize the world, rob it of denotation; but instead she succeeds in unrealizing herself, making herself famished, incoherent, mad, a necrophiliac in love with her own corpse. The finest example of the second kind of refuge is perhaps Yeats's *The Wanderings of Oisin* (1889), in which Oisin drifts for three hundred years through various dreams of perfected satisfaction, hollow images of desire erected like cinema facades on a series of islands, islands not so impenetrably remote that driftwood, memories of a richer, more substantial life, do not keep washing ashore to wake in him an appetite for the real. Oisin ends half-content to be a three-hundred-year-old man, wrinkled and without sinew, if that is the only way he can reside in the honest Ireland in which sexual love culminates in children and battles spill actual blood, but half-wishing for another, better, giddier, more ravingly vital island, where desire is still more spectacularly fulfilled.

Neither the young Tennyson nor the young Yeats seemed confident that he had successfully delimited the precise scope of the operation of fantasy. The Palace of Art turns into a coffin, Oisin's islands pop like balloons, but both leave open the possibility that if the walls, the shorelines, were drawn in a different fashion, if finer adjustments of boundary, better rules for determining admissibility could be legislated, then the Palace of Art might be eminently habitable, Oisin's archipelago the site of a splendid hotel. Tennyson, Yeats, Keats in the "Ode on a Grecian Urn"—all three poets were in their early twenties when they wrote the poems in question—investigate the aesthetic refuge for the sake of making implicit or explicit denunciations of it; but on another level they are practicing their poetic art in a place of disembodied imaginativeness, where Prospero's fact-demanding mouth has been temporarily stopped so that Ariel may have free rein, as a kind of preparation for a more serious investigating of the relations between imagination and the given world around us. The aesthetic refuge is overlyrical; there nothing impedes poetical fantasy in its ceaseless figurations and transfigurations, its inventions of airy half-worlds in which everything is permissible except perhaps ugliness. But without careful exploration of the overtly too lyrical it is impossible to know the exact component of lyricality in the outer world, its precise degree of susceptibility to imaginative transformation. To declare that beauty is truth, truth beauty, is to deny oneself any honest understanding of either truth or beauty;

and always there is some slightly infantile, blurred, or meaningless aspect to the aesthetic refuge.

It is a training field for artists, not a mature domain; no artist can discipline himself, build his muscles, where nothing offers resistance to any passing whim or delirium that might seize him. Drayton, an Elizabethan poet oddly surviving into an era of Caroline frivolity, was in his sixties when he wrote *The Muses Elizium* and certainly had no need to train himself as an artist; he had already written his almost inconceivably long topographical poem *Poly-Olbion*, in which he rehearsed almost every square foot of English countryside in order to find such genii loci as might dwell in Britain. *The Muses Elizium* was, I take it, a kind of antidote to the *Poly-Olbion*, an old man's nostalgia for a purely imaginary world, a pastoral unmenaced by the asperities of the real England; at the first gust of harsh wind Drayton averts his face, terminates his poem. The younger artificers of refuges have far more incentive to denounce them, for they need to put behind themselves a childish freedom, a paradise of referencelessness where all art is music.

In general it may be said that an aesthetic refuge is easiest to abandon or scorn or shatter when it is most obviously aesthetic, unnatural. It is no difficult matter to see that the chaste, cold pastoral on Keats's Grecian urn is somewhat life-denying; and in such later sophistications as Swinburne's "The Garden of Proserpine" (1866) the frisson of morbidity, the waxiness of the fruit, is presented as a chief attraction. To understand that living things will not grow on the imperishable mosaic of the Venice of Ruskin or the Byzantium of Yeats, both holding back the formless sea as best they can, takes no especial keenness. Far trickier are those aesthetic refuges that seem to include pedestrian and prosaic satisfactions, to offer a certain homey comfort as well as dizzying sublimity or gaunt hardness of being. Oisin's islands are clearly ghostly, narcotic; but Innisfree is an island perfectly amenable to cultivation, if one has a packet of seeds and the book that inspired Yeats to write the poem, Thoreau's *Walden:*

I will arise and go now, and go to Innisfree,

And a small cabin build there, of clay and wattles made:
Nine bean-rows will I have there, a hive for the honeybee,
And live alone in the bee-loud glade.

Yeats struggled for many years to realize such fantasies, especially in his project, conceived in 1895—five years after writing "The Lake Isle of Innisfree"—of founding a cell to study the radical truths of symbols, with Maud Gonne and his astrologer uncle George Pollexfen. Indeed, I am not sure Yeats ever outgrew the hope of living in an aesthetic refuge—the famous Norman tower that he bought and dwelt in was certainly a development of this theme. It is possible that the natural landscapes of Yeats's poems, even when most detailed, inviting, plebeian, are only aesthetic refuges in disguise, refuges from an inner unsettledness, incoherence; as "Meditations in Time of Civil War" 2 and "Coole and Ballylee, 1931" prove, he was incapable, when looking out his window, of seeing roses that were not symbolical, lakes that were not emblematical.

If the lyrical mode is properly divided into areas ruled by Ariel and by Proteus—the former an implacable swerving into a single perfect image, the corpse of Alonso metamorphosed into coral and pearls, the latter an endless shifting from one shape into another, a universe of provisional and interchangeable forms—then we may distinguish a Protean aesthetic refuge from one governed by Ariel. Ariel's taste is gratified by the Palace of Art, by jewels, mosaic, sculpture, vitreous images in which immaterial form assumes a material immediacy; Proteus prefers Circe's island Aeaea, where the whole population, the flora and fauna, are so bewitched and rebewitched that there is no hope of recovering any original shape; and human eyes peek dolefully from every living thing:

Panthers rise from their lairs
In the forest which thickens below,
Along the garden stairs
The sluggish python lies;
The peacocks walk, stately and slow,

And they look at us with the eyes
Of men whom we knew long ago.
(Eliot, "Circe's Palace")

In the past century and a half of English poetry, the refuges of Ariel and Proteus have both been elaborated to unheard-of extremes; it is as if, in the absence of a compelling lyrical vision—a vision like Shelley's that could seize at once every mutable state and the final entelechy, could keep in focus both the wreck of the Sensitive Plant and its eternal perfection—all subsequent poets must take a part of the lyrical mode and try to make of it a whole. The breakdown of every refuge is a failed attempt to make it more complete, more thorough. For every post-Romantic poet who, like Rossetti or Wilde or Yeats, tries to fill a chapel with incense and every chryselephantine glory of art, and who ends blinking like a bat in the light of day, holding in his hands a few shards of glass, there is another poet who esteems natural vitality and robust health and tries to construct a paradise of animism in which every protozoon is visible, writhing:

['Will sprawl, now that the heat of day is best,
Flat on his belly in the pit's much mire,
With elbows wide, fists clenched to prop his chin.
And, while he kicks both feet in the cool slush,
And feels about his spine small eft-things course,
Run in and out each arm, and make him laugh:
And while above his head a pompion-plant,
Coating the cave-top as a brow its eye,
Creeps down to touch and tickle hair and beard . . .
[He] talks to his own self, howe'er he please . . .]
("Caliban upon Setebos," lines 1–9, 15)

Here is the exact opposite of the Palace of Art. Browning's Caliban is a parody, a reduction to absurdity, of something dear to Browning, a secret island in which every amoeba is rammed with life and every created form trembling on the brink of metamorphosis; and the poet himself partakes of all his giddy vivacity, himself little discriminated from the plants and animals around him. It is the materialistic analogue of the Romantic vision of the sublime that states, *I am what I behold.* But just as Tennyson knows that Ariel's paradise, the Palace of Art, is unfit for human habitation, so Browning realizes the deformity latent in Proteus's paradise: to indulge oneself in this endless slosh of mutation is to become a hunchback, a monster, a fish, to regress into protoplasm. What both Tennyson and Browning envy is the confidence of Shelley, who could hold nature and art in balance without settling for denatured art or artless nature; indeed, Browning's whole career is informed by his wretched inability to be Shelley:

> The air seems bright with thy past presence yet,
> But thou art still for me as thou hast been
> When I have stood with thee as on a throne
> With all thy dim creations gathered round
> Like mountains, and I felt of mould like them,
> And with them creatures of my own were mixed,
> Like things half-lived, catching and giving life.
> (*Pauline*, lines 161–67)

These lines, addressed to the "Sun-treader" Shelley in Browning's first published poem, are as astonishing as any lines written by one poet to another. Browning here feels like something invented by Shelley, a demiurge revolving about Shelley, a subsidiary creativity whose creations are secondhand, slightly factitious, derived from Shelley's original force. Shelley is pure light, while Browning is a lens that focuses this light, makes sharper, dimmer images on a level of reality lower than Shelley's imageless splendor. While Shelley transcends nature, Browning is mired in the natural world; this is what Browning means in his essay on Shelley when he praises Shelley as the subjective poet who struggles toward "Not what man sees, but what God sees—the *Ideas* of Plato, seeds of creation lying burningly on the Divine Hand" (Yale Browning 1:1002); Browning is, at least compared with Shelley, an objective poet, less intense but more fully detailed. For Browning and his followers, the world on which their imaginations operate is low, vigorous, somewhat squalid; they are Calibans who rarely deal with any locus of creativity more ideal than Prospero's isle.

Yeats once remarked that "Descartes, Locke, and Newton took away the world and gave us its excrement instead. Berkeley restored the world" (*Explorations*, p. 325). Browning may be regarded as a more-or-less happy Cartesian, investigating without particularly satirical intent the possibilities of excrementitious fantasy.

As the strain of adhering to a vision of Romantic sublimity becomes greater, some poets seek the lyrical in the seethe of protoplasm, others in the small compass of a Fabergé egg; but as we approach the twentieth century we find in places a certain revulsion against every aesthetic refuge, both Ariel's and Proteus's, a deliberate repudiation of the rhetoric of sublimity. D. H. Lawrence began his career, conventionally enough, with a smashup of the Palace of Art:

> The world is a painted memory, where coloured shapes
> Of old, spent lives linger blurred and warm;
> An endless tapestry the past has woven, drapes
> The halls of my mind, compelling my life to conform. . . .
> There's a breach in the walls of the past, lets the daylight
> through.
> Fluent figures of men go down the upborne
> Track of the railway, alive, and with something to do.
> ("Dreams Old and Nascent: Nascent," lines 1–4, 18–20)

A little later he turns against Circe's palace as well:

> everything was tainted with myself,
> skies, trees, flowers, birds, water,
> people, houses, streets, vehicles, machines,
> nations, armies, war, peace-talking,
> work, recreation, governing, anarchy,
> it was all tainted with myself, I knew it all to start with
> because it was all myself.
> When I gathered flowers, I knew it was myself plucking my
> own flowering.
> When I went in a train, I knew it was myself travelling by
> my own invention.
> When I heard the cannon of the war, I listened with my own
> ears to my own destruction.

When I saw the torn dead, I knew it was my own torn
dead body.
It was all me, I had done it all in my own flesh.
("New Heaven and Earth" 2)

Lawrence in the First World War looks out on a world hopelessly personal, hopelessly distained with Lawrence. The permeability of the skin of Browning's Caliban, the parasitic intimacy, the pannatural autoeroticism, the nervous spurtings and tremblings of flesh have here elaborated into a savage cosmos where lilies and armies alike are beheld as possible variations of one's own body, where one's hand is liable to sprout a cannon, one's foot a locomotive, where identity smears out from earth to sky and war is merely a magnified self-loathing. Mind and sense stultify in the absence of an external world, and Lawrence cannot be rid of this horror until he abjures this overextended self in favor of smallness and clean bounding lines; as the poem continues Lawrence is saved by his wife, the anti-Circe who disenchants him by offering him a genuine Other, a telos.

But not every poet escapes with such dispatch from Circe's prison camp. T. S. Eliot suggests that sublime diffuseness of being ends in self-cannibalism, a death that, unlike that of Lawrence in "New Heaven and Earth," leads to no easy resurrection:

He walked once between the sea and the high cliffs
When the wind made him aware of his limbs smoothly passing
each other
And of his arms crossed over his breast.
When he walked over the meadows
He was stifled and soothed by his own rhythm.
By the river
His eyes were aware of the pointed corners of his eyes
And his hands aware of the pointed tips of his fingers. . . .
First he was sure that he had been a tree,
Twisting its branches among each other
And tangling its roots among each other.

Then he knew that he had been a fish
With slippery white belly held tight in his own fingers,

Writhing in his own clutch, his ancient beauty
Caught fast in the pink tips of his new beauty.

  Then he had been a young girl
Caught in the woods by a drunken old man
Knowing at the end the taste of his own whiteness . . .
Because his flesh was in love with the burning arrows
He danced on the hot sand
Until the arrows came.
As he embraced them his white skin surrendered itself to the
  redness of blood, and satisfied him.

"The Death of St. Narcissus" (1915), by coincidence written at almost exactly the same time as Lawrence's "New Heaven and Earth," goes far toward imagining the full horror of an extremely distended coenesthesia. Odysseus's men had to fear only an unwelcome passage into swinehood; Saint Narcissus must mutate into everything he beholds, must reel down the phylogenetic chain until he is a clenched guppy, a self-engrossed tree. One of the key words of the poem is "stifled," for Saint Narcissus walks along in an agony of self-circumscription, confused by his own ramifications, caught fast in his own fist, raped by himself. Well might the poet call Saint Narcissus's eyes and fingers "pointed," for he is continually self-stabbed, violated by a billion rods, hooks, hands, penises, arrows, all of his own devising. Elsewhere among the papers reproduced in *The Waste Land* facsimile, Eliot adapted a passage from the *Bhagavad-Gita:*

I am the Resurrection and the Life
I am the things that stay, and those that flow.
I am the husband and the wife
And the victim and the sacrificial knife
I am the fire, and the butter also.

(p. 111)

The original, of course, does not quote the words of Christ, nor does it have any hermaphroditic suggestion; the tone of Eliot's version is distinctly ironic, as if the Baudelaire of "L'héautontimoroumenos"—in which Baudelaire announces, "I am the wound and the knife"—had decided to rewrite Emerson's "Brahma." Indeed the butter, used in Hindu ritual as a sacred oblation, is somewhat disconcerting in Eliot's lines, with its English-language connotations of fatty domesticity. It is clear from these verses that Saint Narcissus is a cross between Saint Sebastian and an Oriental godhead that is at once the actor and the acted upon, much trivialized by the ludicrousness of his solipsism. Saint Narcissus is a Prufrock drifted further into schizophrenic involution, caught up in the Bradleyan hell that insists on the immitigable privateness of all sensation.

"The Death of St. Narcissus" proves that Circe's island, which seems little like a refuge—indeed seems to offer delirious self-engorgement straining toward infinity—is in fact enervating, claustrophobic. Saint Narcissus beholds his own face in the pool altering, altering, until it assumes every imaginable likeness, but his world is as shallow as the film of water he peers into; he may count himself king of infinite space, but the nutshell in which he is bounded keeps pressing on his body. Circe's isle is vibrant, lush, gaudy, but few poets choose to sustain a lyrical vision grounded in such unreality. It is nature inside a bottle, like the tiny England of Blake's "The Crystal Cabinet" (1803?), in which the poet is locked by a maiden:

> This Cabinet is formd of Gold
> And Pearl & Crystal shining bright
> And within it opens into a World
> And a little lovely Moony Night
>
> Another England there I saw
> Another London with its Tower
> Another Thames & other Hills
> And another pleasant Surrey Bower
>
> Another Maiden like herself . . .
>
> (lines 5–13)

The poetical imagination, perhaps in all poets, keeps inventing and elaborating lovely analogues of the natural world, then shattering them as they grow self-contained, involute, unnatural; as

Auden says, "Nature by nature in unnature ends" ("In Sickness and in Health"). When Blake announces, "I must Create a System, or be enslav'd by another Man's" (*Jerusalem*, 10:20), the unstated corollary is that he is still in danger of being enslaved by his own system unless he keeps creating new ones. The hold of the aesthetic refuge upon poets is finally due to their self-enamoredness, to the spell cast on them by the charms of their own fantasies; and the need to abandon the aesthetic refuge is due to their need to surpass the old delights, to move on to new invention.

If I am right in believing that during the Victorian age the fully lyrical Romantic vision fell asunder into two partial lyricalities, typified by the Palace of Art and Circe's island, then these two begin to converge again in the early Modern era. We have seen that the landscape of "The Death of St. Narcissus," a refuge of the Circe's isle sort, full of overstressed, too-interrelated nature, has a few of the features of the Palace of Art—the airless choking atmosphere, the loss of body fluids. And in the most remarkable of all early-twentieth-century aesthetic refuges, we see that the Palace of Art can grow into something almost exactly like Circe's isle:

> Scattered Moluccas
> Not knowing, day to day,
> The first day's end, in the next noon . . .
> Thick foliage
> Placid beneath warm suns,
> Tawn fore-shores
> Washed in the cobalt of oblivions . . .
> A consciousness disjunct,
> Being but this overblotted
> Series
> Of intermittences;
>
> Coracle of Pacific voyages,
> The unforecasted beach;
> Then on an oar
> Read this:

"I was
And I no more exist;
Here drifted
An hedonist."
(*Mauberley* (1920) 4)

Pound's Hugh Selwyn Mauberley is an aesthete in the Rossetti tradition, whose response to sexual invitation is first to make medallions, then to drift into stupor; he suffers from such a virulent aestheticism that he is finally incapable of art. As his world dwindles, as his scope of imaginative action contracts almost to zero, he changes from an artist to an autist, entertained only by the "Minoan undulation" of his own brainwaves. Mauberley's motto, like that of all dwellers in aesthetic refuges, is Infinite riches in a little room; but that dream is always unattainable, for the imagination becomes impoverished, bankrupt, from the absence of outer stimulation. Mauberley's fantasy keeps constricting until there is nothing in his head but a third-rate Gauguin Tahitiscape, an emblem of the scatteredness, the extreme depopulation, of his intelligence. We know that these putative Moluccas are actually Circe's isle, because the oar-tombstone is an echo of the request of Elpenor, the member of Odysseus's crew who fell from Circe's roof and was left unburied on Aeaea, and whose ghost asked Odysseus to bury him and place an oar over his grave—a story that Pound translated in his first Canto, written shortly before this poem. Mauberley regards the sexual invitation of his model as equivalent to Circe's spell, an obsession that lames, disperses, etiolates his fantasy until it reaches almost perfect emptiness. This is the peril inherent in the lyrical mode, whether governed by Proteus or by Ariel: a nature that is strictly marvelous, strictly phantasmagorical, strictly saturated with the beholder, may be so far removed from our common world that it is craziness. To live on a Grecian urn, to see one's own eyes reflected from every tree and beast, may be to choose death.

Chapter 4

LYRICAL SOCIETY

If, as we have seen, nature undergoes strange distortions under the pressure of the lyrical sensibility, becomes snarled and colluded with the intelligence of the poet, so human society also must mutate when beheld lyrically. Strictly speaking, every introduction of a second or third person into a poem is a step downward from the lyric to the dramatic; and yet the lyric poem, according to its mythic origin in the panegyric, has always presupposed as its object some hero or god, not the poet himself but some figment of splendor before whom the poet swoons. In archaic times this object was typically the victor or nobleman or king who paid the poet's salary; in modern times this object is often the oversoul or *anima mundi*, an absolute secular archetype of the human mind; but in either case the poet dejects himself or catches himself up in some vision of a perfected man. To this extent lyrical society does not look much like a sociologist's report of a few plutocrats sailing gaily on a sea of proletarian blood, as in William Carlos Williams's poem "The Yachts"; it is instead a pantheon of bright, vague majesties spied out dangerously by the poet and his fellow Actaeons, a chess game in which all the pieces are queens.

It has been snidely said of Pindar that he expended the utmost magnificence of imagination to glorify the exploits of mule drivers;

and this lampoon will serve as a little parable for the relation of lyrical society to its lower, coarser referent. The lyric poet takes a secret glee in the uncanny irrelation of the transfigured creature presented in the poem to its homely source; to make a god of Alexander the Great is no grand feat; but the apotheosis of a mule driver is an accomplishment. Shaw said that the ethics of a munitions maker require him to sell his wares to anyone who can pay the price; and similarly the panegyrist is professional, ethical, to the extent that he can write as fine an ode to a toothless weakling as to an emperor. Lyric society maintains its loftiness, its superbity, insofar as it frustrates any penetration to a lower world; for once the panegyrist has got out his best bellows he can inflate anyone and anything with such a dose of *pneuma* that the palsied slave and Jupiter waddle over the clouds on an equal footing. This is the general lyric trait that sly Pindar demonstrated in his Olympian odes: Arbitrariness of Content.

Let us begin by studying the method of characterization that Ben Jonson used in an enthusiastic but sophisticated panegyric, "To the Immortall Memorie, and Friendship of That Noble Paire, Sir Lucius Cary, and Sir H. Morison" (after 1629):

THE COUNTER-TURNE

Alas, but *Morison* fell young:
Hee never fell, thou fall'st, my tongue.
Hee stood, a Souldier to the last right end,
A perfect Patriot, and a noble friend,
But most a vertuous Sonne.
All Offices were done
By him, so ample, full, and round,
In weight, in measure, number, sound,
As though his age imperfect might appeare,
His life was of Humanitie the Spheare.

THE STAND

Goe now, and tell out dayes summ'd up with feares,
And make them yeares;
Produce thy masse of miseries on the Stage,
To swell thine age;

Repeat of things a throng,
To shew thou has beene long,
Not liv'd; for life doth her great actions spell,
By what was done and wrought
In season, and so brought
To light; her measures are, how well
Each syllab'e answer'd, and was form'd, how faire;
These make the lines of life, and that's her ayre.
(lines 43–64)

It may be said that Jonson's basic conceit here is the strife between the discursive and the lyrical. Everywhere in the ode Jonson contrasts what is lengthy, tedious, bulked out (the time waster of four score years in line 27, the oak in line 67) with what is brief, intense, and beautiful (the lily in line 69). Of the exact nature of Morison's heroic deeds, or the cause of his early death, Jonson says nothing; indeed one can learn little of Cary and Morison except that they were friends, and noble, and that one of them is dead. The subject of the poem is not the content of their achievement but the poetry of it; the lyricality of it. Their histories have been denatured, detemporalized, and reprojected upon a heavenly screen, a musical staff: Cary and Morison have been siderealized, "exprest, / In this bright *Asterisme*" (lines 88–89) as the constellation Gemini, and their deeds have been reduced to sheer rhythm, the heavings and subsidings of a metrical scheme. Jonson affects to believe that the poem, the melody, the two-part invention of their heroic acts, is a far finer thing than the vast, lax mass of his own writings for the theater, indeed than the present ode, which is heard as a kind of stuttering echo of the poem their nobility wrote—"Hee never fell, thou fall'st, my tongue" (line 44); "*Friendship*, in deed, was written, not in words" (line 123). If the ode is to avoid the discursiveness, the boredom, that it continually deplores, it can do so only by imitating in its involutions, in its doublings-back, in its turns and counterturns, the sphericality and closure so prized in Morison's career. And so the ode begins with the tale of the Infant of Saguntum, so repelled by the devastation of his town that he crawled back into his mother's womb and refused to let himself be born; and the ode ends with a sowing that is a harvest, a collapsed circle, time and space alike contracted to a single sharp point. This is a model for the presentation of people in lyric poems: people distend into featureless spheres, contract into stars, are brought to a fever of intensity, become governed by the rules of prosody and metaphor, not of biography and chronology. Instead of a recognizable face we are offered a balloon with a light bulb inside.

Some burn damp faggots, others may consume
The entire combustible world in one small room
As though dried straw, and if we turn about
The bare chimney is gone black out
Because the work had finished in that flare.
Soldier, scholar, horseman, he,
As 'twere all life's epitome.
What made us dream that he could comb grey hair?

This is the eleventh stanza of Yeats's "In Memory of Major Robert Gregory," a poem based, like Jonson's, on the contrast between the haltingly historical and the impetuously lyrical. Again, the attempt to characterize Robert Gregory, to point out idiosyncrasy, recognizable feature or fingerprint, is as futile as before: Gregory possesses all genius and finesse, and therefore his image recedes into white light.

Lyrical society has no politics, no sociology, no biology; but it does have a kind of physics. In Marvell's "An *Horatian* Ode upon *Cromwel's* Return from *Ireland*" (about 1650), we see a poet deeply engaged with political affairs, but his political sympathies are famously difficult to judge from the text of the poem, and the political actors have been rendered inhumanly forceful:

So restless *Cromwel* could not cease
In the inglorious Arts of Peace,
    But through adventrous War
    Urged his active Star:
And, like the three-fork'd Lightning, first
Breaking the Clouds where it was nurst,

Did thorough his own Side
His fiery way divide.
For 'tis all one to Courage high
The Emulous or Enemy;
And with such to inclose
Is more than to oppose.
Then burning through the Air he went,
And Pallaces and Temples rent:
And *Caesars* head at last
Did through his Laurels blast.
'Tis Madness to resist or blame
The force of angry Heavens flame;
(lines 9–26)

The gods of the Iliad were vigorous and capricious partisans; Marvell's Cromwell seems far more impersonal, implacable, indifferent—divine—than they. The complicated drama of Cromwell's opposition to King Charles, of his struggles to subdue his friends as well as his enemies, has been abstracted into a sort of meteorology; Cromwell subsists as a nimbus, an electricity before which all the inertia of matter is negligible. He has superseded every moral category—" 'Tis Madness to resist or blame"—for Jupiter himself cannot be bound by the laws he imposes on others. There is nothing particularly unusual in this line of panegyric, though it is slightly lacking in the graciousness, the clemency, that the master likes to hear expressed in his praise; what is odd is that *both* of the major figures in the poem, Cromwell and his great antagonist alike, work actively toward a state of extreme depersonalization and rarefaction. Marvell says of Cromwell that he wishes modestly to redirect his own glory to the House of Commons:

And, what he may, forbears
His Fame to make it theirs:
And has his Sword and Spoyls ungirt,
To lay them at the *Publick's* skirt.
(lines 87–90)

Similarly King Charles at the moment of his execution abdicates more than his crown, attains a state of heroic resignation, simplicity, nonchalance:

> *He* nothing common did, or mean,
> Upon the memorable Scene:
> But with his keener Eye
> The Axes edge did try:
> Nor call'd the *Gods* with vulgar spight
> To vindicate his helpless Right,
> But bow'd his comely Head
> Down, as upon a Bed.
>
> (lines 57–64)

Marvell, in the preceding lines, refers to Charles as the *Royal Actor*; and the king, like Cromwell himself, understands his life as foreordained, governed by a script, himself a kind of artifice. T. S. Eliot has said that Shakespeare's characters, at certain moments of intensity, start to see themselves in a dramatic light (*Selected Essays*, pp. 27, 110). This experience, which we can find in certain plays and poems and perhaps in our own lives as well, seems to be essentially lyrical rather than dramatic. A character in a play is most dramatic when he finds himself most credible as an agent in the little spectacle being enacted before the eyes of the audience —that is, when the situation rouses him to his most telling, most characteristic behavior. But a character who *sees himself* in a dramatic light has lost a certain confidence in the autonomous reality within the proscenium; he has at least a dim understanding that the trees are made of wire and tissue paper, that the light that falls on him is not the light of the sun, that the fourth wall is preposterously open and full of dark gaping faces; the character is asked to acknowledge his enactedness, his mysterious complicity with his playwright, and so the actor becomes a reciter of poetry rather than someone lost in the representation of an imaginary man. The preternatural keenness of King Charles's eye, an eye that can outcut the ax that beheads him, manifests just this stepping above the conditions of mortality. To understand oneself as a lightning bolt, an embodiment of inexorable energies, or to understand oneself as an actor wearing one's regalia as a kind of costume, is to become strangely disidentified with humanity: the actor knows that any finite role is arbitrary and undistinguished, and the lightning bolt will blast or transfigure one thing as happily as another.

The oddity of Marvell's "An Horatian Ode" is that we expect the lyrical hero of a panegyric to thrust forward against a background of lesser, nonlyrical people, just as Jonson contrasts the lyrical Cary and Morison with his blithery nonlyrical self. But Marvell's adversary is as lyrical as his hero; perhaps this represents an advance in the evolution of the panegyric. Strictly speaking, there can be no such thing as a lyrical villain, for either the antagonist of the lyrical hero must have descended out of the lyric into the sodden world of representation and therefore come to manifest a principle of inertia or recalcitrance to flight, or else he must have become as spherical and stellar as the hero himself, the white dwarf in a binary star. Indeed, the elevation of a genre or mode may be judged by the degree of villainy it permits: a Zola novel is exclusively concerned with villains; a romance must supply a dragon for Saint George to slay. An epic cannot treat a true villain, for Turnus must be noble if Aeneas is not to be demeaned by fighting him, and the champion of an alien culture ought to represent different and less-favored values, not necessarily inferior ones. A lyric, insofar as it is concerned with several personages, must apotheosize all of them into a single constellation.

In Marvell's "An Horatian Ode," the process of Cromwell's assimilation from the representational to the lyrical is rapid: the poem begins with the poet's exhortation to the "forward Youth" to "leave the Books in dust, / And oyl th' unused Armours rust" (lines 5–6), for Cromwell is permitted only four lines of privacy and personal leisure before he is summoned to be lightning. But in other, similar poems we can watch a gradual transition from the mundane to the unearthly, the aesthetic. In Yeats's "Easter 1916" (1916), for example, the poem lingers for most of its first half in the prelyrical, a world where the houses were built in the eighteenth century and ordinary clownish fellows make small talk on the streets; it is the locus of common representation, casual and pedestrian, devoid of any special significance. But as the poet considers an assortment of scholars and louts, he marvels at the hidden intensities that led them to take part in the uprising at the Dublin Post Office:

> Hearts with one purpose alone
> Through summer and winter seem
> Enchanted to a stone
> To trouble the living stream.
> The horse that comes from the road,
> The rider, the birds that range
> From cloud to tumbling cloud,
> Minute by minute they change;
> A shadow of cloud on the stream
> Changes minute by minute;
> A horse-hoof slides on the brim,
> And a horse plashes within it;
> The long-legged moor-hens dive,
> And hens to moor-cocks call;
> Minute by minute they live:
> The stone's in the midst of all.
>
> (lines 41–56)

In the midst of the loose, breathless novelties of the natural, a continual random slipping from one state to the next, there is something unnatural, inexplicable, hard. The Easter 1916 rebellion was ostensibly a political act, but as Yeats knew it was an act of desperation unlikely to gain much public good; it more resembled Cuchulain's fight with the sea than a well-considered measure to win independence from England. Here political pressures were wrought to a pitch beyond politics and into the domain of art. In "Easter 1916" Yeats seems to imagine lyrical society as a community of stones, as if the Irish conspirators had evolved into their own tombstones, unforgettable, magnificent, obsessive, lifeless, eternal—it is not far from these stone-enchanted hearts to the "Monuments of unageing intellect" in "Sailing to Byzantium"—a superhuman purposefulness disrupting the ordinary course of events. In a later poem, "The Statues" (1938), which also considers the Easter 1916 rebels and speaks of the statue of Cuchulain erected in the rebels' honor in the Dublin Post Office, Yeats seems to imagine that lyric society has been refined from a community of stones to a community of statues:

> No! Greater than Pythagoras, for the men
> That with a mallet or a chisel modelled these
> Calculations that look but casual flesh, put down
> All Asiatic vague immensities,
> And not the banks of oars that swam upon
> The many-headed foam at Salamis.
> Europe put off that foam when Phidias
> Gave women dreams and dreams their looking-glass.
> (lines 9–16)

It is clear from Yeats's prose draft that the theme of this poem is man's shifting attempts to embody God, as if there was a single deity whom Pythagoras tried to seize by mathematical calculation, whom Phidias tried to manifest as Apollo, who grew fat and shapeless, empty-eyed, Buddhesque, as Indian sculptors altered the divine image that Alexander the Great had brought to the East, who at last was set in the Post Office in the pagan shape of Cuchulain. Civilization seems to be a vast museum populated by images of God, images that serve as *teloi* for human action, types for human sexual passion. In an early poem, "The Indian upon God" (1886), the poet learns that the moorfowl imagines God as a huge moorfowl who makes rain from his dripping wings, the lotus imagines that God is a lotus, and so forth: a convenient congeries of Gods to answer every natural desire. Similarly in "The Statues," images of God multiply with disturbing frequency; and according to Yeats's strange myth of aesthetic eugenics, it is possible that the human race will evolve through increasingly accurate approximations of these statues, these Gods. Where life is most intense, it is most supernatural, most governed by the rules of art. In this sense the casual comedians of "Easter 1916" are sculpting themselves, growing statuelike, as they gather their forces against the tyrant.

We have already examined, in connection with Hermione in

The Winter's Tale, something of what it means, in the lyrical scheme of things, to become a statue. To some poets, like Auden in "In Praise of Limestone" (1948), heaven itself is best imagined as nothing more than an ensemble of pastoral statues, for "The blessed will not care what angle they are regarded from, / Having nothing to hide." It is the undoing of the Fall, when all fig leaves are cast away and the elect present their bodies for overt visual delight. For a poet like Browning, whose relationship to the lyric mode is more equivocal than Auden's, the mutation from man to statue is more sinister. In "The Statue and the Bust" (1855), Browning tells a legend about Ferdinand de' Medici, who committed adultery with a certain lady in his heart, but not his body; after many years he commanded John of Douay to erect an equestrian statue of him in the public square, forever regarding a bust of the lady sculpted by one of the Della Robbias and placed in her window. Interestingly, Pater in his "Winckelmann" essay describes Browning's psychologically engorged and supersubtle style in almost the same terms he uses to describe the terra-cotta work of Luca Della Robbia. Browning does not seem to admire the duke and the lady for their self-restraint, for their pursuit of their love affair through such artful vicars:

> The counter our lovers staked was lost
> As surely as if it were lawful coin:
> And the sin I impute to each frustrate ghost
> Is—the unlit lamp and the ungirt loin,
> Though the end in sight was a vice, I say.
> (lines 244–48)

It was a lyrical hope, the hope of the duke and the lady that a pair of surrogates could consummate the affections their bodies never knew; the hope that the declension from organism to icon or chess piece would lead to some eerier, more enduring love than that possible to mere mortals. It is not hard to imagine Wilde or Yeats retelling this same story in a way that would stress the superior keenness and vertigo of the love between two images as opposed to the sweaty grunting of carnalities—indeed there is a sense in which they do exactly this, Wilde in *Salome* and Yeats in *The King of the Great Clock Tower*, in which severed heads and flesh-hating dancers take the place of statues and busts, become the aesthetic equivalents of disembodied souls. But Browning, with his devotion to imperfect human juices, can find little to praise in the translation from flesh to carved image; and so the lyrical aspirations of his characters are exposed as bloodless, meatless, sentimental.

Every lyrical movement toward stones and statues is, of course, a movement toward death; and to this extent lyrical society is composed of the dead. If we examine the personages found in English lyrics over the course of the language, we find that most of them are indeed dead, or infantile, or frigidly rural, or anonymous, or nothing but names. Many of the usual appurtenances or extrapolations of the lyric mode, such as the aesthetic refuge, also have, as we have seen, a certain whiff of the grave. If Barbara Hardy is right in claiming, in *The Advantage of Lyric*, that one of the central functions of the lyric is to prolong emotions, this stretching of affect will also lead the poet beyond the limits of mortality. We may look to several authorities to confirm Mrs. Hardy's argument. One of them is Shelley:

> A child at play by itself will express its delight by its voice and motions; and every inflexion of tone and every gesture will bear exact relation to a corresponding antitype in the pleasurable impressions which awakened it; it will be the reflected image of that impression; and as the lyre trembles and sounds after the wind has died away, so the child seeks, by prolonging in its voice and motions the duration of the effect, to prolong also a consciousness of the cause. In relation to the objects which delight a child, these expressions are, what poetry is to higher objects. (*A Defence of Poetry*, p. 27)

Another is Yeats:

> The purpose of rhythm, it has always seemed to me, is to prolong the moment of contemplation, the moment when we are both asleep and awake, which is the one moment of creation, by hushing us with an alluring

> monotony, while it holds us waking by variety, to keep us in that state of perhaps real trance, in which the mind liberated from the pressure of the will is unfolded in symbols. . . . I have been swept, when in more profound meditation, beyond all memory but of those things that came from beyond the threshold of waking life. (*Essays and Introductions*, p. 159)

Insofar as he tries to prolong emotion, the lyric poet resembles either a child whirling around until he is dizzy-sick, trying by an act of weak magic to supply from inside himself the cause of his own pleasure, or a conjurer of spirits. Both the child and the magus are involved and uncompanionable creatures; but the magus seems able to surround himself, like Yeats in *A Vision*, with a phantom society of the illustrious dead. The prolongation of emotion is a kind of self-hypnosis, and it is not surprising that such a state will tend to populate itself with characters who little resemble those solid, reasonably finished and autochthonous beings found in a novel by George Eliot; the personages in a lyric poem tend to be hallucinations, mysteriously complicit with the desires and fears of the poet.

We can see another lyrical advantage to the society composed of stones or statues: such entities are little subject to decay or diminution; and if the purpose of writing lyric poems about people is to prolong the emotion felt for them, then when directed toward stone or statue that emotion has discovered an object as fixed and incorruptible as itself. It is of course disturbing to the poet that the image of a man is so poor a substitute for the man himself; but it is also disturbing that the emotion felt for an image is so different in character from the emotion felt for a man—that prolonged emotion changes its quality, its timbre, by the mere act of prolongation. Keats was unusually expert in evaluating the poverty of oversustained emotion, the emotion of the lover on the Grecian urn who never, never can kiss, though winning near the goal; Keats knew that the body's flushes and spasms were much preferable, despite their rapid loss of power, to their aesthetical equivalents. But perhaps among English poets the subtlest student of the relation of prolonged to immediate emotion, as well as the builder of the most extensive and detailed lyrical society, is Wordsworth.

The famous definition of poetry in the Preface to the *Lyrical Ballads* suggests something of the difference in quality of emotion between its raw state and the poet's digestion of it:

> I have said that poetry is the spontaneous overflow of powerful feelings: it takes its origin from emotion recollected in tranquillity: the emotion is contemplated till, by a species of reaction, the tranquillity gradually disappears, and an emotion, kindred to that which was before the subject of contemplation, is gradually produced, and does itself actually exist in the mind. In this mood successful composition generally begins, and in a mood similar to this is carried on; but the emotion, of whatever kind, and in whatever degree, from various causes, is qualified by various pleasures, so that in describing any passions whatsoever, which are voluntarily described, the mind will, upon the whole, be in a state of enjoyment.

The distinction between the original feeling and the intellectual faculty that rehearses it at leisure for the sake of expressing it is far from original with Wordsworth; Dryden, for example, in "The Author's Apology for Heroic Poetry and Poetic Licence" (1677), licenses hyperbole and other extravagant or passionate forms of speech on the grounds that "this boldness of expression is not to be blamed if it be managed by the coolness and discretion which is necessary to a poet." Wordsworth's contribution to English poetics lies in his distinction in tenor between the felt emotion and the evoked emotion: the evoked emotion is always a species of enjoyment, no matter how little enjoyable its original might have been. Wordsworth postulates a separate class of aesthetic emotions, in many ways like their originals but strangely mutated by the very faculty that tranquilizes them, restores them, makes them conducive to joy. Now no poet is less an aesthete than Wordsworth; given his deep distrust of language and his hatred of any art detached from the natural and social world, it is likely that he wished to make the emotions digested by art as similar as possible to their originals, and that he was forced to distinguish between them precisely because no verbal equivalent could conjure in him exactly the emotion as first experienced. He puts the best face he can on the discrepancy; but I think he would have preferred a magical identity of meat and excrement.

To Wordsworth, then, the attempt to write a lyric poem, the attempt to prolong and memorialize emotion, is not a drawing out of emotion into an inhuman tenuity; it is instead a complicated process of freezings and thawings, paralyses of feeling followed by sudden stabs. Many of Wordsworth's poems reenact this drama inside themselves, as if Wordsworth were trying to seize the instant when his imagination was suddenly enabled.

A slumber did my spirit seal;
    I had no human fears:
She seemed a thing that could not feel
    The touch of earthly years.

No motion has she now, no force;
    She neither hears nor sees;
Rolled round in earth's diurnal course,
    With rocks, and stones, and trees.

Here feeling is implicit, anesthesia explicit; nerves are severed, then rejoined, then severed again. First the poet is anesthetized by his delusion of Lucy's immortality; at last he is anesthetized by his empathy with her corpse. That faculty that tranquilizes the spontaneous overflow of feeling is so highly developed, so muscle-bound, that all feeling seems in danger of extinction. Wordsworth wrote this short poem in 1799, one year before he wrote the famous Preface to the *Lyrical Ballads*, and I believe it shows the dark side of the poetic presented so ardently, so exultantly, in the Preface. There are many passages in Wordsworth's poetry in which the poet exercises his faculty of imagination in its highest degree by attributing to rocks and stones and trees a large blunt intelligence:

To every natural form, rock, fruit or flower

Even the loose stones that cover the highway,
I gave a moral life—I saw them feel
(*The Prelude* 3.124–26)

In "A Slumber Did My Spirit Seal" we have the negative inversion of this triumph; the exercise of imagination is equally great, but here the inanimate world seems to suck out the poet's apparatus of feeling into its own numbness, inertia. In Wordsworth's poetry, from beginning to end, there is a current of emotion and there is a counterforce that arrests the current; sometimes Wordsworth expostulates against this counterforce, calls it a demonic spirit of analysis (as in *The Prelude* 2.216) that hacks apart the world with its false discriminations; but mentality, ego, soberness, chilling are necessary to the process that converts experience into poetry. The prevalence of waterfalls has often been noted in Wordsworth's poetry: the coursing of water is one of his central emblems for that unanimous outflow of feeling that animates every created thing; but the stream must freeze, must be held in check at least for a while, if a poem is to be written.

When first, descending from the moor-lands,
I saw the Stream of Yarrow glide
Along a bare and open valley,
The Ettrick Shepherd was my guide. . . .
And death upon the braes of Yarrow
Has closed the Shepherd-poet's eyes:

Nor has the rolling year twice measured,
From sign to sign, its steadfast course,
Since every mortal power of Coleridge
Was frozen at its marvellous source.
(lines 1–4, 11–16)

This is one of Wordsworth's last great poems, the "Extempore Effusion upon the Death of James Hogg" (1835), in which Wordsworth recapitulates the deaths of the famous authors he has known. In each case there is a movement "From sunshine to the sunless land," or from a pastoral valley to a city, or from a flowing to a freezing, or from spontaneous emotion to tranquility; it is as if these great poets and essayists, in their living and their dying, reenact the process of composing a poem. The stanza on Coleridge, full of echoes of "A Slumber Did My Spirit Seal," makes us remember all of Coleridge's poems, such as "Dejection: An Ode," in which the poet was anxious over the tendency toward abstract thought that inhibited his imagination, his poetic gift; but from the perspective of Wordsworth's doctrine in the *Lyrical Ballads*, a certain inhibition of feeling, a certain numbing of feeling for the sake of re-presentation, is indispensable to the writing of poems. In this sense, death of feeling is the mother of beauty. The purpose of elegy is partly to prolong emotion and partly to soothe it, to cauterize by freezing; and in the "Extempore Effusion" Wordsworth peoples a little kingdom of dead poets, both for the sake of rehearsing his love for them and for the sake of dismissing them to get on with the rest of life; spontaneous emotion and tranquility, extemporaneousness and consideration, effusion and death, are raised to the highest possible pitch.

EPITAPHS

One of Wordsworth's greatest prose works is his *Essay on Epitaphs* (1810), which is for our purposes a kind of manual on how to make people into poems, how to construct a lyrical society. Why do people write epitaphs? It is, says Wordsworth, because of an intuition of immortality, because we wish some permanent memorial to the permanence of the individual soul. To confirm the truth of the soul's immortality, Wordsworth appeals to his favorite philosopher, the Infant Babe, who lives in a state of tremulous wonder, half-ignorant and half-knowing, at the miraculous origins and ends of things:

> Never did a child stand by the side of a running stream, pondering within himself what power was the feeder of the perpetual current, from what never-wearied sources the body of water was supplied, but he must have been inevitably propelled to follow this question by another: "Towards what abyss is it in progress? what receptacle can

> contain the mighty influx?" And the spirit of the answer must have been, though the word might be sea or ocean . . . a receptacle without bounds or dimensions;—nothing less than infinity. (*Prose Works* 2:51)

The child knows immediately, just as in the Immortality Ode, that human life is a stream, and that some ocean will gather its waters at last. We have seen that in Wordsworth's aesthetic theory a poem takes its shape from the tension between the spontaneous flow of emotion and some tranquilizing force; and Wordsworth's theory of human identity works in exactly the same way. Human life is a stream; and it will be tranquilized by the grave:

> The passions [in a proper epitaph] should be subdued, the emotions controlled; strong, indeed, but nothing ungovernable or wholly involuntary. . . . Moreover, a grave is a tranquillizing object: resignation in course of time springs up from it as naturally as the wild flowers, besprinkling the turf with which it may be covered, or gathering around the monument by which it is defended. (*Prose Works* 2:60)

It seems fitting that Wordsworth, always laboring to demolish the barriers between life and art, should imagine the shape, the tendency, of the composition of a poem to approximate as closely as possible that of human life. It may be said that the epitaph is Wordsworth's ideal poetic form, for in the epitaph spontaneous emotion and tranquility are inevitable, natural, as if the author of the poem were no one in particular, but the whole community of suffering mankind—as if human life breathed its sorrow and consolation without intervening artifice, almost without words. It is also true that a great many of Wordsworth's best poems are, at least in the loosest sense, epitaphs.

The *Essay on Epitaphs* is largely an expostulation against and a reply to Samuel Johnson's peculiar manual of epitaph writing placed at the end of his life of Pope. Johnson, unwilling to compose his own official epitaph on Pope, is there content to show the feebleness of Pope's epitaphs; but his criteria for judging their quality rankled Wordsworth considerably. Unlyrical soul that he was, Johnson liked best those epitaphs in which the lamentation was most specific and exact, in which the unique character of the subject was most concisely manifest.

> The difficulty in writing epitaphs is to give a particular and appropriate praise. This, however, is not always to be performed, whatever be the diligence or ability of the writer; for the greater part of mankind *have no character at all*, have little that distinguishes them from others equally good or bad, and therefore nothing can be said of them which may not be applied with equal propriety to a thousand more. . . . whenever friendship, or any other motive, obliges a poet to write on such subjects, he must be forgiven if he sometimes wanders in generalities, and utters the same praise over different tombs. (*The Lives of the Poets* 2:338)

Wordsworth uses Gray's "Elegy Written in a Country Churchyard" to confute Johnson:

> however general or even trite the sentiment may be, every man of pure mind will read the words with pleasure and gratitude. . . . a pious admonition to the living, and a humble expression of Christian confidence in immortality, is the language of a thousand church-yards; and it does not often happen that anything, in a greater degree discriminate or appropriate to the dead or to the living, is to be found in them. This want of discrimination has been ascribed by Dr. Johnson . . . to two causes; first, the scantiness of the objects of human praise; and, secondly, the want of variety in the characters of men. . . . The objects of admiration in human-nature are not scanty, but abundant; and every man has a character of his own, to the eye that has skill to perceive it. The real cause of the acknowledged want of discrimination in sepulchral memorials is this: That to analyse the characters of others, especially of those whom we love, is not a common or natural employment of men at any time. (*Prose Works* 2:56)

Indiscriminateness, triteness, therefore become proofs of sincerity and almost of poetic excellence. Again and again in the *Essay*

Wordsworth quotes a wretched specimen of an epitaph and admires its sincerity of feeling, even while he cringes at its clumsiness of expression. Are all epitaphs, then, of equal merit? No, for Wordsworth vituperates those in which the poet calls attention to his own rhetorical trickiness, artful wit. According to Wordsworth's scheme, both the author and his subject must be indistinct, oceanic, half-absorbed into the final receptacle of the human race. Every attempt to particularize shows the taint of mortality, egoism.

Taken far enough, this doctrine would suggest that it ought to be possible to write a single all-purpose epitaph, as valid for king as for yeoman; but Wordsworth resists this extrapolation:

> [The excellence of an epitaph] will be found to lie in a due proportion of the common or universal feeling of humanity to sensations excited by a distinct and clear conception, conveyed to the reader's mind, of the individual, whose death is deplored and whose memory is to be preserved; at least of his character as, after death, it appeared to those who loved him and lament his loss. The general sympathy ought to be quickened, provoked, and diversified, by particular thoughts, actions, images. . . . But the writer of an epitaph is not an anatomist, who dissects the internal frame of the mind; he is not even a painter. . . . The character of a deceased friend or beloved kinsman is not seen, no—nor ought to be seen, otherwise than as a tree through a tender haze or a luminous mist, that spiritualises and beautifies it. . . . The composition and quality of the mind of a virtuous man . . . ought to appear, and be felt as something midway between what he was on earth walking about with his living frailties, and what he may be presumed to be as a Spirit in heaven. (*Prose Works* 2:57–58)

The luminous mist suggests all the sudden veilings in ether in *The Prelude* and elsewhere, atmospheric effects that manifest the workings of the august Imagination. An epitaph is supposed to depict a man caught in the very act of being transfigured, hovering with a rapid beat of wings between his earthly outline and the high figure he will make in heaven. Again, the man and the poem attain a magical similarity of design, for the poem's mimesis is directed not toward the warts on the face, the broken blood vessels, the thousand stains of character, but toward the process of his assumption into paradise—a kinema, not a static portrait in oils.

An epitaph is bad insofar as it calls attention to itself, for all its imaginative energies must be directed outward toward the emparadising of its object. It is not surprising, then, that the *Essay* contains Wordsworth's most savage attacks on language, for overt wit destroys the illusion that he most cherishes, that an epitaph is an expression of the general sympathy, the fellow feeling, of the human race. Poor Pope, damned by Johnson for his repetitiousness and his indiscriminate generalities, is damned by Wordsworth for the opposite reason, for his captious antitheses and specious precisions.

> "*The Saint sustained it but the Woman died.*" . . . Why was not this simply expressed; without playing with the Reader's fancy to the delusion and dishonour of his Understanding, by a trifling epigrammatic point? But alas! ages must pass away before men will have their eyes open to the beauty and majesty of Truth, and will be taught to venerate Poetry no further than as She is a Handmaid pure as her Mistress—the noblest Handmaid in her train! (*Prose Works* 2:79)

But this is mild compared with a later passage in which Wordsworth condemns all language that exuberates apart from its reference, that takes on itself a spurious independence and a febrile, unnaturally vigorous private life:

> If words be not . . . an incarnation of the thought but only a clothing for it, then surely will they prove an ill gift; such a one as those poisoned vestments, read of in the stories of superstitious times, which had power to consume and to alienate from his right mind the victim who put them on. Language, if it do not uphold, and feed, and

> leave in quiet, like the power of gravitation or the air we breathe, is a counter-spirit, unremittingly and noiselessly at work to derange, to subvert, to lay waste, to vitiate, and to dissolve. (*Prose Works* 2:85)

A proper epitaph is the expression of the irresistible impulse of a man toward his entelechy, his heavenly goal; it is a celestial body put on a man to enable flight; a bad epitaph is a shirt of Nessus that depraves and eats up its subject. It is as if the language, caught up in self-admiration, usurps the energies that ought to impel its object to heaven. In these passages we see the magical function that Wordsworth assigns to epitaph writing; insofar as the epitaph is written by an act of the same communal imagination that sustains and elevates the whole natural and social world, it is no mere human testimonial to a virtuous man, but an active participant in his ascension into the circle of the blessed.

Elsewhere in the *Essay* Wordsworth alleges that the antithetical style of Pope is an instrument perfectly suited to the analysis of the damned, for evil passions are necessarily oblique, incoherent, inauthentic, self-thwarting, "at war with each other and with themselves" (p. 80); whereas the style that he himself recommends is appropriate to depict the elect:

> a perfect image of meekness . . . might easily lead on to the thought of magnanimity: for assuredly there is nothing incongruous in those virtues. But the mind would not then be separated from the Person who is the object of its thoughts: it would still be confined to that Person . . . that is, would be kept within the circle of qualities which range themselves quietly by each other's side. Whereas, when meekness and magnanimity are represented antithetically, the mind is not only carried from the main object, but is compelled to turn to a subject in which the quality exists divided from some other as noble, its natural ally—a painful feeling! (*Prose Works* 2:81)

Wordsworth claims no one should write an epitaph about an evil man; but he might go a little further and claim there is no such thing as an evil man, only a manure pile of evil traits that fail to constitute a self. The antithetical style deflects the reader's attention from the person at the center of the description to the internecine traits he manifests; Wordsworth's style, on the other hand, causes the finite traits to recede into luminous mist, so that the subject will impend, make himself felt, all the more strongly. In the bad Augustan epitaph, the adjectives of character description will generate their own antitheses without regard to the sanctity of the subject; person will vanish into paronomasia, and the poem will feed monstrously on its own verbality; but in the good Romantic epitaph the words become transparent, hide themselves demurely as they thrust forward the image of a man.

Wordsworth does not mind the rough-hewn awkwardness of the epitaphs in the country churchyard because he wants a kind of epitaph that is scarcely made of words at all. When he himself writes epitaphs he sometimes impinges on a condition of languagelessness. The *Essay upon Epitaphs* concludes with a specimen epitaph by Wordsworth, a poem too long to be engraved on a tombstone, but a thoughtful, detailed celebration of a virtuous cottager "gathered from enquiries concerning the Deceased made in the neighbourhood":

He grew up
From year to year in loneliness of soul;
And this deep mountain valley was to him
Soundless, with all its streams. The bird of dawn
Did never rouze this Cottager from sleep
With startling summons: not for his delight
The vernal cuckoo shouted; not for him
Murmured the labouring bee.

(*Prose Works* 2:94)

The man and the tribute are perhaps both unremarkable; but it is of interest that Wordsworth chose to write his specimen epitaph on a deaf man. To Wordsworth poetry was essentially an acoustic act: his habit of chanting his poems outdoors in the process of invention, his peculiar aversion to pen and paper, are well known. The deaf man, indefatigable reader though he may be—"books / Were ready comrades whom he could not tire"—is necessarily deprived of much of the experience of the poem; the epitaph seems to aspire toward the state of wordless reverie in which the cottager spent his days. Just as the deaf ear extinguishes all the noises of nature, so the poem seems to hush itself, to tranquilize its own music, to work toward a pure contemplation of its object. The cottager, in his extreme enclosedness, was as if already dead, blissfully involute in his will to do good.

A slow disease insensibly consumed
The powers of nature; and a few short steps
Of friends and kindred bore him from his home . . .
To the profounder stillness of the grave.
(*Prose Works* 2:95)

In his deafness he carried his own grave with him. If the aim of the epitaph writer is to display his subject midway between earthly and heavenly life, this deaf man was well over halfway to heaven at the moment of his birth.

In many ways Wordsworth populates the body of his poetry with a lyrical society of creatures similar to this deaf man, half-resorbed into the imagination's mist. The many children in his poems, all trailing clouds of glory, have of course not quite congealed into humanity; but it will be worth our while to examine briefly Wordsworth's treatment of a colorful adult, the sort of man who, in other hands, could be a quirky Dickensian old coot, as far removed as possible from what we have called the lyrical: I mean the leech gatherer in "Resolution and Independence" (1801), an example of suffering and deformity, whose "body was bent double, feet and head / Coming together in life's pilgrimage." In this poem the poet is disconsolate because so many poets have died young; he asks the cheerful leech gatherer how he maintains himself; the leech gatherer explains, but somehow the poet does not quite understand what he says:

The old Man still stood talking by my side;
But now his voice to me was like a stream
Scarce heard; nor word from word could I divide;
And the whole body of the Man did seem
Like one whom I had met with in a dream;

> Or like a man from some far region sent,
> To give me human strength, by apt admonishment.
> (lines 106–12)

We have proceeded from a consideration of the deaths of poets to a situation in which words have dissolved into some superhuman incomprehensibility; the stream freezes, the stream flows. The poet knows only English, not Angelish, so he must ask the leech gatherer to repeat his life story. The leech gatherer, whose outward appearance is that of a "huge stone," has a voice like "a stream"; by this manipulation of similes, Wordsworth makes him seem like the genius loci of the whole landscape, an icon of half-animate nature. The greatest poetry, it seems, consists not of words but of nature noise, inarticulate deep-meaning rumbles and whispers; and the leech gatherer is an image of how the speaker of this poetry might be personified, with his lowliness, his wet, palpable closeness to earth, his immanence. He is, unexpectedly, a satisfactory replacement for Chatterton and Burns, because they, like Wordsworth, aspired to the tactile, celestially mundane language he represents. The leech gatherer, like the deaf man, like Lucy, like most of the personages in Wordsworth's poems, has turned out to be one of the blessed, has taken on a certain ghostliness, an iconicity, a transparence—the reader can see through him mountains and pools and streams; and so lyrical society shows itself to consist of characters who flatten and heave themselves into all manner of inhuman shapes.

ELEGIES FOR DEAD POETS

> Elegy is the form of poetry natural to the reflective mind. It *may* treat of any subject, but it must treat of no subject *for itself*; but always and exclusively with reference to the poet himself. . . . Elegy presents every thing as lost and gone, or absent and future. (Coleridge, *Table Talk*, 23 Oct. 1833)

Coleridge's notion of the elegy is a lyrical notion; indeed it almost seems that Coleridge regards the elegy as the essential lyrical act.

As we have seen, it is considered desirable in elegy or epitaph to distinguish one's subject, at least to some degree, from the general mass of humanity; but in the high elegy—and the highest sort of elegy is the elegy for one's predecessor, the most recent great poet—biography is nearly superfluous. Every attempt to characterize the subject is a step down from lyricality into representation:

> . . . thou hadst small *Latine*, and lesse *Greeke*
> (Jonson, "To the Memory of . . . Shakespeare," line 31)

> You were silly like us; your gift survived it all:
> The parish of rich women, physical decay,
> Yourself.
> (Auden, "In Memory of W. B. Yeats" 2)

> . . . you won't think me imposing if
> I ask you to stay at my elbow
> until cocktail time: dear Shade, for your elegy
> I should have been able to manage
> something more like you than this egocentric monologue,
> but accept it for friendship's sake.

This last passage, the end of Auden's "The Cave of Making (*In Memoriam Louis MacNeice*)," is an apology to the dead MacNeice for Auden's treating "of no subject *for itself*; but always and exclusively with reference to the poet himself," as if Auden thought Coleridge's prescription was bad advice. Yet, as one reads through the canon of elegies for dead poets, one is struck by how seldom the elegist even attempts to manage something more than an egocentric monologue. Sharp, telling portraits, and even affectionate rehearsal of the dead poet's foibles, are almost nonexistent. This is partly because, as Wordsworth says in the *Essay upon Epitaphs*, "The mighty benefactors of mankind . . . do not stand in need of biographic sketches" (*Prose Works* 2:61); but no discourse read at a wake or a funeral would ever be permitted to ignore the specific nature and achievement of its subject to the extent usually practiced by the elegy.

Why is this avoidance of the particular considered seemly? The answer lies, I think, in the magical function of elegy writing. The purpose of an elegy is to effect a metamorphosis of its subject from the human into something superhuman; and every reminder that MacNeice loved "women and Donegal" ("The Cave of Making, line 19), or that Keats was remarkably sensitive to bad reviews, becomes a kind of ballast that impedes the effort toward transfiguration. The only data from the subject's life relevant to the elegy are data that pertain to his own magical gift, his artistic ability to render imperishable the perishing earthly things he loves. But insofar as the matter to be discussed in an elegy is not the dead poet's history, or even the dead poet's poems, but instead the dead poet's genius, the elegiac subject will be individuated only to a very slight degree, will be perceived as someone more or less identical to every other great poet. The magical hope of the elegy is that the dead poet's genius will finally be brought to bear not on the actual poems he has written, but upon his own apotheosis, and that the genius of the elegist will be a kind of ancilla helping, tactfully directing the genius of the dead poet during its last movement from pupa to psyche—uttering the incantation that the dead poet, being dead, cannot utter for himself. The efficacy of the spell demands that it be spoken almost in the same words whenever it is performed, and so we have from Bion and Moschus to Auden a series of elegies of growing richness and splendor, and yet nearly interchangeable.

In the peculiar symbiosis of the elegy, the dead poet receives from his successor a vehicle into the heaven of language, in return for which the dead poet agrees to act as a male muse for the living. Milton calls Shakespeare the "Dear son of memory" ("On Shakespeare, 1630," line 5), and, since the Muses are the daughters of Memory, that makes Shakespeare the Muses' brother; even the shade of Louis MacNeice, the presiding spirit of the Cave of Making—that is, the study in which Auden writes his poems—is an agreeable muse of the hour before cocktails; and of course the several metempsychoses of Sidney, Keats, Clough, and Yeats all offer an inspiration, all provide their elegists with a poem. In most elegies the living poet prostrates himself before his predecessor; but there is usually a secret countermovement, in which the living poet struggles to assimilate the dangerous energies of the dead poet, to compel his magic for his own ends, to change defunct Prospero into functioning Ariel.

In almost every great elegy there is tension between the role of the dead poet as a transmuted entity safely in heaven and the role of the dead poet as muse. In his former role the dead poet achieves a terminal image—the symbol maker is changed into a symbol; in his latter role the dead poet is turned into an invisible, continuous selfless presence, guiding the imagination of the living poet. The former role is a triumph, but the latter is a species of genteel slavery. To the extent that Coleridge is right that every elegy is egocentric, a reflex of the elegist, the dead poet who is the ostensible subject must become an arbitrary minor actor in the all-engrossing dialogue of the elegist with himself.

Insofar as the genre of the elegy presupposes a movement from the historical self of its subject to some satisfying unhistorical or posthistorical condition, an elegy will enact a movement from the nonlyrical to the lyrical. To describe the nature of this lyric shift we may summon our old helpers Ariel and Proteus—even literary critics may dabble with familiars. Ariel, as we have seen, likes to effect transformations once and for all, enjoys the spectacle of dead Alonso as a confection of coral and pearls. Ariel therefore may be said to govern the innumerable elegiac transmutations of the dead poet into some beautiful terminal image—the species of elegiac transmutation for which the story of the metamorphosis of the gored Adonis into a flower is the model. A fine specimen of the Ariel elegy is Spenser's *Astrophel* (1595), a belated elegy on the death of Sidney; in it Spenser transposes many aspects of Sidney's life into rustic affairs of shepherds and shepherdesses, so that the history of Sidney's death in battle in the Netherlands is modified into a tale of a great hunter, perhaps too emulous of praise (line 90), who seeks out a mighty boar and is gored to death. When his beloved Stella finds his corpse she indulges in a good deal of theatrical lamentation, and at last dies:

> The gods, which all things see, this same beheld,
> And pittying this paire of lovers trew,
> Transformed them, there lying on the field,

Into one flowre that is both red and blew:
It first growes red, and then to blew doth fade,
Like Astrophel, which thereinto was made.

And in the midst thereof a star appeares,
As fairly formd as any star in skyes,
Resembling Stella in her freshest yeares,
Forth darting beames of beautie from her eyes;
And all the day it standeth full of deow,
Which is the teares that from her eyes did flow.
(lines 181–92)

Spenser is here straining at the limits of the resources of metaphor, inventing a flower-star that comprises the hero's body, in its full round from red vigor to blue rigor, and the hero's beloved, captured forever at her emotional peak, always beautiful and always weeping. The flower-star—a note to my edition of Spenser says it may be the sea starwort, *Aster tripolium*—suggests some postnatural collapse of the ephemeral and the permanent, flower and star; its motto is the same as that of Spenser's other, greater Adonis in *The Faerie Queene* 3:6.47, "eterne in mutabilitie." Spenser cleverly manages this terminal symbol to hint at a consummation in which a great man is united with what he desires, in which he becomes Star-lover and Star, Adonis and Venus in one.

The elegist is not an especially vivid presence in *Astrophel*; indeed, Spenser's poem is but an introduction to a collection of elegies written by others, as if Sidney in death diffused into a general force field of inspiration instead of becoming the muse of one particular genius. But in many later elegies on dead poets Coleridge's idea that the elegy chiefly refers to the elegist is fully demonstrated. If there is a gamut from concentration on the dead poet—referentiality to the subject—to concentration on the elegist—self-referentiality—Spenser's *Astrophel* lies at the first end of the scale; and perhaps all elegies that depend on full elaboration of the terminal image, the triumph of the dead poet, will also tend in the same direction.

In the other kind of elegy—the Proteus elegy, not the Ariel elegy—the emotional center of gravity will lie not in the dead poet's achievement of final blessedness, but in some scene in which the dead poet persists as a presence on earth, enabling the living poet to write and perhaps assisting others as well. This species of elegy may be called Protean, because the dead poet never achieves the satisfaction of a fixed form, an aesthetical perfection, but instead lingers as an indefinite hovering thing, a spirit much praised but seemingly slightly forlorn, never capable of dismissing itself into full beatitude. If *Astrophel* is a specimen of the Ariel elegy, we can find a pure example of the Proteus elegy in one of the most famous of all English lyrics, Milton's *Lycidas.* Sidney was a poet whom Spenser well may have regarded as a genius comparable to his own; but Edward King, the subject of *Lycidas,* was a poet of such slender accomplishment, and dead so young, that it is not surprising that the self-referential quality of the elegy would wax monstrously, that Milton would put his own gift on display while King kept tumbling in the seaweed, never petrifying into coral and pearls, never ascending into any but the lowest of godheads.

We have seen, in our discussion of Wordsworth's "Extempore Effusion," that the elegy is a genre of fits and starts, of freezings and thawings; the imagination becomes fluent for a while, even prodigal, and then some stab of grief, some exhaustion, paralyzes the movement of the verse. There is a sense in which the elegy is a literary mode designed to be self-terminating, designed to stop itself so that, by an act of magic, the painful emotion it rehearses will cease as well. In this sense the elegy is a long, difficult approach to one final overwhelming image, like the flower-star in *Astrophel,* that, when attained, will dismiss any further need to speak. The elegist, therefore, is in the peculiar situation of finding his own imaginative fluency something of a burden, insofar as every burst of invention detains him from his goal, which is silence, relief, catharsis.

The reason *Lycidas* has often been regarded as insincere is not because of its pastoral conventions, not because of its frigid mingling of classical and Christian elements, but because the elegist so rejoices in the profusion of his invention and is so distressed whenever the milk of imagination fails to overflow. The "sincere" elegist is glad of an opportunity to end, while Milton wishes only a further and wider field on which his genius can operate—"Tomorrow to fresh Woods, and Pastures new." Everywhere in the poem there is an odd sense that Lycidas, the ostensible hero, has no real part to play, is a kind of unwanted intruder in the text:

> Where were ye Nymphs when the remorseless deep
> Clos'd o'er the head of your lov'd *Lycidas?*
> For neither were ye playing on the steep,
> Where your old *Bards*, the famous *Druids*, lie,
> Nor on the shaggy top of *Mona* high,
> Nor yet where *Deva* spreads her wizard stream:
> Ay me, I fondly dream!
> Had ye been there—for what could that have done?
> (lines 50–57)

The motif of the helplessness of the nature sprites to avert the hero's death is conventional in the Greek elegy; but I do not think that Theocritus or Bion ever gives the sense, as Milton does, of being irritated that he must cease his lovely embroidery of the landscape and return to his chosen subject. Lycidas, throughout the first part of the poem, is a spirit of disenchantment, a sober spoilsport, who checks Milton's poetical invention, wakens him from his happy fables of nymphs and river gods, bards and wizards, the pagan high priests of imagination. Edward King was a young clergyman as well as a poet; and in the first part of *Lycidas* it seems likely that Christian rigor will render the whole genre of pastoral elegy impossible, will prevent the identification of its subject with a conveniently metamorphosable god, the necessary strategy for the elegiac discharge of emotion. It seems that, if the poet permits himself the luxury of classical fantasy, of constructing a grotto where one may sport with Amaryllis in the shade, an angel will arise to smite it with a two-handed engine, utterly despoiling the work of imagination. Everything that Peter, the pilot of the Galilean lake, tells the elegist tends to blast and shrivel the pleasing fictions concocted earlier in the poem; and the elegist's reaction to Peter's long speech about the ruin and perversion of the clergy is to try as best he can to extenuate it, to cover the horror of truth with further bouquets of fable:

> . . . Return *Sicilian* Muse,
> And call the Vales, and bid them hither cast
> Their Bells and Flowers of a thousand hues. . . .
> Bid *Amaranthus* all his beauty shed,
> And Daffadillies fill their cups with tears,
> To strew the Laureate Hearse where *Lycid* lies.
> For so to interpose a little ease,
> Let our frail thoughts dally with false surmise.
> Ay me!
>
> (lines 133–35, 149–54)

Milton descends from Christian severity to classical ornament because of the danger that biblical rage will freeze the power of imagination, render the act of poem-making worthless; but it seems in vain, for classical mythology cannot validate itself, cannot lift itself from "false surmise" into true. Yet this flurry of flower strewing is performed only so that Milton may accomplish the last and subtlest of his elegiac tricks. On both occasions when the elegist says "Ay me!" (lines 56 and 154), there is a sudden deflation of mythology—with that stab of exclamation he pricks his own balloon; but one order of myth is dispelled only so that another order will seem perfectly valid. If Milton had oriented *Lycidas* entirely on the Christian plane, had dispensed with the apparatus of pastoral mythology, the reader might well have questioned the propriety of a Christian fabulizing in which a dead clergyman was allowed to become "the Genius of the shore" (line 183), a tutelary spirit guiding sailors away from shipwreck. Indeed, even in Milton's strange sort of Protestantism one may still question the propriety of such a resolution; but by the strategy of ripping his way through an attractive but overtly preposterous mythology Milton makes his doubtful outcome seem plausible by comparison. Christianity, which seemed in the first part of the poem sternly antimythological, debunking, at last settles into a myth, an agency for elegiac apotheosis. The imaginary and the "real"—that is, the Christian—become conjoined, and the battle between fictive easing effusiveness and high paralysis at last appears to be resolved. And yet, when Milton near the end of the poem mentions Lycidas's appearance in heaven—"With *Nectar* pure his oozy Locks he laves" (line 175), we may feel that Lycidas's transfiguration is incomplete, if he is still dripping mud and seaweed onto the celestial floor. To call attention to Lycidas's drowned body reminds us that he is far from having undergone the perfecting magic that changed Astrophel and Stella into a single flower, and the vision of Lycidas as an invisible lighthouse protecting "all that wander in the perilous flood" may suggest a kindly ghost tarrying at the scene of its ruin, still bound to earth and unable to pass into some more devastating consummation of being. As a mild Genius of the shore, himself not much more than a naiad, Lycidas seems to have value chiefly for his ability to inspire Milton to write a poem; and so we see what happens in a truly self-referential elegy, in which the subject simply takes whatever temporary form best suits the convenience of the elegist. As a corpse Edward King permitted Milton to criticize his own processes of invention, to investigate the sorts of inventions permitted by Christian belief; and so Lycidas changes from a pretext for a grief immitigable by fiction into a provisional statement of the ultimate hope of every poet, the true fiction.

The fact of Edward King's death both provokes Milton's imagination and stifles it, for the imagination can do nothing to alter fate, to bring the dead poet back to life, despite all its manipulations of surrogates. There is, however, a magical argument that some elegists use in order to claim that the dead poet has attained resurrection: that the dead poet survives as an animating presence in the mind of the elegist himself. Milton does not explicitly make this claim in *Lycidas*, but in "On Shakespeare, 1630" we can see something of the process of transference of identity between dead poet and living:

For whilst to th' shame of slow-endeavoring art,
Thy easy numbers flow, and that each heart

Hath from the leaves of thy unvalu'd Book
Those Delphic lines with deep impression took,
Then thou our fancy of itself bereaving,
Dost make us Marble with too much conceiving;
And so Sepulcher'd in such pomp dost lie,
That Kings in such a Tomb would wish to die.
(lines 9–16)

Milton envisages his faculty of imagination as a kind of womb, no longer capable of parthenogenesis, for the superior masculine force of Shakespeare has deprived it of the power of bearing any children but his. Shakespeare's fury of image making seems to paralyze the mind of any competing author and send it reeling into exhaustion as it tries to follow, to reconstitute what Shakespeare has achieved. It is not simply that the death of Shakespeare was a tragedy for art—a common panegyrical theme—but that his successors find themselves stultified, petrified, both by the energies released in his writing and by the removal of the human source of these energies, as if the death of Shakespeare-Adonis meant we must all dwell in a perpetual winter of the spirit. Shakespeare's death seems to infect all subsequent writers with a kind of rigor mortis.

In this poem the dead poet does not turn into a star or a flower; instead the living poet, turned into a marble statue, becomes a sort of terminal image assumed by the dead poet. In other elegies the collusion of genius between the living and the dead becomes stranger still. For example, in Thomas Carew's "An Elegie upon the Death of the Dean of Paul's, Dr. John Donne" (1633), Carew alleges that Poetry has been "widowed" (line 1) by Donne's death, and that the elegy Carew now writes must, like every other poem subsequent to Donne's death, be defective, uninspired, out of breath:

Oh, pardon me, that break with untun'd verse
The reverend silence that attends thy hearse,
Whose awful solemn murmurs were to thee
More than these faint lines, a loud Elegie,
That did proclaim in a dumb eloquence

The death of all the Arts, whose influence
Grown feeble, in these panting numbers lies
Gasping short-winded accents, and so dies;
So doth the swiftly turning wheel not stand
In the instant we withdraw the moving hand,
But some small time maintain a faint weak course
By virtue of the first impulsive force:

(lines 71–82)

Of Donne's fate after death, of his reception into heaven, Carew has nothing to say; but on the subject of Donne's power to transmute and invigorate the English language he is eloquent. Carew imagines our language as inert, sluggish, shapeless, recalcitrant until Donne's overwhelming "masculine expression" (line 39) forces it into higher obedience.

Our stubborn language bends, made only fit
With her tough-thick-ribb'd hoops to gird about
Thy giant phansie . . .

(lines 50–52)

Greek and Latin are too dulcet and liquid, overrefined, for Donne's mighty conceptions; only English is sturdy enough, coarse enough, to retain the shapes Donne impressed on it. Because the inertia of English is so great, it continues in motion after Donne's death; a less massive and substantial language would relax after the plastic stress imparted by a great poet disappears, but English continues to inflect itself, to alter and grow shapely, simply because its heft is too great for sudden stops. Carew himself, then, has no intrinsic poetical power; he is only the accidental transmitter of Donne's residual energies in Donne's absence. Indeed Carew's imitation of Donne's verbal style, with all its agility, its felicities of contortion, its impetuosities, its scarified or scabrous texture, is so uncannily accurate that one can almost credit the conceit that the dead Donne seized on Carew as a medium to write an elegy for his own funeral. Donne is at last no flower, no star, no genius of the shore, only an urge within the English tongue; and Carew's elegy is governed by Proteus in that it postulates no final form for its subject—Donne survives flickeringly as a presence informing the heavings of language, the heavings of the corpse of language.

The Proteus elegy, as we have seen, attempts to abolish the division between the dead poet and the living; the term *Proteus elegy* is admissible only insofar as we can discover an elegiac mode in which there is behind the text no clear division of elegist and subject but instead a splayed hybrid thing, indeterminate between living and dead, as if poetical genius were one multiform spirit that on some occasions assumed the shape of Donne or Shakespeare, on other occasions the shape of Carew or Milton. Some elegies have characteristics of both the Ariel elegy and the Proteus elegy. If we consider Shelley's *Adonais* (1821), we see a poem that seems to be a classical Ariel elegy, like Spenser's similarly Adonean *Astrophel:* Shelley begins with the spectacle of Keats's corpse and ends with the spectacle of Keats fully stellified, beaconing from the abode where the eternal are. This is exactly the sort of perfected terminal image I have associated with Ariel throughout this book. But elsewhere in the poem there are hints of a different vision of Keats, a Keats who does not pass into effortless starriness but instead grows oddly confused with Shelley, congruent to him; a Protean Keats. As the elegist studies the corpse of Adonais, the little scene of the bier becomes animated with the dead poet's faculties:

> Oh, weep for Adonais!—The quick Dreams,
> The passion-wingèd Ministers of thought,
> Who were his flocks, whom near the living streams
> Of his young spirit he fed, and whom he taught
> The love which was its music, wander not—
> Wander no more, from kindling brain to brain,
> But droop there, whence they sprung; and mourn their lot
> Round the cold heart, where, after their sweet pain,
> They ne'er will gather strength, or find a home again.
>
> And one with trembling hand clasps his cold head,
> And fans him with her moonlight wings, and cries,
> "Our love, our hope, our sorrow, is not dead;
> See, on the silken fringe of his faint eyes,

> Like dew upon a sleeping flower, there lies
> A tear some Dream has loosened from his brain."
> Lost Angel of a ruined Paradise!
> She knew not 'twas her own; as with no stain
> She faded, like a cloud which had outwept its rain.
> (lines 73–90)

This elfin consort is much elaborated in the subsequent stanzas: one washes Adonais's limbs with dew, another cuts her hair and throws a wreath of it on him, a third alights on this lips, caresses them, and momentarily sends a flush of inspiration through the poet's dead limbs; and after these Dreams and Splendors there throngs a vast company of Desires, Adorations, Persuasions, Destinies, Glooms, Incarnations, Phantasies, and so forth. These creatures were previously given form, incarnated, in Keats's poetry; and now that Keats is dead they are denied any outlet into other minds, and so, frustrated and inexpressible, they cling balefully around the corpse of the one man who could have realized them. In their present forlorn unreality they have something of the charm of the sylphs in Pope's *The Rape of the Lock*, in a much more pallid and solemn form; they dwindle into fairies because the brain that could have given them intensity and stature is defunct. Imagination has died, and so its images must become necrophiliac.

This doting on the poetical faculties, now sadly liberated, cut free from the poet, is typical of the Proteus elegy; implicit is the theme that these free-floating faculties will find a new home in the mind of the elegist himself. Nowhere does Shelley describe the migration of genius from Keats to Shelley; but when Shelley starts to write about himself, he introduces certain parallels to his description of Keats:

> Midst others of less note, came one frail Form,
> A phantom among men; companionless
> As the last cloud of an expiring storm,
> Whose thunder is its knell; he, as I guess,
> Had gazed on Nature's naked loveliness,
> Actaeon-like, and now he fled astray

With feeble steps o'er the world's wilderness,
And his own thoughts, along that rugged way,
Pursued, like raging hounds, their father and their prey.

A pardlike Spirit beautiful and swift—
A Love in desolation masked;—a Power
Girt round with weakness;—it can scarce uplift
The weight of the superincumbent hour;
It is a dying lamp, a falling shower,
A breaking billow;—even whilst we speak
Is it not broken? On the withering flower
The killing sun smiles brightly: on a cheek
The life can burn in blood, even while the heart may break.
(lines 271–88)

If Shelley is a phantom among men, then he is in the odd position of being himself a member of the company of Dreams and Splendors, Phantasies, who decorated the twilight chamber of Keats's death; the elegist seems too weak and insubstantial for any independent existence, so he becomes a droopy specter haunting the precincts of a more powerful, skillful poet. It is as if Keats's genius, detached from its original and much enfeebled by the loss of the sanity, the physical vigor, of the rest of Keats, turns into Shelley. Keats was an organ of divine expression, able to realize the crew of Dreams and Splendors, to master and embody them; Shelley, on the other hand, sees himself as an Actaeon harassed, worried by his thoughts, pursued as if by raging hounds, for now Genius is too subtle, keen, disembodied, impoverished, to attain any control over its own insights, its glimpses of beauty. Keats's deadness seems to have infected Shelley: Keats's corpse was briefly animated, flushed, when a Splendor caressed its lips, and Shelley too seems to be a febrile, morbid thing, his life only a series of spasms beneath his general withering, extinguishing. Shelley is Keats dead, a heap of fretful poetical faculties unable to cohere. It is a great relief when Shelley turns aside from the description of this poor disabled thing and continues with Keats's memorializing, for we may have felt concern that the elegy would be unable to continue with such a blighted elegist as the author. Insofar as Keats and Shelley are consubstantial, it interferes with the whole elegiac process; the Shelley who reels from Keats's death, half-identifying himself with Keats, is incapable of the sustained force necessary for his project.

Yet in other poems the ability of the elegist to identify himself with the elegized seems to be what gives the elegy its power and magical efficacy. Carew's elegy on Donne is a rare case of a minor poet pretending to be a major poet in order to make a worthy tribute to his subject—there is in music an exact analogue, John Blow's masterpiece the "Ode on the Death of Mr. Henry Purcell" (1696)—but it is still rarer for a major poet to efface himself, to grow transparent, to become a colorless medium for a dead poet's self-presentation. Such is the case in Auden's "In Memory of W. B. Yeats" (1939), which begins with chaste, objective, nonlyrical description of the events surrounding Yeats's death—

The mercury sank in the mouth of the dying day.
What instruments we have agree
The day of his death was a dark cold day—

and ends with a magic spell, for Auden-Proteus takes the exact shape of Yeats, imitates exactly his orotundity, his rhetoric, his metrical vigor:

Follow, poet, follow right
To the bottom of the night,
With your unconstraining voice
Still persuade us to rejoice . . .
In the deserts of the heart
Let the healing fountain start,
In the prison of his days
Teach the free man how to praise.

The rhythm of this concluding section is catalectic trochaic tetrameter, the meter of Shakespeare's "Full fathom five" and the witches' chorus in *Macbeth* and many other magic charms; the grammar of glamour. But in the twentieth century the patent on this meter belongs to Yeats, who uses it in many famous poems, such as

"Under Ben Bulben" and—with many acatalectic lines as well—"Man and the Echo" (1938):

And, all work done, dismisses all
Out of intellect and sight
And sinks at last into the night.
Echo Into the night.
  Man O Rocky Voice,
Shall we in that great night rejoice?

Yeats was fond of the rhyme *voice/rejoice:*

What matter? Out of cavern comes a voice,
And all it knows is that one word "Rejoice!"
("The Gyres," 1937)

I believe that, in rehearsing Yeats's themes in one of Yeats's favorite rhythms and favorite rhymes, Auden is not only investigating the limits of stylistic imitation but also slyly alluding to "Man and the Echo": Yeats is the Man and Auden plays the part of the Echo.

It is misleading to imagine, however, that Auden is subservient to Yeats, that Yeats remains a stark monument while Auden adapts selflessly to his model. Yeats too has undergone a metamorphosis:

The current of his feeling failed; he became his admirers.

Now he is scattered among a hundred cities
And wholly given over to unfamiliar affections,
To find his happiness in another kind of wood
And be punished under a foreign code of conscience.
The words of a dead man
Are modified in the guts of the living.
("In Memory of W. B. Yeats")

Beneath this passage is the myth of the dismemberment of Orpheus. Auden imagines Yeats as the Orphic singer who once guided affection, moved beasts, trees, stones, but now has been torn apart by maenads, by the Dionysiac energies he formerly controlled. Auden was a keen student of Eliot's *The Waste Land*,

and there is a vague sense that the mercury is below freezing because Yeats's death has laid waste the land; and of course in the classical elegy the dead poet is identified with the gored Adonis, whose death saps the vigor of nature. In a classical elegy, however, Adonis is at last transfigured into flower or star; but Yeats enjoys no such aesthetic relief, seems subject to a churning of digestion and modification and reinterpretation with no discernible terminus. Here Yeats's readers seem to perform on the great poet not only a ritual *sparagma* but a ritual cannibalism as well; and Auden seems not only to modify Yeats in his gut but also to eat Yeats, to assume by magic Yeats's faculties. Yeats dissolves waterily into a vague connective medium among isolated readers, a genius of the shores of human contact, a benign spirit of rhetoric, "A way of happening, a mouth," a megaphone through which Auden can bellow.

Again it is as if there were one Genius, which could assume as it chose the person of Yeats or the person of Auden, so close is the convergence between them at the end of the poem. But Auden was somewhat uneasy about becoming a second Yeats, and much of the tension of the elegy comes from this uneasiness. As we know from Humphrey Carpenter's biography of Auden, 1939 was the year Auden was trying to decide how far he ought to engage himself in political issues, that is, whether to be to the fight against fascism what Yeats was to the struggle for Irish home rule. The concluding section of the elegy suggests that Auden will continue Yeatsian political action after Yeats's death ("Teach the free man how to praise"), but part 2, the last-written section of the elegy, composed soon after Auden gave a rousing speech in New York City to support the refugees from the Spanish Civil War, suggests that a poet has no business taking part in public life ("poetry makes nothing happen"). In this way the poem enacts Auden's indecision about the wisdom of adopting Yeats as his muse. Eventually Auden decided against Yeats, and the elegy to Yeats became a kind of memorial to the Yeats-like Auden, forever repudiated. Later in Auden's life, when his friends reproached him for deleting from his canon "September 1, 1939," a poem in which Auden erects a little idol of himself as a moral exemplum to mankind ("May I . . . Show an affirming flame"), he wrote a letter to Stephen Spender defending his decision:

> I am incapable of saying a word about W. B. Yeats, because, through no fault of his, he has become for me the symbol of my own devil of inauthenticity . . . false emotion, inflated rhetoric, empty sonorities. . . . His [poems] make me whore after lies. (Carpenter, p. 416)

As Auden became more confident, assured, about his own poetical persona, the Protean model of the poet, capable of stealing any persona for himself, became less and less attractive. And so Yeats, denied the respite of a terminal image, was at last not permitted to collaborate with Auden's poetical faculties either. There is a sense, therefore, in which "In Memory of W. B. Yeats" is, though it contains every elegiac motif, not an elegy at all, for the elegist can discover no occupation or form for his subject and must relegate him to limbo.

THE ANTIELEGY

Auden's elegy to Yeats appears to be at the furthest reach of the Proteus elegy, yet I know of one poem that goes still further in that direction, indeed that shows Proteus provoking metamorphoses of the dead poet beyond any possible elegiac bound: Eliot's uncanny memorial to Yeats in *Little Gidding* 2 (1942):

> I caught the sudden look of some dead master
> Whom I had known, forgotten, half recalled
> Both one and many; in the brown baked features
> The eyes of a familiar compound ghost
> Both intimate and unidentifiable.
> So I assumed a double part, and cried
> And heard another's voice cry: "What! are *you* here?"
> Although we were not. I was still the same,
> Knowing myself yet being someone other—
> And he a face still forming;

In the published text of *Four Quartets*, the identification of this "dead master" with Yeats is unclear, a matter of hints and guesses; but there is ample evidence in the manuscript drafts and in Eliot's essay on Yeats (1940) to show that Eliot, when writing this passage, had Yeats primarily in mind. Helen Gardner reprints, in *The Composition of Four Quartets* (p. 187), a draft in which no poet other than Yeats can have been meant, though even here certain details are left unspecified:

I also was engaged as you must know,
In fighting for language: here, where I was tutored
In the strength and weakness of the English tongue
And elsewhere: when the political fire had regressed
My alien people with an archaic tongue
Claimed me.

The movement of Eliot's revision is to denature, de-Yeatsify, the dead master, to purge him of any finite identity, to make him an abstract vehemence. In his famous essay "Tradition and the Individual Talent" (1919), Eliot recommends to the artist "a continual self-sacrifice, a continual extinction of personality," a loss of one's own peculiarly inflected mentality in favor of what he calls "the mind of Europe" (*Selected Essays*, pp. 8–9). In the second part of *Little Gidding* the mind of Europe, half-personified in the figure of W. B. Yeats, meets the poet during an air raid patrol in order to suggest certain modifications of the doctrine of "Tradition and the Individual Talent," written before Eliot's conversion to Christianity. It is as if Language were given a tongue of its own, not that of any particular poet, then made to confess its inadequacy to the attainment of salvation; or, as Yeats says,

The Soul. Seek out reality, leave things that seem.
The Heart. What, be a singer born and lack a theme?
The Soul. Isaiah's coal, what more can man desire?
The Heart. Struck dumb in the simplicity of fire!
The Soul. Look on that fire, salvation walks within.
The Heart. What theme had Homer but original sin?
("Vacillation" 7)

At the end of "Vacillation" (1932) Yeats chose the Heart, chose song, language, original sin, instead of fire, purgation, all that would be most welcome in the tomb—knowing, of course, that all such choices are provisional, impoverishing, unsatisfactory; and in *Little Gidding* 2 a newly dead Yeats is compelled to make the opposite choice, the Soul's choice, the choice of fire:

> Those who knew purgatory here shall know
> Purgation hereafter: so shall you learn also,
> Caught in the embraces of that fiery wind
> Where you must learn to swim & better nature.
> (Gardner, p. 187)

In a sense Eliot is activating potentialities in Yeats's work, constructing a Yeats who is no longer caught on the horns of a dilemma but magically allowed to choose mutually exclusive alternatives at the same time; a Yeats not of *either/or* but of *both/and*. In this fashion Eliot's dead master keeps growing rounder, fuller, exhibiting dimensions not available to a mortal, at once a master of language and a master beyond language, at once a scarecrow and the cock of Hades who reorganizes the newly dead into shapes worthy of Byzantium.

Eliot was oddly uncertain about the setting of *Little Gidding* 2, whether it was to be hell or purgatory. In an early draft Eliot wrote not "What! are *you* here?" but "Are you here, Ser Brunetto?"—an allusion to *Inferno* 15, in which Dante finds his beloved old teacher among the company of the damned sodomites. Eliot explained this deletion in a letter to John Hayward:

> I think you will recognise that it was necessary to get rid of Brunetto for two reasons. The first is that the visionary figure has now become somewhat more definite and will no doubt be identified by some readers with Yeats though I do not mean anything so precise as that. However, I do not wish to take the responsibility of putting Yeats or anybody else into Hell and I do not want to impute to him the particular vice which took Brunetto there. Secondly, although the reference to that Canto is intended to be explicit, I wished the effect of the whole to be Purgatorial which is much more appropriate. (Gardner, pp. 64–65)

Eliot did not succeed in solving this problem by suppressing the reference to Ser Brunetto, however. The *Four Quartets* have little meaning apart from the Christian theology that governs them; and so, desirable as it may be for Eliot's purposes to turn the ruins of London into purgatory, or a gateway into purgatory, it is nevertheless true that the unregenerate pagan Yeats, though he wrote a play entitled *Purgatory*, belongs in no region of the afterlife other than hell. In the *Divine Comedy* Virgil, dwelling in the gentlest possible state of damnation, can briefly enter purgatory to give Dante a tour of its precincts; but the dead master of *Little Gidding* seems to be not, like Virgil, a worshiper of a false god, distinguished in many ways from his Christian successor, but instead someone in exactly the same situation in which Eliot, after death, will find himself. The dead master has gained such amplitude in death that he is uncategorizable as either a Christian or a pagan—as if every great poet reached out unconsciously toward the truths of Christian salvation, whatever his religion might be.

If *Little Gidding* 2 were an elegy to Yeats of the Ariel type, it would show Yeats in heaven, or in some state of aesthetic bliss, caught in an image sharper, more focused, than any available here on earth. All of Yeats's irresolution, indecision, blurriness of being would be eliminated, and he would display himself in some form more telling, more characteristically Yeatsian. Instead, of course, Yeats has been dislimned and shadowed, unrealized, magnified; he has attained no final resting place, been forced to wander, a desolate, implacable thing, through the limbo of this world and the limbo of the next:

> . . . the passage now presents no hindrance
> To the spirit unappeased and peregrine
> Between two worlds become much like each other . . .

Insofar as purgatory is a place appropriate for unfinished creatures, for painfully twiformed beings moving imperceptibly toward beatitude, it is the proper state for this shapeless Yeats. As Eliot's poem evolved through its drafts, Yeats not only suffered a certain loss of particularity, he became compounded with other dead poets as well: the lines

> To purify the dialect of the tribe

and

> . . . the laceration
> Of laughter at what ceases to amuse

suggest that elements of Mallarmé and Swift (more precisely, Yeats's translation of Swift's epitaph) have been agglomerated into the dead master; as Eliot makes the texture of the dead master's speech a tissue of allusion, correspondingly the dead master himself starts to become every-poet, a being who sums up in himself all genius, a human anthology. In his essay on Yeats Eliot discusses, for the second time in his career, the process through which a poet impersonalizes himself:

> I have, in early essays, extolled what I called impersonality in art, and it may seem that, in giving as a reason for the superiority of Yeats's later work the greater expression of personality in it, I am contradicting myself. It may be that I expressed myself badly . . . but I think now, at least, that the truth of the matter is as follows. There are two forms of impersonality: that which is natural to the mere skilful craftsman, and that which is more and more achieved by the maturing artist. The first is that of what I have called the "anthology piece," of a lyric by Lovelace or Suckling. . . . The second impersonality is that of the poet who, out of intense and personal experience, is able to express a general truth; retaining all the particularity of his experience, to make of it a general symbol. And the strange thing is that Yeats, having been a great craftsman in the first kind, became a great poet in the second. (*On Poetry and Poets*, p. 299)

Eliot has enacted in *Little Gidding* an analogy of this second impersonality: instead of the process by which a poet turns his personal experience into literature, into general symbol, we have the process by which a poet himself metamorphoses from a personality into an impersonality, retaining only the ghost of the particularity of his experience. In his essay Eliot discusses Yeats as a symbol maker; in *Little Gidding* Eliot discusses Yeats as a symbol, a vague surrogate or vicar for all poets, a human abyss that can swallow up every language wielder, including at last Eliot himself.

In Eliot's earlier poetry there are moments of strain when it seems that the usual barriers that separate poet, poem, and reader, that articulate the relationships among them, are breaking down. By the end of "The Burial of the Dead" in *The Waste Land,* for instance, we have heard a single voice—the original title of the whole poem was *He Do the Police in Different Voices*—impersonating a European countess, the prophet Ezekiel, the sailor whose song opens *Tristan und Isolde,* and many other roles; but when the Voice utters the final line it is still a shock:

"That corpse you planted last year in your garden,
"Has it begun to sprout? Will it bloom this year? . . .
"You! hypocrite lecteur!—mon semblable,—mon frère!"

If we readers are the likenesses, the twins, of the speaker, then we must face the uncomfortable possibility that we ourselves are part of the repertory of the Voice; that it can mimic each of us as effortlessly as it can mimic all the other personages. In *Little Gidding* there is a similar breakdown, not between poet and reader, but between living poet and dead poet; between Eliot and the reservoir of genius. This is the reason he speaks both of the dead master as a "familiar compound ghost" and of himself as assuming a "double part" and hearing "another's voice cry" when he himself speaks: the intimacy, the strangeness-in-intimacy of the poet and the dead master, is so great that the poet is losing his ability to distinguish self from other. The dead master seems to be a voice for his own deepest being, while at the same time he endures a spasm of self-estrangement. The last compound within the familiar compound ghost is T. S. Eliot himself; for the poet stands on the threshold of absorption into this big Yeats, distended into a receptacle commodious enough to hold every master of language. Auden, in his elegy on Yeats, honors his great predecessor by assuming his voice; but here it seems not just that the elegist will grow congruent with the elegized, but that the elegist and the elegized will alike vanish into some smoke or fire, some phantom of skill, some great stark, tenuous intelligence into which every finite mind must sink. In a note to Hayward, Eliot said that he liked the word "re-enactment" in the dead master's speech because it meant "to take the part of oneself on a stage for oneself as the audience" (Gardner, p. 194); and if all of the scene of the ghost and the air raid patrol is part of a monodrama, then it is impossible to speak of *Little Gidding* 2 as an elegy, for there is no one to lament, no one to bury.

WOMEN

Whenever Eliot introduces certain large reverberations into his poetry, he is attempting to display a persona as vast, blurred, and impressive as that ascribed to Yeats in *Little Gidding* 2. There is a famous passage in "Gerontion" (1919), for example, that describes the disintegration of mankind:

> What will the spider do,
> Suspend its operations, will the weevil
> Delay? DeBailhache, Fresca, Mrs. Cammel, whirled
> Beyond the circuit of the shuddering Bear
> In fractured atoms.

Not only do DeBailhache, Fresca, and Mrs. Cammel crumble into galactic dust, but Gerontion too starts to grow large and incoherent, for his discourse is growing resonant, overresonant, with echoes, echoes of Chapman and, behind Chapman, Seneca, because Gerontion is alluding to Chapman's *Bussy d'Ambois* and Chapman in turn was alluding—Eliot explains all this in *The Use of Poetry and the Use of Criticism* (p. 147)—to Seneca's *Hercules Oeteus* and *Hercules Furens*. By this means Eliot hopes to produce a kind of literary vertigo in the voice of Gerontion himself comparable to the gooseflesh produced by the whirls and tumbles of these figures, disfigures, lost among the stars.

But the great master of this effect of allusion in a regression of mirrors was not Eliot but Ezra Pound, who at his moments of greatest intensity liked to display himself not in propria persona but substantiated, upheld, glorified by the images of other gifted poets who preceded him; Pound is happiest when he can feel stirring in his work the genius of the illustrious dead. Thus he begins his *Cantos* with Odysseus's descent into hell, a translation not of Homer but of Divus's Renaissance Latin translation of Homer; and he begins the *Homage to Sextus Propertius* (1917) with a passage in which Propertius invokes the shades of Callimachus and Philetas, the distinguished Greek lyric poets whose work he is adapting to Latin meter, Latin temper. Plato speculates in the *Ion* that poetic genius is a magnetic chain whose end is in heaven; and Pound too seems to hope that he can connect himself to prehistoric godhead through a chain of poets stretching from himself immemorially back. Pound, more than any other poet I know, espouses an ideal of compoundedness, as if he were most comfortably himself when sprouting from his body the various heads, the various limbs, of Confucius, Homer, Ibycus, Flaubert, Sappho, and others. No voice is ever unmixed; each must be thick with harmonics:

> If possible I shd. even have wished to render a composite character, including something of Ovid, and making the portrayed figure not only Propertius but inclusive of the spirit of the young man of the Augustan Age, hating rhetoric. (*Selected Letters*, p. 150)

It is as if every great poet possessed some fragment of a primary Genius and a modern poet ought to try to swallow as many fragments as possible. Pound's work may suggest, then, that the lyric poet should aspire to be every poet, should labor toward a grand synthesis of his predecessors within his own being.

> If I wrote of personal love or sorrow in free verse, or in any rhythm that left it unchanged, amid all its accidence, I would be full of self-contempt because of my egotism and indiscretion, and foresee the boredom of my reader. I must choose a traditional stanza, even what I alter must seem traditional. I commit my emotion to shepherds, herdsmen, camel-drivers, learned men, Milton's or Shelley's Platonist, that tower Palmer drew. Talk to me of originality and I will turn on you with rage. I am a crowd, I am a lonely man, I am nothing. Ancient salt is best packing. (Yeats,

"A General Introduction for My Work," 1937, in *Essays and Introductions*, p. 522)

There are times when it seems that many of the most powerful descriptions of poetical identity in the twentieth century are only elaborations of Keats's doctrine of negative capability. Lyric genius, like dramatic genius, seems to be a power of universal self-identification, universal self-disidentification, a hovering discreet *posse* that descends only provisionally, disdainfully, into *esse*.

I believe that this model of lyric genius, as a jumble of all previous lyric geniuses, or as an omniform vocality, can easily be adapted into a model for that sort of woman found everywhere in lyric poems, the beloved, the object on which lyric genius acts. The student of Renaissance sonnet sequences, as is well known, can scarcely distinguish Delia from Stella, Stella from Diana; if literary criticism can, through a heroic effort, differentiate the personalities of these ladies, all cruelly fair, fairly cruel, it nevertheless has always admitted that they are more alike than different. But my point is not just that impassioned rhetoric tends toward a high convergence of all its possible female objects, toward the erasure of idiosyncrasy; it is that these objects are synthetic in exactly the same manner as the genius that pursues them is synthetic. From before the Renaissance to Yeats and beyond, the beloved has been constructed through a process of choosing the best features of famous women:

> I seem to pen her praise that doth surpass my skill;
> I strive to row against the tide, I hop against the hill.
> Then let these few suffice: she Helen stains for hue,
> Dido for grace, Cresside for cheer, and is as Thisbe true.
> (Gascoigne, "Gascoigne's Praise of His Mistress," 1575)

In the nineteenth century, after the invention of photography, attempts were made to piece together the ideal woman from the various superb features of several admired beauties; but this search for perfection by means of the composite was only a modern visual analogue of the age-old practice of poets. It is easy to see why this technique permits little individuation: each characteristic or pungent attribute is systematically purged from the image, so that the image perfects itself by becoming blander, more polished and artificial, less memorable, until it is at last only a celestial vapidity, a Chlorinda or Phyllis whose feet have never touched earth.

Among these lyrical women we can find our twin spirits, Ariel and Proteus, again at work. Ariel presides over the sort of lyric in which the beloved turns into a doll, a sheer artifice; just as he delighted in mutating King Alonso into pearls and coral, so he delights in the Midas touch that turns women into gold—imperishable, unembraceable:

> Queene Vertues Court, which some call *Stellas* face,
> Prepar'd by Natures cheefest furniture:
> Hath his front built of Alablaster pure,
> Golde is the covering of that statelie place.
> The doore, by which sometimes runnes forth her grace
> Red Porphire is, which locke of Pearle makes sure:
> Whose Porches rich, with name of chekes indure,
> Marble mixt red and white, doe enterlace.
> (Sidney, *Astrophel and Stella* 9, 1591)

> There is a Garden in her face,
> Where Roses and white Lillies grow . . .
> Those Cherries fayrely doe enclose
> Of Orient Pearle a double row,
> Which when her lovely laughter showes,
> They looke like Rose-buds fill'd with snow.
> Yet them nor Peere nor Prince can buy,
> Till Cherry ripe themselves doe cry.
> (Campion, *Fourth Booke of Ayres* 7, 1617)

I suspect that the uncomfortableness modern readers feel about such poems as these is not due to loss of ease with old conventions, for these poems clearly had a disquieting effect upon their contemporary readers as well: there are deliberately hideous Renaissance engravings of women with hair made of wire, teeth of pearls, and so forth; and Shakespeare wrote a remarkable sonnet of protest, a conventional repudiation of a convention:

> My mistress' eyes are nothing like the sun;
> Coral is far more red than her lips' red:

If snow be white, why then her breasts are dun;
If hairs be wires, black wires grow on her head . . .
And yet, by heaven, I think my love as rare
As any she belied with false compare.
(Sonnet 130)

One should notice that, though Shakespeare sweeps away the fossilized apparatus of simile, his mistress is in this poem made no more individual or vivid than the mistresses of the inferior poets he mocks. Shakespeare will not let Ariel transform his mistress to coral and pearls, but for that reason Shakespeare cannot realize her, cannot present her at all; and so, although she grows black and dun, fleshly, seems in danger of sinking out of the lyric mode, she still dances away from our grasp, from his embrace. If she cannot be made into a Petrarchan doll she has little business as the heroine of a sonnet sequence. It is because the imagination reels at the translation of a woman into the facade of a building, or into a cherry garden—to visualize it is to see an Arcimboldo face composed of artichokes, berries, zucchini—that these images are appropriate for fully lyrical women. They must be artificialized to the greatest possible extent if they are to be the objects of the highest rhetoric. If art is magic—and in a seduction poem, like a funeral elegy, the poet always hopes that art will be magic—then the poet and his beloved must both endure a metamorphosis into an unnatural realm where concinnity is law and passion is equivalent to rhetorical ingenuity, where words and images are indistinguishable from what they signify, from what they are images of. Apollo's mistake with Daphne was his failure to understand that, within the confines of a legend, a tree is far more wooable, more amenable, more whittlable than a human woman.

As lyrical rhetoric grows intense it deforms its object, makes her aesthetic, susceptible to charms and glamours; and this transfiguration appears from the point of view of the natural world to be only a disfigurement. I believe that, subliminally, Sidney and Campion and other poets intended that their women seem grotesque; only the grotesque is sufficiently unnatural. Few social situations can have been stranger than that of a woman handed an Elizabethan sonnet sequence and told, "Here, this is about you"—in an essay Auden tries to imagine how Shakespeare's Mr. W. H. might have felt when reading the sonnets addressed to him—for to connect oneself with such a voodoo doll, such a rhetorical surrogate as Stella or Delia, would have been no easy matter.

He call'd her beauty lime-twigs, her hair net;
She fears her drugs ill laid, her hair loose set.
(Donne, "Satyre IV," lines 195–96)

The beloved who turns into palace or orchard is exactly equivalent to the dead poet who turns into flower or star; either transformation is governed by Ariel. The poet who mutates his beloved in Proteus fashion does not assign to her a single fixed image but instead celebrates her resistance to fixity, the waywardness of charm that is as ungraspable as a cloud. One of the greatest lyrics of this sort in English is Herrick's "Corinna's Going a-Maying" (1648):

Rise; and put on your Foliage, and be seene
To come forth, like the Spring-time, fresh and greene;
    And sweet as *Flora*. Take no care
    For Jewels for your Gowne, or Haire:
    Feare not; the leaves will strew
    Gemms in abundance upon you:
Besides, the childhood of the Day has kept,
Against you come, some *Orient Pearls* unwept:
    Come, and receive them while the light
    Hangs on the Dew-locks of the night:
(lines 15–24)

Corinna, as Herrick imagines her, is but a shimmer of dew; and by the end of the poem he compares both her and himself to water droplets, now vibrant but slowly freezing into poetry:

And as a vapour, or a drop of raine
Once lost, can ne'r be found againe:
    So when or you or I are made
    A fable, song, or fleeting shade;

All love, all liking, all delight
Lies drown'd with us in endlesse night.
(lines 63–67)

In a love poem governed by Proteus, the poem's artificiality, its symmetry and closure, is always something of an embarrassment: Herrick and D. H. Lawrence seek some fleeting image of the beloved, some quickness or vivacity that eludes any final decomposition into a poem. This iridescence in the woman, this evasiveness, has an element of erotic teasing: the poet dresses up his beloved in a transparent fabric, a mousseline of Cos, for the sake of half-concealing, half-revealing:

. . . if hair is mussed on her forehead,
If she goes in a gleam of Cos, in a slither of dyed stuff,
There is a volume in the matter . . .
And if she plays with me with her shirt off,
We shall construct many Iliads.
(Pound, *Homage to Sextus Propertius* 5.2, 1917)

In another poem by Herrick, "Upon Julia's Clothes" (1648), the poet speaks admiringly of "That liquefaction of her clothes . . . That brave Vibration each way free"; and in this sort of love poem not only the beloved's clothing but the beloved herself is in a state of liquefaction, brave vibration.

The work of art that perhaps best presents the erotic tension between Ariel and Proteus is not a lyric poem but Federico Fellini's film *Casanova*. There it seems that Casanova is a lover driven by the spirit of Proteus—it may be true of all promiscuous folk—for his appetite can fix on no single woman. His zest for sexual experience lies in the continual transshifting of the object of his attention, so that he must fall in love with—I exaggerate somewhat—arthritic hags, giantesses, amputees, hairy dwarfs; one can even imagine a sequel to the film that takes Casanova into the zoophilous, for his lusts seem to lead him beyond the verge of the human. Indeed, at the climax of the film, its most delicately passionate moment, he has an encounter with a mechanical doll, a clever simulacrum of a woman; this calls attention, of course, to the essential narcissism of his quest for love, but in the context of this chapter's discourse it may also suggest that the fixed inviolable image, what Ariel provides, can act as relief, a terminus to the incoherent pansexuality, the tantalizings of Proteus. With the mechanical doll Casanova is florid, eloquent, swooningly romantic, more so than with any human woman, as if sheer artifice lies at the end point of sexual expertise, perfection of the techniques of seduction, themselves a somewhat mechanical competence. There may be, in the sexual drive itself, something that seeks what Proteus gives, an agreeable rogerable cloud, ever changing its shape in response to the need for variety, and something that seeks what Ariel gives, an ideal in which lover and beloved are caught up in biophysical purity, the absolute rhythm of the machine inside the body. Even at the beginning of the film Casanova likes to measure his coition to the beat of a metal wind-up bird that he carries with him for this purpose; and it is not impossible that many sorts of yearnings for a fixed artificial image of the human body, even in such sophisticated versions as the golden bird in Yeats's "Sailing to Byzantium," have some sexual basis. It would be misleading, perhaps, to say that the best sex is sex between robots, but there is a good deal of literature, including Kleist's essay on the marionette theater, Delibes's ballet *Coppélia*, and Offenbach's opera *Les Contes d'Hoffmann*, that might testify to an obscure fascination with this theme. In our usual dialectic we identify the sexual with the organic; but it may be that glass and marble, pigment and verb, have their concupiscence as well.

I have been speaking up to this point of works of art that treat the artist's attraction to a woman; but works that treat the artist's revulsion show a similar nature. The synthetic woman, compounded of many pieces, can as easily be a motif of satire as a motif of praise; the poet need only present her as a thing composite not of all the shapeliest features of women of former times—Cleopatra's nose, Helen's mouth, Cinderella's foot—but of various unsavory limbs unearthed by ghouls. The satirical equivalent of the love poem governed by Ariel is this:

> *Corinna*, Pride of *Drury-Lane* . . .
> Takes off her artificial Hair:
> Now, picking out a Crystal Eye,

She wipes it clean, and lays it by.
Her Eye-Brows from a Mouse's Hyde,
Stuck on with Art on either Side,
Pulls off with Care, and first displays 'em,
Then in a Play-Book smoothly lays 'em.
Now dextrously her Plumpers draws,
That serve to fill her hollow Jaws.
Untwists a Wire; and from her Gums
A Set of Teeth completely comes.
Pulls out the Rags contriv'd to prop
Her flabby Dugs and down they drop.
(Swift, "A Beautiful Young Nymph Going to Bed," 1731)

The lady prized by the Elizabethan sonneteer was also made of glass and wire; Swift has merely literalized these metaphors, turned them into detachable prostheses under which the reader finds no vision of glory but a purulent slut. All the subliminal grotesquery of the sonneteer's images has been brought into the foreground, made nauseously explicit, as if every attempt to find beauty in human flesh, every attempt to extenuate its sordor, to reform its shapelessness, were a shameful lie and must be exposed; for Swift hates Ariel. There is a sense in which Swift's attack upon cosmetic alteration—he goes so far as to let a cat piss on the plumpers near the end of the poem—is an attack upon metaphor and simile. From time to time such attacks have been made during the course of English literature:

Your thighs are appletrees
whose blossoms touch the sky.
Which sky? The sky
where Watteau hung a lady's
slipper. Your knees
are a southern breeze—or
a gust of snow. Agh! what
sort of man was Fragonard?
—as if that answered
anything.
("Portrait of a Lady," 1918)

William Carlos Williams's lady is slowly divested of the metaphors that falsify her; Swift's lady was slowly divested of her own false self. Williams was a poet who like Lawrence despised fixed images, the artifices that stifled, clogged, crippled the organic—a lyrist of Proteus, not of Ariel—whereas Swift seems to disallow the lyric mode entirely, to use its devices for the sake of ridicule.

I know of only one poem more extreme than "A Beautiful Young Nymph Going to Bed" in its use of lyricality for satire against a woman: Pound's "Portrait d'une Femme" (1912):

> Your mind and you are our Sargasso Sea,
> London has swept about you this score years
> And bright ships left you this or that in fee:
> Ideas, old gossip, oddments of all things,
> Strange spars of knowledge and dimmed wares of price.
> Great minds have sought you—lacking someone else. . . .
> Idols and ambergris and rare inlays,
> These are your riches, your great store; and yet
> For all this sea-hoard of deciduous things,
> Strange woods half sodden, and new brighter stuff:
> In the slow float of differing light and deep,
> No! there is nothing! In the whole and all,
> Nothing that's quite your own.
>   Yet this is you.

Here are Proteus's techniques of glorification turned wretchedly askew. We have examined such poems as Herrick's "Corinna's Going a-Maying" and, in an earlier chapter, Pope's "Epistle to a Lady," poems in which the central charm of the beloved was her evanescence, her rainbow gleams, her strange state of lovely self-contradiction; in this poem the lady is just as inchoate and vague, but trivially vague, blitherily vague, not delightfully vague. Herrick could not guide Corinna, and Pope could not guide Mrs. Blount, into a definite, satisfying image because their ladies were too multiform and subtle, too likely to recede into airy *sourire*, underlaughter, to permit any resolution, any pinning to the wall; but Pound cannot find any metaphor for his lady more exact than the Sargasso Sea because she is a vast bloated, decomposing thing, a human shipwreck.

Pound, perhaps more than any other great poet, espouses the notion that poetical genius is composite, that the poet ought to incorporate into himself the faculties manifest in the work of Propertius, Sophocles, Arnaut Daniel, and so forth; so it is not surprising that he espouses in equal measure the notion that the woman addressed in a poem ought to be composite:

> Anyone who has read anything of the troubadours knows well the tale of Bertran of Born and My Lady Maent of Montaignac, and knows also the song he made when she would none of him, the song wherein he, seeking to find to make her equal, begs of each preëminent lady of Langue d'Oc some trait or some fair semblance: thus of Cembelins her "esgart amoros" to wit, her love-lit glance, of Aelis her speech free-running, of the Vicomtess of Chalais her throat and her two hands, at Roacoart of Lady Audiart "although she would that ill come unto him" he sought and praised the lineaments of the torse. And all this to make "Una dompna soiseubuda" a borrowed lady or as the Italians translated it "Una donna ideale."

This is a note to Pound's poem "Na Audiart" (1908), an early fantasy based on the late-twelfth-century canzone by Bertrans de Born called "Dompna Pois de me No'us Cal," the poem Pound summarizes in this note, itself translated by Pound a few years after "Na Audiart." Since Bertrans borrowed Lady Audiart's torso in his synthesis of the ideal woman, "Na Audiart" is one of the most elaborately midriff-oriented poems in the English language; the poet's eyes never stray a hairsbreadth from Lady Audiart's girdle, for no other limb or feature of her has contributed to the composite confected by Bertrans. "Portrait d'une Femme" is a savage parody of this sort of piecing together of a woman: instead of a discriminating search for the components of sensuous perfection we have fragments shored against a ruin.

Swift's "A Beautiful Young Nymph Going to Bed" and Pound's

"Portrait d'une Femme" both attempt to display a lady who is nothing, a zero woman. But it must be stressed that such defectives are never far removed from the lyric ideal; zero and infinity are always intimate with each other. When Pope, in the "Epistle to a Lady," wrote that "Most Women have no Characters at all," he knew well that this assertion could be used either to praise or to vilify; but he could hardly have expected to receive the commentary that Coleridge offered in his lecture on *The Tempest* and repeated in his *Table Talk:*

> "Most women have no character at all," said Pope, and meant it for satire. Shakspeare, who knew man and woman much better, saw that it, in fact, was the perfection of woman to be characterless. Everyone wishes a Desdemona or Ophelia for a wife,—creatures who, though they may not always understand you, do always feel you, and feel with you. (27 September 1830)

To equate want of prominence, lack of individuation, with beauty, as Coleridge does seriously and Pope does ambiguously, is to raise the disturbing possibility that Swift's dismembered nymph and Pound's lady-who-has-nothing-of-her-own are beautiful; or that beauty and ugliness somehow converge. I will offer one last demonstration of this point. If someone were to ask what sort of poem would result if a poet decided to compare a woman to a vampire, a deep-sea diver, and a haggler for rugs, most people would answer, a satire, possibly of the amorphous sort found in "Portrait d'une Femme"; but that is not necessarily the case:

> She is older than the rocks among which she sits;
> Like the Vampire,
> She has been dead many times,
> And learned the secrets of the grave;
> And has been a diver in deep seas,
> And keeps their fallen day about her;
> And trafficked for strange webs with Eastern merchants;
> And, as Leda,
> Was the mother of Helen of Troy,
> And, as St Anne,

Was the mother of Mary;
And all this has been to her but as the sound of lyres and
flutes,
And lives
Only in the delicacy
With which it has moulded the changing lineaments,
And tinged the eyelids and the hands.

This is the famous sentence on the *Mona Lisa* from Pater's *The Renaissance* (1873); I have transcribed it in Yeats's *vers-libre* lineation, for Yeats published it as the first modern poem in his *Oxford Book of Modern Verse*. Pater was responding here to the fact that the spectator of Leonardo seems to see the same face in a great many sacred and profane paintings and drawings, as if Leonardo used the same model for every beautiful subject; this suggested to Pater that the critic might abstract from all these visual avatars of beautiful women a single Beauty, free from the constraints of space and time, Beauty independent of any finite beautiful thing. Yeats uses this conceit in many of his poems, such as "The Rose of the World" (1892); but my point is that the compounding of many women into a single Woman here reaches a limit. It is as if there were a lyrical woman who could comprise simultaneously the lady of Pound's "Portrait d'une Femme" and the borrowed lady of Bertrans de Born—vampire, Leda, Saint Anne—all ugliness, all vacuity, all indolence, all strenuousness, all loveliness in one; as if satire and panegyric could somehow collapse into a single lyricality.

PERSONAE

It is clear by now that lyrical society does not much resemble any city or town or rural populace known to us in our daily lives; instead of a society in which distinct people earn their bread by working at well-defined jobs, we have large slurred classes of slaves and the idle rich, gods and zombies and the mighty dead. Useful laborers and contented professionals, shopkeepers and secretaries, seem to belong altogether elsewhere. Because the personages found in lyric poems tend to be few in category and only weakly individuated, we may inquire whether these personages may not all reduce to a single being, possibly to be identified with the poet himself. We have already seen that the elegist and the elegized at times become consubstantial, and in Spenser's *Astrophel* the poet and his beloved are conflated into one flower, attain union in death; so there is reason to speculate whether the characters in the ideal lyric would consist only of nebulous drifting manifestations of a single poet.

> Tiresias, although a mere spectator and not indeed a "character," is yet the most important personage in the poem, uniting all the rest. Just as the one-eyed merchant, seller of currants, melts into the Phoenician Sailor, and the latter is not wholly distinct from Ferdinand Prince of Naples, so all the women are one woman, and the two sexes meet in Tiresias. What Tiresias *sees,* in fact, is the substance of the poem.

This is, of course, the celebrated footnote to line 218 of Eliot's *The Waste Land.* The critic might go even further and suggest that what Tiresias *is* is the substance of the poem; for it is possible to imagine the single speaking voice that impersonates all the characters in the poem as a senile hermaphrodite, omniscient and omnisentient, who has foresuffered, fore-enjoyed, fore-sinned, forgiven all the shenanigans of the various personages. If by an act of critical imagination one could envisage a creature who was simultaneously Eliot's Tiresias and Pater's Mona Lisa, one might hit upon the ideal lyric poet.

And yet, even if on some theoretical level it is possible to allege that all lyrical personae can be resorbed into the poet, it is nevertheless true that some personae seem independent, freestanding, and that others seem more lyrical. What exactly is responsible for these degrees of lyricality? How can we know when it is appropriate for us to perform the maneuver of identifying the character in the poem with the poet himself?

Eliot's answer to these questions is found in his essay "The Three Voices of Poetry" (1953), which claims that lyric poetry is not heard, but overheard—it was J. S. Mill who originated this thesis—while nonlyrical poetry is addressed to an audience. A lyrical persona, then, is simply a device by means of which the poet articulates his feelings to himself, something little elaborated into a personality. Dramatis personae—these constitute what Eliot calls the third voice—are fully humanized creatures, private agents in no way to be identified with the playwright. Between these two extremes is what Eliot calls the second voice, that of the dramatic monologue:

> What we normally hear, in fact, in the dramatic monologue, is the voice of the poet, who has put on the costume and make-up either of some historical character, or of one out of fiction. His personage must be identified to us—as an individual, or at least as a type—before he begins to speak. If, as frequently with Browning, the poet is speaking in the role of an historical personage, like Lippo Lippi, or in the role of a known character of fiction, like Caliban, he has taken possession of that character. And the difference is most evident in his "Caliban upon Setebos." In *The Tempest*, it is Caliban who speaks; in "Caliban upon Setebos," it is Browning's voice that we hear, Browning talking aloud through Caliban. (*On Poetry and Poets*, p. 103)

If we identify the persona with the poet, then, we do not have a drama; and if we can make any discrimination whatever between persona and poet, we do not have a lyric.

I think that Eliot's discussion in this essay of the first voice, the lyrical voice, is one of his intellectual triumphs; but I am less satisfied with his analysis of the second and third voices. The claim that a drama is a little world in which each character has free will to pursue his own ends does not generally hold; it is easy to think of plays in which that is the case, but the *psychomachia* is a clear example of a large dramatic class in which the characters are far from independent of each other; the medieval *Everyman*, for instance, has only one character with the faculty of free will—the other characters are contingent, unreliable half-entities. Auden may go too far in his insistence on seeing almost every play as a psychomachy, but one may nevertheless admit that there is a kind of drama that is a theatrical representation of the "overhearing" process, in which a single self-engaged man enacts his struggle toward enlightenment.

Eliot also offers no firm criterion for knowing whether it is the poet or the persona who is speaking. Is it impossible that the Caliban of *The Tempest* offers any of Shakespeare's own opinions? How can we learn enough about Shakespeare's personal convictions to be certain they are absent from the discourse of his characters? Another troubling matter lies in Eliot's reliance on audience as a factor in distinguishing the lyrical from the nonlyrical: it is surely true that some poems seem to gesture outward toward a public world while others seem introverted, self-involved, but a great many poems do not easily categorize themselves as one or the other. Browning's "The Bishop Orders His Tomb at Saint Praxed's Church," for example, is addressed to second parties, to whom the bishop is giving instructions; but the second parties, the bishop's illegitimate children, are such minor presences in the poem, and the bishop's speech is such a momentous rehearsal of the quality of his life, that one may think of the interlocutors less as hearers than as overhearers, half-embarrassed by incomprehensible revelations. In the case of Eliot's own example, "Caliban upon Setebos," the poem, though at times it sounds like an invocation, is a soliloquy, addressed to no one. Eliot can say with confidence only that Caliban is a fiction; but, as Eliot certainly shows in his own work, a fiction can treat matters of the greatest intimacy and importance. I believe that we should not look to the criterion of audience, or of fictitiousness, to distinguish the lyrical from its opposite.

Intuition suggests that poems uttered by elaborate fictions are not necessarily less lyrical than poems spoken by a bland, inconspicuous *I*; and I think that this intuition can be justified by theory. In every literary work—poems, novels, letters of recommendation, and so on—in which a persona is visible, there are two aspects to that persona: perceptual modality and self-consciousness. By the former term I mean the unconscious and telling manner in which the persona sees, hears, touches, smells, tastes; by the latter term I mean the person that the persona believes itself to be. The former defines the subjective moment of the persona; the latter defines its objective moment. A *persona*, as Ezra Pound explained it, was something spoken through (*per+sonare*), a mask and a kind of speaking trumpet, an assumption of identity and a device to alter vocal tone; so a theory of persona must begin with a description of the donning of a mask. When we put on a mask—this is true not only of poets but of masqueraders—our vision is to some degree impaired; our nostrils are stopped up; our voices become muffled or shrill, hollow or too loud. Our whole perceptual modality changes, and this assists our imagination, our empathy, for it helps us understand how the world presents itself to someone whose real face is shaped like the mask we are wearing. Every persona must be understood not just as a pretending, but as a constriction of being. The eye slits of a mask do not permit a wide range, but instead concentrate the vision on a few objects; the mouth opening of a mask does not permit a full, flexible gamut of tones but instead effects a distinctive monotony. When confronted with a dramatic monologue, literary criticism has the task of describing the shapes of the eye slits and the mouth opening, the particular acuities and bluntnesses that give savor, distinction, to the persona in the poem; this can be called the analysis of perceptual modality. From this point of view I judge a persona lyrical if the slits and openings of the mask are very wide or very narrow: wide, because then the mask interferes little with the free transmission of emotion, the free reception of the outer world—the poet's eye is open to every glint and dazzle, and there are no firm lines of demarcation between himself and the world he moves through; narrow, because then the mask so throttles and encloses the poet that he is thrown back on his own inner resources, to manufacture a hermetic and reflexive species of discourse.

But, as I have said, there is a second element to consider: self-consciousness. Here the measure of the quality of a persona lies in its degree of self-interestedness; the extent to which the persona is looking in a mirror, and the extent to which the image it sees in the mirror is the correct image. In many poems the degree of the speaker's self-interestedness is small:

> And now I in the Spirit see
> (The Spirit of Exalted Poetry)
> I see the *Fatal Fight* begin;
> And, lo! where a Destroying Angel stands,
> (By all but Heaven and Me unseen,)
> With Lightning in his Eyes, and Thunder in his Hands;
> (Swift, "Ode to the King," 1691)

This is one of Swift's earliest poems, in which King William's success in his Irish expedition is treated as a matter as lofty as the combat between angels and devils in *Paradise Lost.* In visionary poetry generally the degree of self-consciousness is not great; the poet is preoccupied with the exalted images he sees and with the supernatural sources of his inspiration, rather than with analysis of his temperament or historical circumstances; and so it is slightly disconcerting in this ode when the poet, right in the middle of an exciting scene, thumps his chest and preens as the special agent of vision. The laboriousness of the ode writing introduces a slight parodic element into the poem; to behold the poet scribbling away at Armageddon deflects our attention from the matter at hand. Swift's intrusion into the poem is not great, but in certain kinds of poems almost any intrusion is too much; and as the poet becomes progressively more self-conscious, he starts to compete with whatever other matter the poem may contain, to insist on his own image at the expense of all else. In many famous dramatic monologues, such as Browning's "My Last Duchess," much of the attractiveness of the poem lies in the speaker's ability to shoulder aside whatever impedes his self-delighting magnificence, to plume, to bull his way across the stage, on which he is the only worthy character. The duke of "My Last Duchess" is an exceptionally self-interested persona; but he is firmly defined, memorable, telling only because he inhabits a poem that contains a great deal of weighty matter besides the speaker. The heavy furniture, the striking artwork, the Renaissance pomp provide a counterelement, a backdrop against which the speaker must struggle to present himself; without the dowry, without Claus of Innsbruck, without a detailed circumjacent world, the speaker's voice would echo in a void, would lack any means for self-characterization, would lack pride, for it would have nothing to be proud of. The persona of "My Last Duchess" lies in the upper-middle range of self-interestedness; in the extreme upper range the persona is aware of nothing but itself, for all its attention is focused on the mirror. Near the limit of self-consciousness the persona contemplates a universe that has dwindled to its own face:

> I should have been a pair of ragged claws
> Scuttling across the floors of ancient seas. . . .
> Shall I part my hair behind? Do I dare to eat a peach?
> I shall wear white flannel trousers, and walk upon the beach.
> I have heard the mermaids singing, each to each.
>
> I do not think that they will sing to me.
>
> (Eliot, "The Love Song of J. Alfred Prufrock," 1911)

Every persona is to some extent in the position of the young Wordsworth in book 4 of *The Prelude*, staring down from his rowboat at a water surface that is half mirror and half pane of glass: his own face impedes his sight of the pebbles and grasses on the lake bottom. The degree of self-consciousness may be measured by the degree of interference from the facial image. J. Alfred Prufrock knows of an urban world of sawdusty restaurants and of salons where women come and go talking of Michelangelo, but he can think of this world only blurred and refracted through the medium of himself; indeed, the yellow fog that swells, swirls, plumps throughout the poem seems to be an emblem for his tincture of Prufrockality, a pervasive, diffuse selfhood. He ponders the possible existence of a second reality, the woman to whom he will put his overwhelming question; but the only genuine object of his attention is himself, endlessly dressed up in fantastical guises, his necktie rich and modest but asserted by a simple pin, or the costume of an attendant lord of Hamlet, or the carapace of a crab, or the white trousers of an Odysseus so puny that no siren will think him worth the trouble of a song. Prufrock is a human inauthenticity, an actor who knows that even the easiest role would be beyond his power; and yet he is fascinated by all these roles that he is too feeble to play.

On the axis of self-consciousness Prufrock is near the top; to find a more self-conscious persona one would have to look to something nearly inhuman, like Beckett's Unnamable. Prufrock is what I would call a lyrical persona; he is the inwardness, the self-concentration, the involution of a certain strain of lyric poetry given a silly name and asked to criticize its solipsistic tendencies. It is well known that the young Eliot felt deeply the influence of French *symbolisme*; but "The Love Song of J. Alfred Prufrock" also shows Eliot's uneasiness about such self-loving or self-hating, in any case self-engaged, serenades as the poems of Laforgue and Mallarmé. When a lyrical persona is present in a poem, the reader may ask himself whether the speaker of the poem is a human being like himself or instead the poem, or the muse, or abstract genius somehow given a voice. In "Tradition and the Individual Talent" (1919), Eliot says that

> the poet has, not a "personality" to express, but a particular medium, which is only a medium and not a personality, in which impressions and experiences combine in peculiar and unexpected ways. (*Selected Essays*, p. 9)

Prufrock is more a medium than a personality, a medium that calls into question its inadequacies—a yellow fog.

The two great masters in English of fictitious personae—I mean personae that no one would confuse with the historical author, as a naive reader might confuse the dumpy, downcast pilgrim "Chaucer" with Chaucer, or the righteously stinging "Pope" of the Epistles with Pope—are Browning and Pound. Are their personae real human beings, case histories impressive to sociologists, or are they lyrical figments? Among the dramatic monologues of Browning, one can find nearly the full range. Browning's personae, despite their apparent multifariousness, are in fact similar to each other in many ways, a gang of artists, lovers, strivers, mesmerists, wallowers in self; but they vary in energy. "Fra Lippo Lippi" (1855) and "Andrea del Sarto" (1855) depict two Renaissance painters as different as possible in temperament and style, the former a sly madcap, a carouser, a hasty billowing genius, the latter a pensive chiarobscure cuckold, careful and exact, uninspired, a "Faultless Painter" damned for his faultlessness; and yet, when the poems are read consecutively—as Browning intended—one suspects that the two painters are the obverse and reverse of the same man. The development of "Andrea del Sarto" is a decrescendo, a steady self-enervation, self-sapping, as the contours of the painter's personality grow more and more acute as the light dims; he recedes into his own gloom, his own failure. The genius, libido, vim that he lacks eventually constitute themselves as his rival Raphael, whose errors are the errors of a superior faculty:

> That arm is wrongly put—and there again—
> A fault to pardon in the drawing's lines,
> Its body, so to speak; its soul is right,
> He means right—that, a child may understand.
> Still, what an arm! and I could alter it:
> But all the play, the insight and the stretch—
> Out of me, out of me! And wherefore out?
> Had you enjoined them on me, given me soul,
> We might have risen to Raphael, I and you!
> Nay, Love, you did give all I asked, I think—
> (lines 111–20)

He half blames his wife for her failure to be an adequate muse, but the real fault lies in his own uninspirability. He is capable of arousing in his weak emotional system a certain degree of self-excoriation, but except for that his sensibility is almost too slack, tensionless, to function at all. On the axis of perceptual modality the persona of Andrea is exceptionally closed; he has some small insight into his relation to the society of painters and husbands, but for the most part he aimlessly frets, lost in his self-dissembling, a mild narcotic. He is enclosed on all sides by his limitations, for he is nothing but a camera helpless, out of place, before the invention of photography, lacking an authentic apparatus of feeling. He is a hand nicely coordinated with an eye, but otherwise defunct. As he discharges, during this tirade, what little energy he possesses, his persona becomes his tomb.

Andrea del Sarto is all mask and no man, an achromatic medium for representation; and in this way he dwindles into a closed lyrical thing, not vivacious enough to seem human. Fra Lippo Lippi, on the other hand, is all energy, vibration, warm pulse, almost too erratic and jerky, shimmering, to settle into a comprehensible persona. On the axis of perceptual modality he is almost disturbingly open: he sees *everything*, nothing is lost to his keen, rapid overdilated eye; his mask in no way deforms or distorts what he perceives. On the axis of self-consciousness he is near zero: his engagement with the outside world is so intense and complicated, spontaneous, that he rarely engages in self-assessment, self-reflection. The only reason he bothers to give an account of himself during his monologue is that a policeman is interrogating him. His persona cannot take on any very firm definition because he lives always at the quick, in a state of sensuous immediate relation to the outer world:

> I could not paint all night—
> Ouf! I leaned out of window for fresh air.
> There came a hurry of feet and little feet,
> A sweep of lute-strings, laughs, and whifts of song,—
> *Flower o' the broom,*
> *Take away love, and our earth is a tomb!*
> *Flower o' the quince,*
> *I let Lisa go, and what good in life since?*
> *Flower o' the thyme*—and so on. Round they went.
> Scarce had they turned the corner when a titter
> Like the skipping of rabbits by moonlight,—three slim shapes,
> And a face that looked up . . . zooks, sir, flesh and blood,
> That's all I'm made of!
>
> (lines 49–61)

Andrea del Sarto was a craftsman, a willing prisoner of his discipline; but Fra Lippo Lippi is an escape artist. It is not simply a matter of breaking free from imposed tasks in order to riot and dally; it is that Lippo refuses to be imprisoned in any finite mask as well, refuses to be incarcerated by his own history. He explains to the guard that his childhood was a long starvation and that the monks of the convent tried to teach him to be chaste and obedient; but he evades every attempt to limit his reach. In Canto 2 (1922) Pound retells Ovid's story of Dionysos impressed into slavery on an Aegean slave ship until the amused god turned his captors into fish monsters, filled their ship with grape bunches, ivy tendrils, aerial panthers, a wilderness of metamorphoses; and Browning's Lippo is a minor Dionysos, subverting his jailers' every attempt to assign him a role:

> I drew men's faces on my copy-books,
> Scrawled them within the antiphonary's marge,
> Joined legs and arms to the long music-notes,
> Found eyes and nose and chin for A's and B's,
> And made a string of pictures of the world
> Betwixt the ins and outs of verb and noun,
> On the wall, the bench, the door. The monks looked black.
> (lines 129–35)

He cannot move without imposing genius on the world; nothing can resist his powerful facility, the pressure of design. Against the rectitude and rule of the monks Lippo seems instinct with chaos, a fecund chaos that keeps resolving outlandishly into visual form. There is a sense in which he is too urgent, stormy, venereal to be confined to a merely human shape, and so it is not surprising to discover him in heaven at the end of the poem:

> Then steps a sweet angelic slip of a thing
> Forward, puts out a soft palm—"Not so fast!"
> —Addresses the celestial presence, "nay—
> He made you and devised you, after all,
> Though he's none of you! Could Saint John there draw—
> His camel-hair make up a painting-brush?
> We come to brother Lippo for all that,
> *Iste perfecit opus!*" So, all smile—
> I shuffle sideways with my blushing face

Under the cover of a hundred wings
Thrown like a spread of kirtles when you're gay
And play hot cockles . . .
(lines 370–81)

He knows he is no saint, and he seems far too lascivious and sly to belong in a Christian heaven; but he in fact is busy extending into a broader domain a great Christian mystery, the Incarnation. Wherever the sensuous world assumes the aspect of beauty, there, says Lippo, is soul; soul is not an abstract, unrepresentable thing (line 187) but is continually manifest in flesh. It is as if the things of this world are momentary coalescences of an energy felt everywhere and Lippo is an organ of this plastic stress, rearranging things for his, its, own ends. As a painter Lippo's eye is sharp, but as a persona he is not sharply defined, despite his electric bristliness. He is too unselfconscious, too ignorant—

Flower o' the clove,
All the Latin I construe is, "amo" I love!
(lines 110–11)

has too great a tendency to break off his own discourse in favor of song. A volatile, fuming intelligence, he overflows any constraint of a historical self, a mask. It may seem odd to regard "Fra Lippo Lippi" as a lyric, but the poem can accurately be described, I think, as a portrait that keeps trying to break free of circumstantial precision, to veer off into the lyrical; and Lippo himself can be called a kind of naked genius, a Proteus whose clothes are arbitrary, undefining.

A dramatic monologue seems least lyrical when its subject's clothes fit him well. The duke of "My Last Duchess" is comfortable in his rich apparel and attains a Rembrandt-like exactitude of magnificence; but Lippo seems to yearn for undress, promiscuity. But the nakedest of Browning's personae—and here is the gist of my argument against Eliot—is Caliban:

['Will sprawl, now that the heat of day is best,
Flat on his belly in the pit's much mire,
With elbows wide, fists clenched to prop his chin.

And, while he kicks both feet in the cool slush,
And feels about his spine small eft-things course,
Run in and out each arm, and make him laugh:
And while above his head a pompion-plant,
Coating the cave-top as a brow its eye,
Creeps down to touch and tickle hair and beard . . .
[He] talks to his own self, howe'er he please . . .
Letting the rank tongue blossom into speech.]
"Caliban upon Setebos" (1864), lines 1–9, 15, 23)

Freud, noting that the adult sexual urge was concentrated on the genitals, hypothesized an immature sexual condition called polymorphous perversity, in which every square inch of skin was equally excitable, vivid. Browning's Caliban is a perfect preexample of Freud's fanciful infancy: his physical and intellectual life is nothing but a long tickling, by efts, by tendrils, by theological speculation. He is little discriminated from his environment, seems scarcely capable of telling inside from outside; his tongue is a vegetable, rankly blossoming into speech. He is a kind of amphibian, wallowing in slush, adaptable in almost any direction, but a form of life too low and indestructible to allow for any specialization; a literary pre-man, with aspects of both a Neanderthal and a baby; fetal slime given a voice. An intrauterine Lippo Lippi would sound a little like this, radically open, selfless; Caliban, of course, does not have oils or canvas, so the only medium on which his artistic instinct can work is his own body:

Then, when froth rises bladdery, drink up all,
Quick, quick, till maggots scamper through my brain;
Last, throw me on my back i' the seeded thyme,
And wanton, wishing I were born a bird.
Put case, unable to be what I wish,
I yet could make a live bird out of clay:
Would not I take clay, pinch my Caliban
Able to fly?—for, there, see, he hath wings,
And great comb like the hoopoe's to admire,
And there, a sting to do his foes offence

(lines 71–80)

Caliban imagines a drunken god reshaping a Caliban, making a new improved model. It does not seem wholly impossible, given his imaginative malleability, his sense that all animal and vegetable forms are latent within him, that the Caliban of this poem might actually sprout wings and fly. If he is a sort of fetus, who knows what he might grow into? The joke of the poem is that Caliban conceives of a god who is nothing but a Caliban writ large; and this further confirms our sense of the boundarilessness of Caliban and his island, for wherever Caliban looks, inside, outside, he sees nothing but pullulating undifferentiated stuff, protoplasm resentful of its inability to find a satisfying lovely form. Caliban is shapeless and stimulated, self-stimulated, incoherent, *lyrical.* Caliban is Proteus.

In his essay on Shelley Browning opposes the Shelleyan artist, gazing upward at the One and inward at his own soul, "the nearest reflex of that absolute Mind," to the artist observant of facts, tactilely faithful to the world of experience. There are hints in this essay that Browning regards his artistic mission as a synthesis of these two orientations; and that is proper, for the dramatic monologue must lie at the boundary between them. The subject of a dramatic monologue is essentially a man caught on a stage set, among the low, heavy accouterments of the world of experience, but restless, gathering force, spilling out at last into a kind of transcendence, an unseizable dynamism of spirit. Lippo's operatic tendencies, his *stornelli*, baritone serenades, are only one manifestation of this; but a good many of Browning's personae want to sing, want to elevate themselves into the lyrical.

Ezra Pound's use of personae is similar to Browning's but more extreme. Like Fra Lippo Lippi these personae tend to equate artistic and sexual prowess, and they tend to burst into song:

> I have sung women in three cities. . . .
> . . . eh? . . . they mostly had grey eyes,
> But it is all one, I will sing of the sun.
> " 'Pollo Phoibee, old tin pan, you
> Glory to Zeus' aegis-day,

Shield o' steel-blue, th' heaven o'er us
Hath for boss thy lustre gay! . . ."
("Cino," 1908)

In an unpublished letter written to his mother in the same year as "Cino," Pound says that he likes dramatic poetry because dramatic poets such as Browning, Theocritus, and Ovid in the *Heroides* "proceed from a center outward, not from one point of the circumference to another." This comment exactly defines what Browning does in "Fra Lippo Lippi" and what Pound does in "Cino": the persona is erected and inflected with lavish historical detail, but as the poem continues the scope of sensibility and intellect grows too broad to be confined by any discrete mask; Cino, for example, loses interest in his social identity, his subtle but slightly humiliating adulteries with noblewomen, and turns his attention to the sky, becomes an impudent minstrel of the gods. The wider, the more inclusive a persona becomes, the more it tends toward a blurry lyricality. In a later letter, now in a collection at Cornell University, Pound tries to define his relation to his personae:

> I agree that the present lit. disease in USA is a confusion of self-expression with art . . . while "HSP," Seafarer, Exile's Letter and Mauberley are all "me" in some sense; my personality is certainly a great slag heap of stuff which has to be excluded from each of this [*sic*] crystalizations. And an expression of the "personality" wd. be a slag heap and not art. (To F. M. Ford, 7 September [1920?])

Possibly Browning would have agreed with this formula: a persona is some small aspect of an author's personality isolated, refined, pickled, made absolute. In the broad middle ground between the too faint and the too energetic, between Andrea del Sarto and Fra Lippo, such a persona will have a distinctness and an economy of gesture superior to those of any real human being; but at the fringes, as the persona proceeds too far outward from its central germ, its primary explosion, it will start to become vast, amorphous, too complicit with the slag heap of the author's genius.

Thus it is to be expected that Cino, Bertrans de Born, the crazy Piere Vidal seem to converge into an inextricable tangle of vitalities, a single rambunctiousness dressed up in many costumes.

Most of the personae in Pound's early poetry seem to be laboring to supersede themselves, to create an identity and then cast it away. This casting away of self is the lyric moment in each poem:

> In the "search for oneself," in the search for "sincere self-expression," one gropes, one finds some seeming verity. One says "I am" this, that, or the other, and with the words scarcely uttered one ceases to be that thing.
>
> I began this search for the real in a book called *Personae*, casting off, as it were, complete masks of the self in each poem. (*Ezra Pound and the Visual Arts*, p. 202)

This is from the great Vorticism article of 1914. Pound imagines an infinite series of tiny defective, partial Pounds, each uttering itself and then extinguishing itself so that the author can proceed to the next in the sequence. But Pound makes sure that each persona somehow alludes to the higher shapelessness in which it is contained, genius catching itself at the instant of inspiration, as if he hopes the whole series will magically constitute what none can constitute by itself, self-expression.

I have been speaking so far of poems in which Pound invents personae of a perceptual modality even wider than any of Browning's, personae of such impetuousness, such vehemence, that they howl from their radical openness to sensation. Some of them, like Bertrans in the "Sestina: Altaforte," are madly transpierced by sun and lightning; but all of them are intense, rapid, nerve-exposed, almost maskless, indeed almost skinless. But there is another sort of persona in Pound's work as well, which goes to the opposite extreme of perceptual modality. The persona of *Hugh Selwyn Mauberley* (1920) is an Andrea del Sarto taken still further toward the limit of contraction, of narrowness. This mask chokes the delicate creature inside it behind a foot-thick wall of wood, with eye slits and a mouth opening each only a millimeter wide; it is no wonder Mauberley grows psychotic, delirious, self-engorged, self-entombed, stupefied with his own smell. When a persona grows too highly developed it reduces to a set of mechanical gestures, tics, twitches, goggles, so that the limit of this method produces a persona so little spontaneous that it is for all purposes dead. But, as we have seen, dead people are appropriate subjects in lyric poems. It is only in the wide middle ground of personae—agreeable, convincing representations of recognizable human beings—that we find the unlyrical.

Chapter 5

MUSIC AND METAPHOR

WE have seen some of the quickenings, the transformations, the deformities that happen to the poet's themes under the aspect of the lyric; and now it is time to turn our attention away from theme and toward technique. The primary technical question that faces a lyric poet is, To what degree can a poem resemble music? Can verbal discourse approximate the condition of wordless intonation? It has always been clear that verbal rhythm and musical rhythm are closely related; indeed the names of the poetical feet—trochee, iamb, anapest, and so forth—were originally musical terms as well. But there is not now and never has been any consensus about the possibilities for embodying in a poem any of the nonrhythmical aspects of music. Ezra Pound, for instance, lays down, or almost lays down, a law forbidding the poet to attempt harmonic effects:

> The term harmony is misapplied to poetry; it refers to simultaneous sounds of different pitch. There is, however, in the best verse a sort of residue of sound which remains in the ear of the hearer and acts more or less as an organ-base. ("A Few Don'ts by an Imagiste," 1913)

T. S. Eliot, on the other hand, claims that something very like simultaneous sounds of a different pitch can be produced in verse:

> The music of a word is, so to speak, at a point of intersection: it arises from its relation first to the words immediately preceding it and following it, and indefinitely to the rest of its context; and from another relation, that of its immediate meaning in that context to all the other meanings which it has had in other contexts, to its greater or less wealth of association. . . . a "musical" poem is a poem which has a musical pattern of sound and a musical pattern of the secondary meanings of the words which compose it. ("The Music of Poetry," 1942)

It may be objected that the effect Eliot is describing here is not harmony, a genuine acoustic phenomenon, but only the semantic illusion of harmony; for Eliot seems to imagine a poem as a single line, a discursive movement through space, which at certain moments of heightened tension starts to grow homophonic, thick with reverberations of meaning, wealthy. But illusion is perhaps enough. A poem cannot actually become a consort of viols; but much of the history of the technical progress of poetry has always been inspired by attempts to usurp or counterfeit its sister arts, to attain the visual immediacy of painting, the carnality and kinesis of dance, the agility, the harmonic richness of music.

Of course music too has borrowed much from poetry: Stravinsky's *Apollon Musagète* (1928) was composed almost entirely in iambic rhythms, and its composer said of it, "The real subject of 'Apollo' is versification . . . [a] supremely arbitrary set of prosodic rules." The student of lyricality often feels that there are moments in which poetry so strains to be music and music so strains to be poetry that a complete breakdown is possible, that an oboe will speak, a line of poetry turn into sheer humming. G. M. Hopkins, as musically sensitive as any English poet, tried to develop a theory of metrics that would permit something that seems on the face of it impossible, rhythmic counterpoint, to be achieved by reversing feet against the background of a standard metrical form, so that the ear perceives a shadowy polyphony:

> since the new or mounted rhythm is actually heard and at the same time the mind naturally supplies the natural or standard foregoing rhythm, for we do not forget what the rhythm is that by rights we should be hearing, two rhythms are in some manner running at once and we have something answerable to counterpoint in music. ("Author's Preface," 1883)

Here we have the utmost ingenuity in impressing in poetry what seems to be a purely musical device. In the next century Benjamin Britten seems to have taken this confusion one step further by writing a fugue for unaccompanied cello in which the counterpoint-monody of Hopkins's poetical theory is transferred back to musical style; I quote from Peter Evans's description of the second movement of the Second Suite for Cello, op. 80 (1967):

> Because of the placing of the rests in its subject, the player is able to set against this a countersubject and then to execute *stretti* (closely overlapped entries of the subject) of two and eventually three "voices," all without ever sounding more than one note at a time. (Notes to London recording CS 6617)

It is an eerie effect; one can by this means actually hear a succession of single tones as a simultaneous representation of two different themes, or of the same theme in two different phases of itself. I feel often in lyric poetry just this impossible richness of texture; as if a line of words hung in a verbal space far deeper and wider than the usual universe of discourse, hung and turned and curved back upon itself, at once a melos and a mobile spun in the wind.

> "as the sculptor sees the form in the air . . .
> "as glass seen under water . . .
> and saw the waves taking form as crystal,
> notes as facets of air,
> and the mind there, before them, moving,
> so that notes needed not move.
>
> (Pound, Canto 25, 1928)

There are critics who think that the best of lyric poetry has long since been accomplished; but I think that the musical possibilities of language have only begun to be explored, that a thread of English may curl into whole orchestras of concord and dissonance, panpipes and percussion, Ariel's stillness, the Shakespeherian rag.

MUSIC AS ANTIWORLD

John Hollander has studied for many years, with erudition and scholarly panache, English poems that treat the theme of music. In his *The Untuning of the Sky* (1961) he discovers a gradual shift in emphasis, in poems written from 1500 to 1700, from the theme of music as transcendental harmony, a heavenly ratio that controls the orbits of stars and tempers the minds of men, to the theme of music as a dangerous arouser of passions, less disembodied reason than disembodied will. I will not rehearse all his evidence or his arguments, but I will note that, whether music sobers or whether it ravishes, whether it is ideal pattern or sensuous beckoning, it is to a large degree antithetical to the world we know; mysterious; wyrd. If music is order, that order is not like our order; if music is chaos, that chaos is not like our chaos. The great locus of imaginative effort on the theme of music in poetry is the body of odes and songs written for Saint Cecelia's Day, or in imitation of such odes:

As from the Pow'r of Sacred Lays
The Spheres began to move,
And sung the great Creator's Praise
To all the bless'd above;
So, when the last and dreadful Hour
This crumbling Pageant shall devour,
The TRUMPET shall be heard on high,
The dead shall live, the living die,
And MUSICK shall untune the Sky.
(Dryden, "A Song for St. Cecilia's Day," 1687)

Sooth'd with the sound, the king grew vain;
Fought all his battles o'er again;

And thrice he routed all his foes; and thrice he slew the slain.
The master saw the madness rise;
His glowing cheeks, his ardent eyes;
And, while he heav'n and earth defied,
Chang'd his hand, and check'd his pride.
He chose a mournful Muse,
Soft pity to infuse . . .
(Dryden, "Alexander's Feast or, The Power of Music; An Ode in Honour of St. Cecelia's Day," 1697)

By Musick, Minds an equal Temper know,
Nor swell too high, nor sink too low.
If in the Breast tumultuous Joys arise,
Music her soft, assuasive Voice applies;
Or when the Soul is press'd with Cares
Exalts her in enlivening Airs.
(Pope, "Ode for Musick, on St. Cecilia's Day," c. 1708)

As Conscience, to the centre
Of being, smites with irresistible pain,
So shall a solemn cadence, if it enter
The mouldy vaults of the dull idiot's brain,
Transmute him to a wretch from quiet hurled—
Convulsed as by a jarring din;
And then aghast, as at the world
Of reason partially let in
By concords winding with a sway
Terrible for sense and soul!
(Wordsworth, "On the Power of Sound," 1828)

O ear whose creatures cannot wish to fall,
Calm spaces unafraid of wear or weight . . .
Restore our fallen day; O re-arrange.
O *dear white children casual as birds,*
Playing among the ruined languages . . .
O wear your tribulation like a rose.
(Auden, "Anthem for St. Cecelia's Day," 1940)

In many of these poems the antithetical relation of our world to the locus of music is clear: the natural world is chiefly inhabited by despots, sinners, idiots, and children, ineffectual and innocuous, puppetlike—even Alexander the Great is a doll obedient to the strings of Timotheus's lyre—while music posits some region of fiery simplicities, shudders, tremors, gravities, stabbings, supernal calm. In these odes one finds a peculiar physics, according to which the frame of the earth, the stamina of things, is supported by celestial tensions and resonances, as if the screwing up of a fiddle string or the pressure of air in an organ pipe were the proper emblem for the god who upholds and informs the world. The mundane is a pressure point on which immense energies are brought to bear from the realm of music; but to be enraptured, transported out of this world, absorbed into music is to experience a sudden liberation, relaxing, because the kingdom of sheer music is wider and airier than the earth we know: on Judgment Day the archangel's trumpet blast will untune our sky; and near the end of "L'Allegro" (c. 1631) Milton speaks of untwisting "the chains that tie / The hidden soul of harmony," as if terrestrial music were unpleasantly constricted by the rules of consonance, by the involvements of the inner ear, by the narrowness of vibrating columns of air. Extremes meet; in the antiworld of music there is at once the greatest tension and the greatest relaxation.

There is not only a strange physics in the domain of the musical, but a strange biology as well. All rationality, all irrationality, all volition, all conation, all affect are stripped away from the world we know and reassigned to Saint Cecelia's precincts in the sky; without music men are not men, they are not even animals, they are just inert clay until made reasonable or passionate or tranquil by the power of music. Alexander is simply an instrument on which Timotheus plays, a vehicle for the conjuring of horrid specters or for the burning of Babylon or for other forms of public entertainment; Timotheus, like the gods of Lucretius, regards every display of passion as the occasion for aesthetic delectation. There is a sense, of course, in which Pope's ode is an unwriting of Dryden's, for Pope congratulates Saint Cecelia for helping to reduce all extremes of emotion to the mean, whereas Dryden prizes the highest mania, the deepest depression;

but in another sense Pope and Dryden are agreed, in that both claim, or at least pretend to claim, that whatever agency intensifies emotion or tempers it lies outside the human orbit, in the realm of music. Yeats's doctrine of the Moods, that the emotion we feel is not our own but some spidery dispatch from eternity, is similar to the ethos of the Saint Cecelia ode: as Auden expresses it in his Toller elegy, We are lived by powers we pretend to understand. We are vicars; ourselves the organs that Saint Cecelia constructs, that Saint Cecelia plays. This is the reason, I think, why Auden depicts Saint Cecelia, at the beginning of his anthem, not only as a traditional pious icon, reverent and calm, but as the exciter, the mistress, of Botticelli's Venus, born out of the sea, borne on a shell:

> Blonde Aphrodite rose up excited,
> Moved to delight by the melody,
> White as an orchid she rode quite naked
> In an oyster shell on top of the sea . . .

Dryden, embarrassed at Cecelia's Dionysiac potentialities, substituted the fable of the un-Christian Timotheus; but Auden is content with a Cecelia at once chaste and sexual, the witch bewitching all our strings.

If our passions are not our own but reside in an exterior chroma, the domain of music, the same is true of our faculty of reason, indeed our whole sensibility. Wordsworth, in the passage cited above, seems to imagine the diatonic scale, the ratio of tightened string lengths, the entire proportionate, intervallic system of music, as a great outer mind, as if an idiot, listening to Mozart, could become capable of thought, as if a sonata-allegro could do his thinking for him. This notion helps explain one of the central problems in the history of the lyric, why a poetic style originally associated with an actual musical accompaniment, by means of lyre or cithern, became in due course a poetic style that tends to resist musical setting because of its dense and complicated introversion. A lyric, that is, a "musical" poem, will thread its way through labyrinths of intellection, of feeling-nuance; if music and mind are the same thing, the most musical poet will be the poet who attends most carefully to the processes of his own sensibility. Shelley, in a passage near the beginning of *A Defence of Poetry* (1821), tends to confirm this view:

> Man is an instrument over which a series of external and internal impressions are driven, like the alternations of an ever-changing wind over an Aeolian lyre, which move it by their motion to ever-changing melody. But there is a principle within the human being . . . which acts otherwise than in the lyre, and produces not melody alone, but harmony, by an internal adjustment of the sounds or motions thus excited to the impressions which excite them. It is as if the lyre could accommodate its chords to the motions of that which strikes them, in a determined proportion of sound. (pp. 26–27)

The poet is the ghost within the lyre. Music and mind are neither strictly outside the poet nor strictly inside him, but instead come into being through a complex homeostasis, an interadjusting of the poet and the sensations that stimulate him, the ideal forms he intuits within him. Thinking and harmonizing are almost synonyms, for the sensibility of the poet keeps modifying, modulating what it feels and knows toward ever greater clarity, proportion, consonance. The ghost inside the lyre, like Maxwell's demon, sorts out into proper category the bloomings and buzzings that arise around it. In this way the lyrical mode abandons dealing with actual sounds in favor of unheard melodies, the operations of the mind, grows self-involved, self-admiring. This is not speech intended to be sung but the speech of Song itself, words passing out into twitters, breezes, humidity, subvocal inflections of thought. It is not far from singing angels, the winged consort of medieval illuminations, to the blind and inward-lucid angel of Rilke.

WORDS AS NOTES

To some extent every lyric poet is in the position of the dear white children of Auden's "Anthem," playing among the ruined languages, and hoping that song will somehow atone for that ruin. One may go still further and speculate that the lyric poet deliberately contrives the ruin of language, the destruction of denotation and reference, so that his singing will be all the purer. How can a lyric poet use his language in a manner that will make words lose consciousness of their own verbality, appear to be nothing more than the blank notes of a musical scale, arbitrary and referenceless? One clue is offered by Mr. Hollander, who observes that

> From a purely formalistic point of view, the "music of poetry" would be confined to patterns of linguistic redundancy, of those elements which, the poem being treated as a coded message, would be beside the point. (*The Untuning of the Sky*, p. 8)

If we know the meaning explicitly, or at least satisfy ourselves that further study of the denotation would not yield much, then other aspects of language—textures and hefts, fallings and risings of stress—make themselves felt. It is as if repetition of meaning prepares the poem, sensitizes it for other repetitions, such as assonance, consonance, regularity of accent. To be sure of meaning requires no further attendance to the semantic properties of words; and so the sememes recede into the background, grow tactful and unobtrusive, while the phonemes grow vivid, self-assertive. This is why almost all great composers of songs—Schubert perhaps most notably—show a disconcerting preference for simple poems, as if good poems were less lyrical than bad poems.

Another method for denaturing language is to introduce into the poem some languageless thing and to identify that thing to some degree with the poet. This is half a matter of content and half a matter of technique, for it requires the poet to denominate a wordless singer and then produce a kind of verse appropriate to it. The most prestigious of such singers is, of course, the bird:

> Mean while the Mind, from pleasures less,
> Withdraws into its happiness:
> The Mind, that Ocean where each kind
> Does streight its own resemblance find;
> Yet it creates, transcending these,

Far other Worlds, and other Seas;
Annihilating all that's made
To a green Thought in a green Shade. . . .
Casting the Bodies Vest aside,
My Soul into the boughs does glide:
There like a Bird it sits, and sings . . .
(Marvell, "The Garden," 1681)

Now more than ever seems it rich to die,
To cease upon the midnight with no pain,
While thou art pouring forth thy soul abroad
In such an ecstasy!
Still wouldst thou sing, and I have ears in vain—
To thy high requiem become a sod.
(Keats, "Ode to a Nightingale," 1819)

Hail to thee, blithe Spirit!
Bird thou never wert . . .
What thou art we know not;
What is most like thee? . . .
Like a poet hidden
In the light of thought,
Singing hymns unbidden,
Till the world is wrought
To sympathy with hopes and fears it heeded not:
Like a high-born maiden
In a palace tower,
Soothing her love-laden
Soul in secret hour
With music sweet as love, which overflows her bower:
Like a glowworm golden
In a dell of dew,
Scattering unbeholden
Its aërial hue
Among the flowers and grass which screen it from the view! . . .
Sound of vernal showers
On the twinkling grass,

Rain-awakened flowers,
All that ever was
Joyous, and clear, and fresh, thy music doth surpass.
(Shelley, "To a Skylark," 1820)

The dust of the lark that Shelley heard . . .
Maybe . . . rests in the loam I view . . .
Go find it, faeries, go and find
That tiny pinch of priceless dust,
And bring a casket silver-lined,
And framed of gold that gems encrust;

And we will lay it safe therein,
And consecrate it to endless time;
For it inspired a bard to win
Ecstatic heights in thought and rhyme.
(Hardy, "Shelley's Skylark," 1887)

In this sequence we see the outlines of a myth about the evolution of lyricality, how it begins as a faculty in the poet's vigorous imagination; how it detaches itself from the poet, grows autonomous, leaps into the branches of a tree to sing; how it becomes increasingly remote and estranged from the poet; how its excellence of songfulness becomes a reproach to the earthbound; how it passes out of his ken entirely; how the poet's imagination becomes a shrine, a cenotaph in its absence.

In each of these poems we see many of the usual features of the lyrical. In Marvell's "The Garden" the annihilation of the created world shows, just as energetically as the trumpet that untunes Dryden's sky, the strange violence that the lyrical can exert against the nonlyrical; for the garden is governed by a new space and a new time, a condition of withdrawal into an imaginative profusion where hours are reckoned on a sundial made of flowers. Coleridge's Limbo is to some degree a neurotic eversion of Marvell's garden. In Keats's "Ode to a Nightingale" there is a much starker line of demarcation between the lyrical and the nonlyrical: Marvell's garden is a seductive locus of contemplation that seems available to any indolent, thoughtful fellow; but access to Keats's bower seems to be granted only to the most strenuous and starving imaginers, for it is a region of such intensities that it leaves the rest of the world wan and drab. It is no wonder youth grows pale and specter thin and dies, for every vivacity and keenness has been locked up by the nightingale in some thicket where no human foot can tread, no human eye can see. Keats makes his tentative trial, his experiment in easing his sensibility into the nightingale's domain, but withdraws hastily when he finds himself amid uncontrollable emotions. If a poet could identify himself with Lyricality, he would find himself in a state of intolerable excitement, alternating between the highest highs and the lowest lows, ecstasy and requiem, frenzy and sloth and despair. Keats's quick fall from the pinnacle to the abyss illustrates once again that there is no single emotion proper to the lyric, that the lyrical condition is a contentless agitation, or a contentless anesthesia. If each human feeling has its exact musical equivalent, as theorists once believed, then to verge too closely on a purely musical zone of being is to approach dangerous overstimulation, overfeeling.

In Shelley's "To a Skylark" we see, perhaps more clearly than in any other poem in English, the difficulties of writing the ideal lyric. Shelley is in a sense the ultimate deconstructive poet, the author most intently engaged in ridding his work of every trace of corpulence, gravity, inertia, ugliness, the nonlyrical; the last line of "The Cloud" (1820)—"I arise and unbuild it again"—will serve as a general motto for his project as a poet, his ceaseless destruction of the corporeal, construction of the incorporeal. "To a Skylark" begins with a famous apostrophe to a bird, informing it that it is not a bird; and later the poet, having promoted the skylark to an unknowable nonentity, wonders what he can compare it to. He discovers, in a succession of stanzas, that he can compare it to a poet, a maiden, a glowworm, and a rose. This is all exhilarating, but it is disturbing as well, for something that can be likened to these four things, which have little in common, may be likened to anything at all. Like Intellectual Beauty, the skylark is an open simile; it is like anything, it is like everything, it is like nothing. This is why Shelley makes the skylark invisible, makes it recede to the vanishing point of the horizon: as it approaches zero it approaches a condition of infinite predicability; any theorem can be proved on the null set.

By forcing the aperture of simile so wide that no logical relation can obtain between the parts, Shelley suggests an important truth about lyricality as an abstract ideal. In his remarkable book *The Rule of Metaphor* (1975)—a whole Sahara of insight, full and featureless—Paul Ricoeur treats metaphors as fields of semantic torsion, infundibula through which the not thought and the not spoken enter the domain of the thought and the spoken; this continues a line of inquiry familiar to readers of Nietzsche, and of Shelley:

> Their [poets'] language is vitally metaphorical; that is, it marks the before unapprehended relations of things and perpetuates their apprehension, until the words which represent them, become, through time, signs for portions or classes of thoughts instead of pictures of integral thoughts; and then if no new poets should arise to create afresh the associations which have been thus disorganized, language will be dead to all the nobler purposes of human intercourse. (*A Defence of Poetry*, p. 29–30)

There is indeed a kind of vitally metaphorical language, found in the works of Shelley and many other great poets, that is continually eroding into definition and knowledge; that is, as Ricoeur would have it, the equivalent in speculative discourse of the explaining-model in science. But such vitally metaphorical language is not to be found in "To a Skylark." There the metaphors are, in a sense, *too* vital; where metaphorical energy keeps spilling out in all manner of aimless and random paths, one cannot hope for cognitive purpose. We have crossed the line from the unapprehended relation to the nonrelation; and that, I believe, is the realm of the lyrical, for musical notes have just such an arbitrary and undiscursive relation to each other as can be found in a simile that compares a skylark to a maiden or a glowworm; a lovely absurdity. These radical similes, in which reason cannot find a rule that makes the comparison sensible, are analogous to music and therefore lyrical. Such a metaphor is simply a leap, an interval, an engaging dissonance.

Many commentators have worried endlessly over what is called metaphysical poetry, because of the difficulty of following its transitions, its violent yoking of heterogeneous ideas. I propose that metaphysical poetry is difficult precisely because we are not used to reading such extremely lyrical poetry. There is a passage in which Donne gives away his method:

> If all things be in all,
> As I think, since all, which were, are, and shall
> Be, be made of the same elements:
> Each thing, each thing implies or represents.
> Then man is a world; in which officers
> Are the vast ravishing seas; and suitors,
> Springs, now full, now shallow, now dry; which, to
> That which drowns them, run . . .
> ("Satyre V," c. 1598)

This is the limit of poetic license. If each thing represents each thing, then any metaphor is valid: X=Y, for any X and any Y. We are near the heaven of language, a state of superequivalence where things slip and slide like figures of speech and all words rhyme. Donne has liquefied the world of experience; and any hope for finding logical relations among its parts has drowned in the general thaw. Most poems by Donne should be read in a spirit of intellectual delirium; Donne continually uses the language of logic, of analogy, but it is only a game in which the mind delights in the reeling sensation it feels as it gropes for logical relations amid a pervasive alogicality. The imagination is always moving faster than reason, which keeps struggling for syllogistic design as it falls further and further behind.

In the lyric assault against denotation, Donne works by a constant multiplication of term: no metaphor is allowed to settle, to stabilize into reasonableness, no predicate is allowed to fix, weigh down the poem's subject, for the poet touches on one only to cast it aside, to bound forward eagerly into further acts of predication. Shelley is more radical, in that he offers for contemplation a nonthing and then illustrates the failure of every attempt to define it, to lift it into thinghood. The skylark is nothing but a wordless canorosity, and so it is fitting that it resists any attempt to verbalize it; the poet can only state his puzzlement in ever giddier language. Shelley's Skylark is just another version of his Cloud, half-ornithologized: a nebulous locus of simile. A nonentity, it sings of a nonworld:

> What objects are the fountains
> Of thy happy strain?
> What fields, or waves, or mountains?
> What shapes of sky or plain?
> What love of thine own kind? what ignorance of pain?

This series of questions effectively conveys the objectlessness of the domain where the skylark resides. As the poem proceeds, the poet's ignorance becomes increasingly luminous, urgent; the skylark and its world undo themselves, become thinning films of air in a private sunset, a private dawn.

Not every lyric poet calls into question the apparatus of metaphor with Shelley's violence; but most lyric poets do show a certain density of metaphor in their work. If it is the business of the lyric poet to refine the subject of his work until it approximates the airiness, the agility, the worldlessness of music, then it is useful to replace objects with metaphors, whether radical or otherwise. A metaphor is not a thing, but a twist of meaning between two things—a half-object, a chord of two notes. If we study a simple metaphor like Marvell's "iron gates of life," we may say that Marvell is qualifying the idea of life, embodying, specifying a certain harshness and implacability in our mortal state; or we may say that, from a certain technical point of view, he is deflecting our attention from iron and from life at once, toward an unreal point halfway between them, resting suspended in an imaginary semantic space. No reader can focus exactly on a metaphor, for it is a weightless, vague construction hovering between realities; it dances away from vision. A poem wealthy with metaphors does not tend to constitute a world, but instead floats in its own air.

NONSENSE

At the opposite pole from redundancy, the excess of sense, is nonsense; and surely any attempt to make words approximate music too exactly is liable to verge on the nonsensical, for the tones of the musical scale present an absolute absence of meaning. In the great bird poems in English one sometimes finds, at the center, an attempt to represent the bird's song, a straining of every resource of metaphor and onomatopoeia toward the nonverbal:

> A clear unwrinkled song, then doth she point it
> With tender accents, and severely joint it
> By short diminutives, that being reared
> In controverting warbles evenly shared,
> With her sweet self she wrangles; he amazed
> That from so small a channel should be raised
> The torrent of a voice . . .
> There might you hear her kindle her soft voice . . .
> Till a sweet whirlwind (striving to get out)
> Heaves her soft bosom, wanders round about,
> And makes a pretty earthquake in her breast,
> Till the fledged notes at length forsake their nest;
> Fluttering in wanton shoals, and to the sky
> Winged with their own wild echoes prattling fly.
> She opes the floodgate, and lets loose a tide
> Of streaming sweetness . . .
>
> (Crashaw, "Music's Duel," 1646)

> Left hand, off land, I hear the lark ascend,
> His rash-fresh re-winded new-skeinèd score
> In crisps of curl off wild winch whirl, and pour
> And pelt music, till none 's to spill nor spend.
>
> (Hopkins, "The Sea and the Skylark," 1877)

> He rises and begins to round;
> He drops the silver chain of sound,
> Of many links without a break,
> In chirrup, whistle, slur, and shake—
> All intervolved and spreading wide,

Like water-dimples down a tide
Where ripple ripple overcurls
And eddy into eddy whirls;
A press of hurried notes that run
So fleet they scarce are more than one,
Yet changingly the trills repeat
And linger ringing while they fleet—
(Meredith, "The Lark Ascending," 1881)

In back of all lyricality there seems to be one enormous vowel striving to get out, a huge pressure of wind. Crashaw's nightingale is one terminus of an invisible organ pipe, a Saint-Cecelia-contraption contracted into the figure of a single bird; Crashaw continually wonders at the immense force pent up behind that tiny throat, as if all the bellows of Aeolus were surging through the eye of a needle. The bird's larynx imposes on that great flow a certain discipline, chops it into musical phrases, introduces bar lines, a metric, by punctuating it with consonants, alliteration. In these three passages there is nothing that is positively nonsensical, but the verbal texture is refining itself into something little more than musical notation, staves, clefs, mordants, trills, pitch signs, tablature. Hopkins imagines his skylark as an animated pen drawing staff lines, phrase sweeps, curlicues of musical notation in the air; Meredith feels himself borne down a river of coloratura; and Crashaw envisages the notes of the bird's song as little birds themselves, as if crotchets and quavers visibly flew across the music paper of the sky. As the poem starts to resemble an obscure set of cues, performance instructions for reproducing the melody of a bird's twitter, it becomes giddy, self-delighting, hilarious, a kind of aria.

Passages like these, in which poetry approaches the echoey limit of self-embellishment, musicality, will help to demonstrate another paradox about the lyric mode, that in extreme conditions the expressive and the inexpressible converge. It is clear in all these bird poems that expressiveness is near its peak, that great emotion is here isolated and purified, caught on the wing; there is a vehemence in these birds, almost a ferocity. Novelists too share the lyrical hope for a wordless language of cries, a medium more point blank, more expressive than our poor decorous, syntax-cramped English:

> I need a little language such as lovers use, words of one syllable such as children speak . . . I need a howl; a cry. When the storm crosses the marsh and sweeps over me where I lie in the ditch unregarded I need no words. (Virginia Woolf, *The Waves*, pp. 381–82)

> that's how it will end, in heart-rending cries, inarticulate murmurs . . . I'll laugh, that's how it will end, in a chuckle, chuck chuck, ow, ha, pa, I'll practice, nyum, hoo, plop, psss, nothing but emotion. (Beckett, *The Unnamable*, p. 408)

And yet, as language abandons grammar and sense, grows melodious, slurrily urgent, it becomes difficult to say exactly what quality of emotion is being represented; there is a general expressiveness in the absence of any particular expression. Nyum and hoo and plop may be vivid beyond language, but what grimace accompanies nyum? How does one flail one's arms during hoo? What satisfactions arise from plop? The reader can only guess. In the bird poems also, the precise tenor of the bird's emotion is hard to determine:

> The woods and brooks, the sheep and kine,
> He is, the hills, the human line,
> The meadows green, the fallows brown,
> The dreams of labor in the town;
> He sings the sap, the quickened veins,
> The wedding song of sun and rains
> He is, the dance of children, thanks
> Of sowers, shout of primrose banks . . .
> (Meredith, "The Lark Ascending")

The lark's song is so commodious and capable that one can only speculate on what it is not, what it cannot do; it has widened into such a level of generality that it seems to present every musical mode at once, Dorian, Phrygian, Lydian, and so forth. It is difficult to imagine a song that is simultaneously intense, insistent, and yet vague, insistent on nothing in particular; at once epithalamium, nursery tune, and hymn of thanksgiving.

Furthermore, in the lyric mode a great deference is accorded to the unexpressive. In poems actually intended to be set to music one can often find texts such as this one, from Campion's first *Booke of Ayres* (1601), 14:

> Blame not my cheeks, though pale with love they be;
> The kindly heate unto my heart is flowne,
> To cherish it that is dismaid by thee,
> Who art so cruell and unsteedfast growne:
> For nature, cald for by distressed harts,
> Neglects and quite forsakes the outward partes.
>
> But they whose cheekes with careles blood are stain'd
> Nurse not one sparke of love within their harts,
> And, when they woe, they speake with passion fain'd,
> For their fat love lyes in their outward parts:
> But in their brests, where love his court should hold,
> Poore Cupid sits and blowes his nailes for cold.

The authenticity of the singer's feeling is proved by its inability to rise into expression: it remains tacit, heart-hidden, trembling, motionless. The song makes a ceremony, an elaborate show, of its refusal to sing; if the beloved were to hear it, it would in a sense defeat its own premise, which accords value only to the unspoken, the inarticulate. Instead of fat love we have an exceptionally thin and inward-turned lyric. The phrase "fat love" is taken from Ovid, but it seems to be unusually significant in Campion's imagination: for instance, in his famous *Observations in the Art of English Poesie* (1602) Campion prints a nimble specimen of an anacreontic and comments as follows:

> Some eares accustomed altogether to the fatnes of rime may perhaps except against the cadences of these numbers; but let any man judicially examine them, and he shall finde they close of themselves so perfectly that the help of rime were not only in them superfluous, but also absurd.

Rhyme is like the blush on the lover's cheek, blatant, heavy-handed, gaudy, overexpressive; Campion prefers a technique more lithe and agile, more subtle. It is as if a poem is most lyrical when it least calls attention to its own technical excellence; when it whispers; when it conceals. The celebrated birds in English poetry are, of course, hidden too: the one theme that justifies the outrageous similes in Shelley's "To a Skylark" is the common reticence of the poet, the maiden, the glowworm, and the rose, each of which is screened away, secretly splendid for the sake of its self-entertainment, impinging on the outer world only by the overflowing abundance of its discourse with itself. We conceive expression as a public act, a pressing out of emotional juices for consumption by the many; yet it seems that when expression is screwed to its highest pitch it retreats from the outer world, as if at the extremity the expresser himself must constitute the public he addresses. Eliot's theory of the poet who makes lyrics out of his wrestling with a private angel, a private demon, is only a dramatization of the self-engagement of such entities as Shelley's skylark. A lyric poem is less fat than another sort of poem insofar as it remains involute, half-expressed, unexpressive, teasing, like a saucy fellow who exasperates by humming a little tune, knowing full well his audience craves an explicit informative statement.

If unexpressiveness is a criterion for the lyrical, it seems that nonsense would be the ultimate lyrical act. Possibly this would be true if nonsense could really exist, but in practice denotation is almost impossible to frustrate, even with the invention of private languages. Paul de Man, in a fine essay in *Forms of Lyric,* edited by Reuben Brower, has refuted the view that the poems of Mallarmé, even at their giddiest, lack solid representationality; few powers are harder to slay than the world-indicating virtue of language. The collected works of such experts in nonsense as Lewis Carroll, Edward Lear, and T. S. Eliot (in *Old Possum's Book of Practical Cats*) display a number of intriguingly indefinite objects, such as the Snark and the Jumblies, but almost no nonsense, if by nonsense is meant an unconstruable verbal field: an indefinite object is still an object, and Carroll, Lear, and Eliot are, as Yeats said of Blake, literal realists of imagination. "The Walrus and the Carpenter" constitutes a world, even if its world, governed by the axiom that zero = infinity, is organized by postulates different from those of our world. There is one quatrain in which Carroll approaches something like real nonsense:

TWAS BRYLLYG, AND THE SLYTHY TOVES
DID GYRE AND GYMBLE IN THE WABE:
ALL MIMSY WERE THE BOROGOVES;
AND THE MOME RATHS OUTGRABE.

This was first published in 1855, under the title "Stanza of Anglo-Saxon Poetry"; it is better known, in slightly different form, from its later appearance in "Jabberwocky." In its original version Carroll wrote it out in a rhomboidal fake-uncial script, as if it had been found in an archaic manuscript. It also came outfitted with a glossary, later adapted by Humpty Dumpty:

> BRYLLYG (derived from the verb to BRYL or BROIL). "the time of broiling dinner, i.e. the close of the afternoon" . . . OUTGRABE, past tense of the verb to OUTGRIBE. (It is connected with the old verb to GRIKE or SHRIKE, from which are derived "shriek" and "creak.") "Squeaked."

These explanations differ from Humpty Dumpty's in that there is a pretense of philology. Humpty Dumpty is an airy aesthete who makes words mean whatever suits his convenience; but the scholar of the earlier stanza is a sober pedant who claims to see here a starker, more potent language than modern English, a primal tongue where words mean more intensely than is possible today. It is as if the outward-moving vocabulary of modern English could be traced to a point of convergence, where *shriek* and *creak* and *squeak* were all the same word. Carroll's method seems to vivify and activate, bring forward, the sememes usually invisible in discourse; in the bird poems cited above the phonemes grew prominent, substantial, compelling, and perhaps in nonsense verse the individual sememes, the basic meaning units, try to become flighty, lyrical. This stanza can be read as a parody of that general nineteenth-century tendency to clear away from English the Latinate abstractions that enfeebled it—Hugh Kenner in *The*

Pound Era cites the example of a scholar who seriously believed that "degrees of comparison" ought to be called "pitches of suchness"—to find in our medieval past a language more muscular and significant than our own. We see, then, that in nonsense poetry there may be a strange co-presence of the meaningless and the too-freighted-with-meaning; and certain later examples bear this out. In Eliot's *The Waste Land* (1922) the Thunder speaks the syllable *DA* to represent the salvific, the pan-significant word, the aboriginal Indo-European root; but part of the shock of its appearance lies in its resemblance to an infant's coo—dada—and to the babble of a fool, perhaps a holy fool like Parsifal. Joyce's *Finnegans Wake* (1939) is, of course, the richest trove in English of language too meaningful to mean anything, at once hypersignificant and painfully defective; and Joyce's debt to Lewis Carroll is everywhere notable, particularly in "The Ballad of Persse O'Reilly" (p. 45):

Have you heard of one Humpty Dumpty
How he fell with a roll and a rumble
And curled up like Lord Olofa Crumple
By the butt of the Magazine Wall . . . ?

The attempt to shatter language into its constituents, into random vocables too small to signify anything, never seems to achieve pure unmeaning, a bird's eerie cry. Even though all the king's horses and all the king's literary critics cannot quite put language back together again, it still retains mighty powers of denotation, of pointing to a world.

The most lyrical nonsense I know, however, is not by Carroll or Joyce, not for the amusement of children—or in Joyce's case for the amusement of angels—but for the sake of satiric derision:

I.
So notwithstanding heretofore
Strait forward by and by
Now everlastingly therefore
Too low and eke too high.

II.
Then for almost and also why

Not thus when less so near
Oh! for hereafter quite so nigh
But greatly ever here.

This is a "Lyric for Italian Music" (1720), by Richard Steele, a part of the *Spectator*'s campaign against the nonsensicality of Italian opera. In its way it is as virtuosic, as remarkable, as the arias it ridicules. Even Joyce usually keeps English syntax and grammar reasonably undisfigured—one can generally tell in *Finnegans Wake* what is a noun, what a transitive verb, and so on—but Steele, while preserving the integrity of the word, makes the part of speech difficult to guess. The sheer nounlessness of the two stanzas is disturbing; it seems that a poem ought to be devoid of *things* if it is to be a lyric. Verbs also are missing. In a poem without objects, without motion, nothing is left but perpetual qualifications in the absence of anything to be qualified; a series of gliding approximations—*near* and *nigh* versus *now* and *here*—hovering in a heaven of adverbs. Some of the terms suggest the range of pitches of the singers' voices, but it seems the music lies too low and eke too high at once, beyond any sensible world of discourse. It may be that Steele was by temperament as unlyrical a writer as any published in English; but he seems to have testified accurately to the nature of the lyric, to its unreferentiality, to its singing line.

THE ORTHOGONAL PRINCIPLE

We are now at the end, and it is time to say that the model of lyricality offered throughout this book is only a provisional one. I have asked myself many times exactly what the criteria are for identifying a given poem as a lyric; I have been unable to draw up a satisfying list. I have asked myself many times why it is difficult to do this, to separate lyrical works from unlyrical ones, and I think I know the answer. It is because nothing is in itself either lyrical or otherwise; it presents itself as lyric only in contrast to some general background of unlyrical discourse. We all of us have a general sense of the great prose of being: from newspapers and magazines, from business talk, from household instructions we infer a sort of dim commonplace discourse, what is ultimately prosaic, the *rhetoric degree zero* of linguists. It is against this ground that a lyric, with its greater inflectedness, its greater intensities, its greater torpors, constitutes itself; for a lyric attains its lyrical character only by some perpendicular motion out of the plane of the nonlyrical. I have described the conditions of the lyric, its extradimensional qualities, as opposed to the world invented by sociologists, politicians, and sentimentalists, that is, what we usually call *the world*. But it is possible to imagine a planet governed by the principle of music instead of the principle of statistical legislation—where solid objects are rare and uncanny, while fantastical dissolving things are commonplace; where the lyrical and the nonlyrical are reversed. In this lyrical heaven, what would seem songlike? I have been spared the need of working this all out myself, because Alfred Tennyson did it for me, in the 1850 and 1851 versions of *The Princess*. That long poem is a fable that insists on its fabulousness at every turn, a preposterous farrago of sexual reversals, heavenly intimations, fairy-tale incongruities, so willfully unreal that its hero is subject to seizures in which he feels himself to be a shadow. In the midst of these talky nuages, these umbral cartoons, Tennyson inserted a series of lyrics that show, I think, what would seem lyric in a fully lyricized world:

> Home they brought her warrior dead:
> She nor swooned, nor uttered cry:
> All her maidens, watching, said,
> "She must weep or she will die."
>
> Then they praised him, soft and low,
> Call him worthy to be loved,
> Truest friend and noblest foe;
> Yet she neither spoke nor moved. . . .
>
> Rose a nurse of ninety years,
> Set a child upon her knee—
> Like summer tempest came her tears—
> "Sweet my child, I live for thee."

In its context in *The Princess*, a long tale of airy confabulations, unstrenuous blather, this song has weight, sobriety, grave meaning. At the beginning of the song the woman seems to be a marble statue, wounded beyond expression, unworldly, what we have been calling lyrical; but by the end of the poem she thaws, becomes physical, ordinary, content to be weak. It is as if earth's seriousness suddenly makes itself felt among all the gauzy nothings, a cannonball breaking through a gossamer web. The world of the song is prosaic, unexceptional, a place where men die, women weep, children console; but in the midst of a hallucination the prosaic itself seems songlike. Where all is subjunctive, optative, jussive, moody, contrary to fact, a simple declarative sentence sounds like music. Perhaps Ariel, staring down at us from the heaven of art, finds our opacities, our stolidities, our bluntnesses, our ignorances, lyrical.

Bibliography of Works Cited

Auden, W. H. *Collected Poems.* New York: Random House, 1976.

———. *The Dyer's Hand.* New York: Random House, 1962.

———. *Secondary Worlds.* New York: Random House, 1968.

Beckett, Samuel. "Dante . . . Bruno. Vico . . Joyce." In *Our Exagmination Round His Factification for Incamination of Work in Progress.* New York: New Directions, 1972.

———. *Three Novels.* New York: Grove Press, 1965.

———. *Watt.* New York: Grove Press, 1959.

Blake, William. *Poetry and Prose.* Edited by David V. Erdman. New York: Doubleday, 1965.

Brower, Reuben, ed. *Forms of Lyric.* New York: Columbia University Press, 1970.

Browning, Robert. *Poems.* Edited by John Pettigrew. 2 vols. New Haven: Yale University Press, 1981.

Byron, George Gordon, Lord. *Poetical Works.* London: Oxford University Press, 1945.

Campion, Thomas. *Works.* Edited by Walter R. Davis. London: Faber and Faber, 1967.

Carpenter, Humphrey. *W. H. Auden: A Biography.* Boston: Houghton Mifflin, 1981.

Carroll, Lewis. *Alice in Wonderland.* Edited by Donald J. Gray. New York: W. W. Norton, 1971.

Chaucer, Geoffrey. *Works*. Edited by F. N. Robinson. Boston: Houghton Mifflin, 1961.

Coleridge, Samuel T. *Complete Works*. Edited by W. G. T. Shedd. 7 vols. Vol. 4. *Lectures upon Shakespeare and Other Dramatists*. New York: Harper and Brothers, 1884.

———. *Selected Poetry and Prose*. Edited by Elisabeth Schneider. New York: Holt, Rinehart, and Winston, 1951.

Conrad, Joseph. *Heart of Darkness*. New York: W. W. Norton, 1971.

Da Ponte, Lorenzo, and W. A. Mozart. *Don Giovanni*. Translated by W. H. Auden and Chester Kallman. New York: G. Schirmer, 1961.

Day Lewis, C. *The Lyric Impulse*. Cambridge: Harvard University Press, 1965.

Di Cesare, Mario. *George Herbert and the Seventeenth-Century Religious Poets*. New York: W. W. Norton, 1978.

Dickinson, Emily. *Complete Poems*. Edited by Thomas H. Johnson. Boston: Little, Brown, 1966.

Donne, John. *Selected Poetry*. Edited by Marius Bewley. New York: New American Library, 1966.

Drayton, Michael. *Works*. Edited by J. William Hebel. Oxford: Shakespeare Head Press, 1961.

Dryden, John. *Literary Criticism*. Edited by Arthur Kirsch. Lincoln: University of Nebraska Press, 1966.

———. *Selected Works*. Edited by William Frost. New York: Holt, Rinehart, and Winston, 1967.

Eliot, T. S. *Complete Poems and Plays*. New York: Harcourt, Brace and World, 1962.

———. *Knowledge and Experience in the Philosophy of F. H. Bradley*. New York: Farrar, Straus, 1964.

———. *On Poetry and Poets*. New York: Farrar, Straus, 1957.

———. *Poems Written in Early Youth*. New York: Farrar, Straus and Giroux, 1967.

———. *Selected Essays*. New York: Harcourt, Brace and World, 1960.

———. *To Criticize the Critic*. New York: Farrar, Straus and Giroux, 1965.

———. *The Use of Poetry and the Use of Criticism*. London: Faber and Faber, 1933.

———. *The Waste Land: A Facsimile and Transcript*. Edited by Valerie Eliot. New York: Harcourt, Brace, Jovanovich, 1971.

Emerson, Ralph Waldo. *Poems*. Boston: Houghton Mifflin, 1882.

Erasmus, Desiderius. *The Praise of Folly.* Translated with commentary by Clarence H. Miller. New Haven: Yale University Press, 1979.

Gardner, Helen. *The Composition of Four Quartets.* New York: Oxford University Press, 1978.

Hardy, Barbara. *The Advantage of Lyric.* Bloomington: Indiana University Press, 1977.

Hardy, Thomas. *Complete Poems.* Edited by James Gibson. New York: Macmillan, 1976.

Herrick, Robert. *Complete Poetry.* Edited by J. Max Patrick. New York: W. W. Norton, 1968.

Hollander, John. *The Untuning of the Sky.* New York: W. W. Norton, 1970.

Hopkins, Gerard Manley. *Poems.* Edited by Robert Bridges and W. H. Gardner. New York: Oxford University Press, 1965.

Johnson, Samuel. *The Lives of the Poets.* 2 vols. London: Oxford University Press, 1952.

———. *Poems.* Edited by E. L. McAdam, Jr., with George Milne. New Haven: Yale University Press, 1964.

Jonson, Ben. *Complete Poetry.* Edited by William B. Hunter, Jr. New York: W. W. Norton, 1963.

Joyce, James. *Finnegans Wake.* New York: Viking Press, 1966.

———. *A Portrait of the Artist as a Young Man.* New York: Viking Press, 1963.

———. *Stephen Hero.* Norfolk, Conn.: New Directions, 1963.

———. *Ulysses.* New York: Random House, 1961.

Justice, Donald. *Selected Poems.* New York: Atheneum, 1979.

Keats, John. *Poems.* Edited by Miriam Allott. London: Longmans, 1977.

Kenner, Hugh. *The Pound Era.* Berkeley: University of California Press, 1971.

Lang, Cecil Y., ed. *The Pre-Raphaelites and Their Circle.* Boston: Houghton Mifflin, 1968.

Lawrence, D. H. *Complete Poems.* Edited by Vivian de Sola Pinto and F. Warren Roberts. New York: Viking Press, 1971.

Lonsdale, Roger, ed. *The Poems of Gray, Collins, and Goldsmith.* London: Longmans, Green, 1969.

Marvell, Andrew. *Complete Poetry.* Edited by George deF. Lord. New York: Modern Library, 1968.

Milton, John. *Complete Poems and Major Prose.* Edited by Merritt Y. Hughes. New York: Odyssey, 1957.

Ovid. *Metamorphoses*. Translated by Arthur Golding. London: Willyam Teresin, 1565.

Peacock, Thomas. *The Four Ages of Poetry*. Edited by John E. Jordan. Indianapolis: Bobbs-Merrill, 1965.

Pope, Alexander. *Poems*. Edited by John Butt. New Haven: Yale University Press, 1963.

Pound, Ezra. *The Cantos*. New York: New Directions, 1977.

———. *Ezra Pound and the Visual Arts*. Edited by Harriet Zinnes. New York: New Directions, 1980.

———. *Personae*. New York: New Directions, 1926.

———. *Selected Letters*. Edited by D. D. Paige. New York: New Directions, 1971.

Puttenham, George [attrib.]. *The Arte of English Poesie*. Menston, England: Scolar Press, 1968.

Rhys, Ernest. *Lyric Poetry*. London: J. M. Dent, 1913.

Ricoeur, Paul. *The Rule of Metaphor*. Toronto: University of Toronto Press, 1981.

Rilke, Rainer Maria. *New Poems*. Translated, with introduction and notes, by J. B. Leishman. London: Hogarth Press, 1964.

Schultz, Robert D. Ezra Pound's Developing Poetics, 1908–1915: The Critical Prose. Dissertation, Cornell University, 1981.

Sencourt, Robert. *T. S. Eliot: A Memoir*. Edited by Donald Adamson. New York: Dodd, Mead, 1971.

Shakespeare, William. *Complete Plays and Poems*. Edited by William Allan Neilson and Charles Jarvis Hill. Cambridge, Mass.: Riverside Press, 1942.

Shelley, Percy B. *A Defence of Poetry*. Edited by John E. Jordan. Indianapolis: Bobbs-Merrill, 1965.

———. *Poetical Works*. Edited by Thomas Hutchinson. London: Oxford University Press, 1967.

Sidney, Philip. *An Apology for Poetry*. Edited by Forrest G. Robinson. Indianapolis: Bobbs-Merrill, 1970.

———. *Astrophel and Stella*. Menston, England: Scolar Press, 1970.

Solve, Melvin T. *Shelley: His Theory of Poetry*. Chicago: University of Chicago Press, 1927.

Spenser, Edmund. *Complete Poetical Works*. Cambridge, Mass.: Houghton Mifflin, 1936.

———. *The Faerie Queene*. Edited by A. C. Hamilton. London: Longmans, 1977.

Swift, Jonathan. *Poetical Works*. Edited by Herbert Davis. London: Oxford University Press, 1967.

Tennyson, Alfred. *Poems*. Edited by Christopher Ricks. London: Longmans, Green, 1969.

Webbe, William. *A Discourse of English Poetrie*. Edited by Edward Arber. English Reprints. London: 5 Queen Square, Bloomsbury, 1870.

Whitman, Walt. *Complete Poetry and Selected Prose*. Edited by James E. Miller, Jr. Boston: Riverside Press, 1959.

Wilde, Oscar. *Complete Works*. Introduction by Vyvyan Holland. London: Collins, 1966.

Williams, John, ed. *English Renaissance Poetry*. Garden City, N.Y.: Anchor Books, 1963.

Williams, William Carlos. *Complete Collected Poems*. Norfolk: New Directions, 1938.

Woolf, Virginia. *The Waves*. New York: Harcourt, Brace and World, 1959.

Wordsworth, William. *Poetical Works*. Edited by Thomas Hutchinson; revised by Ernest de Selincourt. London: Oxford University Press, 1969.

———. *The Prelude: 1799, 1805, 1850*. Edited by Jonathan Wordsworth, M. H. Abrams, and Stephen Gill. New York: W. W. Norton, 1979.

———. *Prose Works*. Edited by W. J. B. Owen and Jane Worthington Smyser. Oxford: Clarendon Press, 1974.

Yeats, William Butler. *Collected Plays*. New York: Macmillan, 1965.

———. *Essays and Introductions*. New York: Macmillan, 1961.

———. *Explorations*. New York: Macmillan, 1962.

———, ed. *The Oxford Book of Modern Verse*. London: Oxford University Press, 1936.

———. *Poems*. Edited by Richard J. Finneran. New York: Macmillan, 1983.

———. *A Vision*. New York: Macmillan, 1961.

Index

PR351 .A4 1985
10800664
STACK
Lyricality in Englis